Advance praise for *Reading the Bible with the Damned*

"When one has read the Bible for a hundred years as most engaged Christians have, it is easy to have the Bible become stale, domesticated, and predictable according to our preferences. It is not always obvious how to come to a fresh, faithful reading. But one chance for such newness from the Spirit is to read the Bible in a different socio-economic environment that insists on a different set of questions for interpretation.

This book by Ekblad does exactly that. It moves the Bible away from safe, conventional church venues and reads afresh among the alienated and marginalized. The effect of such a new interpretive context is that the text takes on a poignancy and sharpness that bespeaks the stirring of God's spirit. We may be led by Ekblad to read the Bible yet again, as if for the first time."

—Walter Brueggemann, Professor Emeritus,
Columbia Theological Seminary, and author of several
Westminster John Knox Press books, including
*An Introduction to the Old Testament: The Canon and
Christian Imagination* and *Reverberations of Faith:
A Theological Handbook of Old Testament Themes*

"Bob Ekblad is more like Jesus than most people I know—eagerly welcoming to the insights of those our culture marginalizes, hungrily yearning to bring good news to the poor, respectfully receptive to the faith of society's 'least,' adept in advocacy, and compassionate in acts of mercy. How different the world will be when more of us share Christ's life and heart in this way. I say *when*, not *if*, because this book will hasten the transformation. Be careful: Bob's readings of Scriptures unleash the power of the kingdom of God. You and your church might wind up upended!"

—Marva J. Dawn, Teaching Fellow in Spiritual Theology,
Regent College, Vancouver, British Columbia, and
author of *Unfettered Hope: A Call to Faithful Living
in an Affluent Society* and *Powers, Weakness,
and the Tabernacling of God*

"Bob Ekblad has raised an ominously serious question: What does the Bible mean for the suffering? But the urgency of the question, especially for academics, is that Ekblad does not ask the version of the question: What does the Bible mean for the suffering "over there"—over in another country or in the foreign news stories. Ekblad asks a more unsettling question: What does the Bible say to the suffering down *our* street—across *our* town and city—and out in the fields where *our* supermarkets get *our* produce? The responses are both enlightening and challenging, and Ekblad has written a wonderful book to teach all of us about the Bible, faith and liberation, and the realities of our social system."

—Daniel L. Smith-Christopher, Professor
of Old Testament and Director of Peace Studies,
Loyola Marymount University, Los Angeles,
and author of *A Biblical Theology of Exile*

Reading the Bible
with the Damned

Reading the Bible with the Damned

Bob Ekblad

WESTMINSTER
JOHN KNOX PRESS
LOUISVILLE · KENTUCKY

Unless otherwise identified, Scripture quotations are from the New Revised Standard Version of the Bible, copyright © 1989 by the Division of Christian Education of the National Council of the Churches of Christ in the U.S.A., and are used by permission.

Scripture quotations marked NASB are taken from the *New American Standard Bible,* © 1960, 1962, 1963, 1968, 1971, 1972, 1973, 1975, 1977 by The Lockman Foundation. Used by permission.

For more information on Tierra Nueva and the People's Seminary, see www.peoplesseminary .org, contact info@peoplesseminary.org, or call (360) 755-5299.

Book design by Sharon Adams
Cover design by designpointinc.com

First edition
Published by Westminster John Knox Press
Louisville, Kentucky

This book is printed on acid-free paper that meets the American National Standards Institute Z39.48 standard. ∞

PRINTED IN THE UNITED STATES OF AMERICA

06 07 08 09 10 11 12 13 14 — 10 9 8 7 6 5 4 3 2

Library of Congress Cataloging-in-Publication Data is on file at the Library of Congress, Washington, D.C.

ISBN-13: 978-0-664-22917-7
ISBN-10: 0-664-22917-4

Dedicated to

Juan Garcia Jr.
Seferino Manjares
Francisco Reyes
Douglas Gilkey
Gustavo San Martin

And to all who have died in the midst of the struggle
to be freed by a Gospel that does have the power to save.

To all those who have heard good news in Bible studies
who remain at large, still outside the sheepfold.

To pastors who follow Jesus in seeking
for lost sheep until they are found.

You have not strengthened the weak, you have not healed the sick, you have not bound up the injured, you have not brought back the strayed, you have not sought the lost, but with force and harshness you have ruled them. So they were scattered, because there was no shepherd; and scattered, they became food for all the wild animals. (Ezek. 34:4–5)

I myself will be the shepherd of my sheep, and I will make them lie down, says the Lord GOD. I will seek the lost, and I will bring back the strayed, and I will bind up the injured, and I will strengthen the weak. (Ezek. 34:15–16a)

They shall be secure on their soil; and they shall know that I am the LORD, when I break the bars of their yoke, and save them from the hands of those who enslaved them. They shall no more be plunder for the nations, nor shall the animals of the land devour them; they shall live in safety, and no one shall make them afraid. (Ezek. 34:27b–28)

You are my sheep, the sheep of my pasture and I am your God, says the Lord GOD. (Ezek. 34:31)

Contents

Acknowledgments   ix

Preface   xiii

Chapter 1:   Reading Scripture for the Liberation
of the Not-Yet-Believing   1

Chapter 2:   New Beginnings Require New Readings:
Reading Genesis in and out of Jail   11

Chapter 3:   Getting Back into the Garden   25

Chapter 4:   God Empowers the Down and Out:
Nonheroic Reading of the Patriarchal Narratives   61

Chapter 5:   Encountering God in Exodus
and at Today's Margins   93

Chapter 6:   God's Empowering Call to the People:
Reading Isaiah with Exiles   113

Chapter 7:   Reading and Praying the Psalms   127

Chapter 8:   Reading the Gospels with Tax Collectors
and Sinners   155

Chapter 9:   Following Jesus, the Good Coyote:
Reading Paul with Undocumented Immigrants   179

Notes   **197**

Acknowledgments

I am forever grateful to Willie Cienfuegos, Jose Israel Garcia, Dominic Barton, Julio Montalvo, Ramiro Aguilar, Andres Vega, Jose Flores, Bobby Baldwin, Mario Salinas, Jeff Peters, Zack Joy, Arnold Garcia, Marcial Nemecio, Eugenio Benitez, Epifania Garcia, Jesus Garcia, the late Juan Garcia Jr., and the thousands of inmates and immigrants with whom I have learned to read the Bible for good news. Thanks also to the deputies at Skagit County Jail who have made regular Bible study, worship, and one-on-one counseling available to inmates under their care.

Special thanks to Jaime Farin, who accepted my invitation to read the Torah with me on Kibbutz Regavim and who educated me about the liberation struggles of the poor in Latin America in 1978—initiating me to my vocation. I thank also Catalina Toc and Flavio Ovalle, my Guatemalan language instructors, dialogue partners, and friends, who opened my eyes to the struggles of the poor in Central America. I am especially grateful to Fernando Andrade, David Calix, Jorge Mejia, Hector Giron, and Ramiro and Elia Dominguez, who taught me what good news needs to include to turn the hearts of Honduran campesinos. Thanks also to Francisco Zuniga, Gloria Aguilar, Celio Mejia, Eda Zuniga, and the villagers of Las Delicias and San Isidro de Mal Paso.

I am especially indebted to John Linton and Doug Frank of Lincoln, Oregon, for their provocative teaching and special interest in me and in our ministry. John Linton's Bible studies and mentoring helped me rediscover the Bible as a place where good news abounds. His refusal to dismiss difficult biblical texts and willingness to wrestle grace out of the most notorious passages on behalf of struggling, doubting seekers has helped and inspired me. Doug Frank has taught me to listen and to question from a place of compassion and intellectual honesty. John and Doug's caring for lost sheep has included me at critical periods of my life. I am thankful for their friendship.

Gerald West's writings and teaching style have inspired me greatly. Gerald models a humble yet careful listening that empowers people as their voice is respected and elevated above the voices of dominant culture. Gerald's friendship and encouragement to reflect on and write about my work have been invaluable.

I am grateful to my friend Jonathan Draper for his modeling and encouragement to keep active in both the biblical studies academy and in the parish of the poor. Thanks also to Hans de Wit of the Vrije Universiteit of Amsterdam for his support of reading Scripture at the margins through his leadership in the Intercultural Reading of the Bible Project.

I thank my French mentors in Scripture study and pastoral ministry: Daniel Lys, Michel Bouttier, Jean Ansaldi, Yves Ellul, and Danielle Ellul. I am especially appreciative to the thinkers who first drew me to France: Jacques Ellul, Wilhelm Vischer, and Daniel Lys. Daniel Bourguet's mentorship as my thesis director, prior of the Fraternite Spirituelle Les Veilleurs, and his friendship have continually inspired me to not only carefully read the text but to practice *leccio divina*, praying the words of the Bible with the expectation of contemplating the One to whom the Scriptures bear witness: Father, Son, and Holy Spirit.

I thank Holden Village for providing a mountain refuge and warm community during the sabbatical that launched this project and Robert and Raymonde Pueche for hosting my family for a month of my sabbatical in their home in France. I thank the folks at Lincoln Christian Church and Howard and Ester Claassen for supporting Gracie and me during our years in Honduras. I thank Don Mowatt and the Stewardship Foundation for their encouragement and financial support of Tierra Nueva during the time this book was written.

Thanks also to Roger Capron and Rocio Robles, whose reactions to our discoveries during Bible studies at Tierra Nueva I always trust. Roger's constant quest for good news that has the power to really save has encouraged me greatly. His seeking after lost sheep puts him in the company of Jesus. Thanks also to the many others who work or have worked at Tierra Nueva, served on the board, and participated in our weekly Friday afternoon Bible studies or Sunday worship: among them Rob Mercatante and Eduardo and Luz Maria Cabrera.

Thanks to Regent College, for their willingness to let me teach Reading the Bible with the Damned, Breaking the Chains, and other classes. Special thanks to Loren Wilkinson for his friendship, support of our work, and continual efforts to keep me connected to the lives of Regent students. Thanks to the many students at Regent whose interest has kept this project alive.

Thanks for special encouragement from my friends Letizia Myers, Dave Diewert, Joe Woodbury, John Connell, Brett Greider, Mark Baker, Dave Willis, and Lars Clausen, and for helpful insights from Rich Ward and Rich Lang, who read parts of this manuscript and gave me helpful comments and encouragement. Thanks to Jack Brace, for his proofreading and editing help. Thanks to Bruce Cockburn, for inspiring me to both resist the powers and delight in life through his music and his friendship.

Special thanks to my editor Jon Berquist of Westminster John Knox Press, who brought this project to fulfillment together with the fine copyediting of Esther Kolb and support from Julie Tonini and others at WJK.

My parents, Gene and Ann Ekblad, deserve special thanks for their encouragement and constant desire to hear how people are impacted by weekly Bible studies in Skagit County Jail. Special thanks as well to my brothers Dave and Peter, and to my sister Julie for their love and support, and to my brother and sister-in-law Andy and Mary Ekblad for their cheering me on in this project and in our ministry.

I express my heartfelt thanks to my children Isaac, Luke, and Anna and to my wife, Gracie, for their constant love and support. Gracie's deep friendship and partnership in ministry not only have been necessary for my very survival but are bringing me increasing joy as we grow together in love for God, each other, and humanity.

Finally I give thanks and praise to Jesus Christ for calling me to join him in his ministry to seek out lost sheep until they are found. I feel privileged to work alongside the One who is committed to making us become fishers of people.

Preface

For over twenty-five years I have been reading the Bible in foreign places with unlikely reading partners.[1] I myself grew up as an insider in a mainstream American white, middle-class, Christian family in a wealthy suburb of Seattle. Most of the people I have read Scripture with could be classified as outsiders, marginalized by the dominant classes because of race, ideology, social class, immigration status, behavior, and lack of education.

Over the years that I have read Scripture with people on the margins I have come to appreciate both the tremendous complexities and the obstacles to liberating reading. I continually experience my many limitations as a Bible-study leader, teacher, and pastor—many of which are directly due to the inescapable association with the culture of domination due to my race, nationality, and social class. At the same time I feel privileged to witness breakthroughs when they happen for me and for others.

I am convinced that I learn more than I give during my encounters with fellow readers and the text. I have witnessed many men and women come to believe that God loves them in the midst of many obstacles and hardships. I have seen many people who have felt damned for much of their lives begin to identify God as a liberating, supportive presence. I have heard good news[2] from the people as they come to discover for themselves a God who heals, liberates, and saves. I write this book both to share some of these rich encounters and hopefully to inspire others to enter into this special vocation.

My reading experience has been divided between reading in the south with campesinos in rural Honduras and in the north with undocumented Mexican immigrants, Chicano gang members, and inmates from diverse ethnicities incarcerated in Skagit County Jail in western Washington State. This book presents reflections on reading the Bible and doing ministry with people on the margins of the dominant culture/empire and the mainstream church.

My primary objective is to present approaches to Scripture reading and spirituality that I have found helpful in my work with outsiders and alienated insiders. My hope is that these reflections will help sensitize and form Christians for the specific task of communicating good news to people often submerged in the bad news of poverty, social marginalization, addictions to alcohol and drugs, criminal activities, oppression by the state, self-accusation, feelings of inadequacy, and other difficulties. The "outsiders" I envision are first and foremost fellow human beings who perceive themselves as condemned to poverty or permanent exclusion, beyond repair, unable to change, in bondage—in short, "damned," or as many I currently work with regularly say, "fucked up." On the other hand I hope that alienated "insiders" or those unable to find a home in the church or to remain inside mainstream Christianity will find this book helpful.

Much of this book comes out of a course I teach entitled "Reading the Bible with the Damned."[3] I am convinced, as a result of interaction with graduate students of theology of over twenty nationalities and from many different denominations, that while my reading contexts are specific and limited, the negative images of God that prevail among the marginalized and the approach toward "reading for good news" are applicable to ministry with the underclass[4] in many contexts.

The Gospel writers depict Jesus as placing proclamation of good news and teaching from the Scriptures at the heart of his ministry among the marginalized of his day.[5] Matthew's Gospel presents Jesus as preaching: "Repent,[6] for the kingdom of heaven is at hand" (Matt. 4:17 NRSV note). Jesus went about Galilee teaching in their synagogues, and preaching the gospel of the kingdom (Matt. 4:23; 9:35), and healing all the sicknesses he encountered among the people. According to Mark, Jesus preached the gospel of God and called people to repent and believe in this good news (Mark 1:14–15). Matthew and Mark describe Jesus as consequently calling disciples to a similar mission (Matt. 4:18–22; Mark 1:16–20).

Luke depicts Jesus as quoting Isaiah 61:1 and claiming its fulfillment by his presence. "The Spirit of the Lord is upon me, because he has anointed me to bring good news to the poor" (Luke 4:18), along with proclaiming release to the captives, restoring sight to the blind, letting the oppressed go free, and proclaiming the year of the Lord's favor. Jesus' teaching astonished people because his word had authority (Luke 4:32). Jesus did most of his work at the margins (in Galilee, Samaria) and outside the religious places (as on the road, by the sea, in the fields, on the mountain, by the well). Even in the Temple, Jesus' presence mostly benefited the marginalized (Matt. 21).

Protestant and Catholic laypeople alike are becoming more and more active in desperately needed ministries of service and presence, offering housing, soup kitchens, and clothing banks to the homeless and low-income. However, mainstream Christians are usually held back from (and even embarrassed about) sharing good news through Bible study, prayer, and one-on-one conversations about questions of faith. This is due both to people's personal discomfort in talking about questions of faith and to the daunting barriers related to social class, race, language, and culture. Many differences separate the largely affluent, middle-class church from the underclass. Mainstream people who are generally morally correct, law-abiding citizens are often afraid of people who habitually break the law and the established moral rules. These people are seen as "the problem," because they are "out of compliance." Christians from the dominant culture, who are often educated and English-speaking, are uncomfortable with people on the margins, who have their own street language or foreign tongue and are educated to survive in their contexts but may be functionally illiterate.

Mainstream Christians often support valuable programs that aim at helping the underclass "catch up" with the mainstream. However, most Christians are ill prepared for any kind of ministry of the Word with those outside the institutional church. Those with a message of forgiveness and love, or at least with access to helpful theologies, often keep this "good word" among themselves, leaving the underclass to fundamentalist groups, Jehovah's Witnesses, sectarian evangelicals, and the Mormons—or to whoever is willing to go out into the streets and meet people where they are, often door-to-door. This must change! The survival of the church is dependent on ordinary Christians' rediscovering good news in the Scriptures with and for others and for themselves.

The Mainstream and the Margins Need Each Other

All who follow Christ are called to be bearers of God's good news to the poor. Ignorance of the underclass or immigrants and their world(s) leads to simplistic labeling of people as "poor," "ex-cons," "illegals," "homeless," "underprivileged," "disabled," "poor white trash," "street workers," "runaways," "Mexicans," "disenfranchised," and endless other designations. The church, then, becomes guilty of racial and social-class profiling. We must seek out personal contact, always with an openness to listen in order to understand, recognizing our own tendency to distrust and judge. We must count the cost before naively trying to dismantle barriers that people on the margins have placed there to protect themselves from hurt and abuse.

One of the greatest barriers between mainstream Christians and people on the margins is that mainstream Christians often represent the dominant culture and do little to nothing to distinguish themselves from it. It is not only that many churches include in their membership judges, prosecutors, police officers, probation officers, welfare case workers, landlords, employers, and other active promoters of the system—though this reality alone may keep many of society's "offenders" far from these churches. Few Christians would deny the importance of communicating grace, unconditional love, and forgiveness of sin in Jesus Christ. Yet the church is often silent about issues that directly affect the poor (harsh sentences by the courts, racial targeting by law-enforcement agencies, harsh immigration policies, mistreatment of the poor by landlords and employers, etc.).

When mainstream Christians are absent from the lives of marginalized people, the gap only widens, impoverishing everyone. Unless Christians work deliberately to bridge the gaps, people on the margins will most often assume that Christians stand with the state, the laws of the land, the economic system, over and against the weak and vulnerable. The church's words and witness are too often confused and confusing. As a result of the church's overidentification with the status quo, outsiders find it difficult to hear good, new, surprising, liberating news come mediated by such tainted representatives, who are too often viewed as far away, as God is envisioned as remote.

Drawing closer to marginalized people requires, first, an attitude of humility. This is a long, arduous process that is linked to the experience of conversion itself. Meeting and listening to real people (whether they be illiterate peasants, undocumented farmworkers, drug dealers, street workers, teen runaways, or sex offenders) will complicate our understanding and deeply challenge our dominant ideology and theology. Meeting the people will lead to a newfound solidarity as we identify our common humanity in the other. Awareness of the context of struggle and suffering among the marginalized will help mainstream people become more conscious of the demands on them and the Scriptures in order for a word to be truly good news. Mainstream readers will learn to search the Scriptures for news good enough to make a difference. This search will help the mainstream reader rediscover, or perhaps witness for the first time, the light that shines in the darkness. But we must descend first. Descent into our suffering world may well involve the voluntary setting aside of privilege in the name of sensitive respect for the other. Along the way, we must struggle with obstacles of social class, gender, and race, and of culture, such as domestication, isolationism, sexism, ethnocentrism, and nationalism. We also must face fear-inspiring theologies that lead to harmful approaches to Scripture reading such as literalism, moralism, and heroism.

For me, this descent into the suffering world has become my own life story. My own personal experience of growing alienation within mainstream Christianity, my inability to measure up to the endless demands of a God perceived as celestial sovereign, and my consequent brokenness under the weight of the dominant theology places me to a certain extent among the damned in need of healing and liberation. I have discovered that many of the contradictory images of God that were communicated to me as I grew up inside a mainstream Christian subculture are close to those that keep many of today's "outsiders" alienated from the church and unable to experience God positively. My own experience of God in the midst of suffering during and after my own personal descent within my theological framework involved a discovery of the good news that grounds the Scripture studies with marginalized people recounted throughout this book. My story is clearly specific to my context and represents one version of one person's process of spiritual development. I certainly do not present it as exemplary or in any way universal. This journey is not over, but represents reflections from one stage along the road. I recognize also that the particulars of my reading experiences differ immensely from most other reading contexts. It is my hope that something universal may still shine through my particular reading contexts in ways that will serve readers in a wide diversity of contexts.

Verbatim reporting for the purpose of communicating people's exact perspectives and voices in Bible studies is in most cases impossible. In Honduras many studies take place under mango trees or in crowded community buildings, where the noise of farm animals, children, wind, leaves, crickets, and other distractions make recording nearly impossible. Add to that the fact that larger-group studies often are preceded by small-group discussions, where the best insights are expressed beyond the range of recording devices. Taping or video recording is not permitted in Bible studies carried out among immigrants in Skagit County Jail. Both in Central American and in North American contexts, recording Bible studies would stifle discussion, as people would not feel free to express their views in a situation where "anything you do or say can and will be used against you in a court of law." Even if verbatim transcriptions were possible, translation from Spanish to English also requires interpretation, as cultural elements and idiomatic expressions must be matched by often inadequate expressions. Due to the impossibility of verbatim reporting, the Bible studies expressed in this book have been reconstructed from notes and from memory. I hope that the following stories will bring readers into new communities of readers and strugglers, whose lives and voices continue to touch and challenge me, transforming my life and theology.

Chapter One

Reading Scripture for the Liberation of the Not-Yet-Believing

At the end of the Gospel of Luke, two disciples of Jesus (including one whom tradition has named Cleopas) leave Jerusalem for Emmaus with heavy hearts, not yet knowing of Jesus' resurrection, when a stranger approaches, travels with them along that road, and asks them what they are talking about. When Jesus breaks bread with them, they realize that he is the risen Christ. This story expresses well the hopelessness many of today's damned feel toward the Bible, the church, and the Christian gospel. Their immobility and sadness (24:17) and Cleopas's words to the incognito Christ, "We had hoped that he was the one to redeem Israel," reflect a disillusionment that is rampant among marginalized people. Many people with whom I read have never had hope in God or have given up even discussing together their disappointments. Jesus, God, and the church may as well be dead to them, as they cease to expect anything of consequence to their lives. This despair is due in large measure to the failure of the church to demonstrate the love of God in word and action. Jesus' coming alongside these two discouraged insiders as one who re-presents their traditions through re-interpreting their Scriptures shows the necessary first steps toward discovering a theology that will speak to the disillusioned. Jesus' rebuke, "Oh, how foolish you are, and how slow of heart to believe all that the prophets have declared!" is an initial slap that awakens them to relearn in a way that would cause their hearts to burn with something so good that they would become mobilized to return to Jerusalem, where they would eventually be mobilized by the Spirit at Pentecost.

"Was it not necessary that the Messiah should suffer these things and then enter into his glory?" asks Jesus, challenging the two men's image of

God's anointed one as immune from abuse by the dominant powers and distanced from the depths of human pain.

Luke's description of what Jesus deemed necessary for disillusioned disciples invites today's church to change our ways of thinking about God.

> Then beginning with Moses and all the prophets, he interpreted to them the things about himself in all the scriptures.

The incognito Christ's liberating interpretation opens these disciples to him, though he is a total stranger, to such an extent that they strongly urge him to stay with them. The disciples' surprise as their eyes are opened with his eucharistic blessing is a strong reminder of the slowness of heart that results when God becomes too familiar and "domesticated."

Common Pitfalls to Liberating Reading of Scripture

There are a number of pitfalls that keep religious insiders of a broad range of reading communities from experiencing the burning heart that mobilizes people toward the excluded other. These pitfalls must be identified and consciously remedied if people are to move beyond alienating ways of reading Scripture.

1. Domestication of God and the Scriptures resulting from isolationism is the most destructive pitfall inhibiting liberating reading of the Bible. Biblical interpretation is never neutral. The Bible is locked up by theologies we absorb from our subcultures, whether we grow up in the church or not. Hidden or consciously embraced theological assumptions and other presuppositions influence our interpretation, causing us to automatically interpret along traditional lines. Left unchallenged, these assumptions will cause us to consciously or unconsciously look for evidence in the Bible to support our ideas.

2. The pitfall of moralism is the common tendency to come to the text looking for information about what we think we are supposed to do to be obedient—compliant with God's perceived demands. This tendency is directly related to false assumptions about God and salvation that overly prioritize right, obedient behavior over the good news of God's gracious, unconditional love toward us. This pitfall is visible in the rich young man's question to Jesus: "What good deed must I do to have eternal life?" (Matt. 19:16). The young man's going away sad shows the saving effects of Jesus' words, which frus-

trated his self-sufficiency and pride, revealing to him that he was unable to save himself through rigorous obedience.

3. Related to moralism is the pitfall of heroism or exemplarism. This pitfall happens when we search the Bible for heroes and other model characters who we think are included in Scripture for us to emulate. While there are calls to follow the example of different biblical personalities, heroism can blind us to the antiheroic nature of many biblical characters (Jacob, Joseph, Judah, David, Peter . . .). One of my professors in France, Daniel Lys, is fond of warning against using the example of Abraham (Gen. 18:22–33) for ideal intercessory prayer.

"When someone tells me they will pray for me like Abraham prayed for Sodom, I tell them, no thank you. Sodom was destroyed. What is important about this story is what it says about God. God always says yes to Abraham's intercession. If Abraham had only been courageous enough to intercede for Sodom in the absence of even one righteous person!"[1]

Challenging Pitfalls to Liberating Reading of the Bible

Those desiring to read Scripture for good news must be deliberate and aggressive in combating pitfalls to liberating reading.[2] Domestication and isolationism can be remedied or avoided by consciously broadening our reading community. We often neglect to include the "damned" among our circle of inquirers—like the Pharisees who wanted tax collectors and sinners excluded from the table with Jesus. We carry on our theological discussions with insiders, following the wide path trodden by the successful religious types who run our religious institutions. If our reading community is limited to scholars, fellow Catholics, Protestants, or other church "insiders," we will be out of touch with the street.[3] We need to leave Jerusalem and take our own journeys toward Emmaus, opening ourselves to encounters with strangers through whom God can open our eyes. Reading with people on the margins in their contexts will challenge our traditional readings. If biblical theology is to speak to the heart of today's "tax collectors and sinners" they must be included in some major way in that theology's elaboration.

My own approach to participatory reading at the margins has been deeply influenced by the grassroots Bible-reading movement pioneered in Brazil and elsewhere in Latin America commonly known as *lectura popular de la biblia* (grassroots or people's reading of the Bible). Carlos Mesters's many writings[4] and important work in the Brazilian base community movement (CEBI) and Ernesto Cardenal's seminal example of *lectura popular* in Nicaragua published as *The Gospel in Solentiname*[5] are the best-known representatives of this approach to popular reading. The return to Scripture after Vatican II and the rise of liberation theology led to an outpouring of reflections.[6] Though a more thorough presentation of participatory reading strategies is the subject of my next project, I will briefly present some reflections on facilitation.

Brazilian pedagogue Paulo Freire has deeply inspired my teaching and preaching, both in Honduras and in North America.[7] Freire's participatory, problem-solving model did much to empower the base community movement in Latin America. Peasants and workers who were once passive receivers of monologue-style preaching, teaching, and liturgies began to read and discuss the Scriptures for themselves—becoming subjects of their own liberation process with the help of priests, women religious, pastors, and lay leaders who functioned more as facilitators than as authorities.[8]

According to Freire, monologuing educators who effectively deposit information alien to people's daily lives into passive-recipient students keep people dependent, passive, and uncritical of the authorities. This dependency-producing education system facilitates domination, with people lacking critical thinking skills needed to be free subjects in a liberation process. In contrast, the liberating educator must seek to empower people through engaging them in careful analysis and discussion of their own contexts. Freire's model of participatory education and literacy training led the way for grassroots Scripture-study facilitators' working out of a hermeneutics of liberation. This approach focuses on reflection from a careful analysis of people's problems, beginning with context rather than text, which is often perceived as alien to these people.

Freire encourages teachers to draw people from the margins into the conscientization process through introducing them to critical thinking and problem-solving skills. Facilitators are urged to constantly create an environment of trust that draws out voices and perspectives of people on the margins that are usually squelched by the powers (that is, those who have a voice). Educators are encouraged to facilitate group analysis and to help people express their opinions through a variety of means that do not depend on literacy (such as, sociodramas, art, music, street theater, poetry, cartoons). This is especially important in contexts where people are illiterate or semiliterate.

Clarity about the facilitator's or teacher's role and objectives go hand in hand with an understanding of the most appropriate means of communication. I envision my role as that of a facilitator and midwife. As a facilitator, I seek to do everything possible to set up an encounter between God and the people, through assisting them to reflect on their own lives, the Scriptures, and each other's experiences and viewpoints.

As midwife I seek to assist during the birthing process that I believe in faith is imminent. At the same time I fully recognize my dependency on the Holy Spirit, who labors in intimate communion with people in the depths of their beings. As midwife I seek to be present as sensitively as I can—getting out of the way, simply being present, or intervening, according to the needs of the moment. I set up the birthing room, as it were, making sure that the interpreting process gets off to the best start with a given group and text. Trust must be established between myself and the participants, the participants and each other, and the group members and the biblical text. The chosen Scripture must be introduced in a way that gives people a place of entry into the foreign world of the Bible. Barriers between reader and story must be addressed through introductory remarks and questions that invite the people to ponder and discuss the biblical story.

Simultaneously I do all I can to help people identify contemporary equivalents to the biblical narrative (location, characters, verbs, and other details) in their own lives and world. I strive to bring people to understand the deeper meaning of the biblical stories as these stories illuminate their own lives and surrounding world. My hope is that people will find themselves relating to people inside the text to such an extent that they themselves may be met or addressed by YHWH, Jesus, one of the apostles, or whoever mediates the message or saving action in the biblical story. I see myself as one who works to bring people together in as safe a place as possible for a potential encounter: a meeting between individuals and God that may result in comfort, conversion, healing, a change of heart, call, hope, and transformation. I am an unknowing midwife at best—unaware of what the encounter will birth.

My hope is that God's meeting with each one would bring them to discern God's call on their life, so they will discover their highest vocation and deepest desire. People receive their vocation as they begin to follow Jesus, who turns common people into disciples and followers into recruiters of yet more disciples, who are sent into every nook and cranny of the world.

The Word and the Streets

I seek to formulate questions that draw people out about issues that directly affect them.[9] Most often I begin with a question about people's lives, and then introduce a biblical story and ask questions that help uncover the deeper truths of the text. Other times I begin with the text—most often the case on Sunday, when I am using the selections from the Common Lectionary.

In preparation for my Bible studies in the jail and elsewhere I seek to first determine what questions or issues the biblical text appears to be addressing. This is often the most difficult task, requiring both careful exegesis and spiritual discernment regarding the text and the group participants. The questions that guide my preparatory reading include: What is the heart of the matter in the text? What question(s) does the biblical text appear to be addressing or in some way answering?[10] Since most texts can be read to address numerous issues, I attempt to identify the multiple levels of meaning, prioritizing the issues most clearly addressed in the text.[11]

The interface between the reading and study of Scripture and contemporary reading of our contexts requires deliberate work and creativity. The following suggestions merely point the way toward a workable methodology, which will be developed in more depth in a future book.

First choose whether you plan to begin with a chosen Scripture or begin with people's (or a particular) question or current struggle. If you plan to come to a group with a text or issue already chosen, begin at #2 below, before determining the question at #1.

1. Begin with a question that evokes the contemporary context and burning issue(s) of the people with whom you read. Sample questions include: "What struggles, trials, temptations, challenges are you [or the other with whom you read] facing?" "What are the external forces that are tempting, oppressing, or in any way obstacles to God's call on your or another's life?"
2. Look for a Scripture text that may speak into the life situation or sickness that you discern as the one that needs to be addressed. How do you determine which text for which situation? *Ask yourself:* What is the heart of the matter in the text? What is the deeper meaning? Attempt to prioritize the issues addressed in the text in your preparation for the Bible study.[12]

While a primary objective of Scripture study is to hear God's voice, another critical objective is for people to discover their own, so they too can communicate. After casting out the legion from the Gerasene demoniac with a word, Jesus declines his request to follow, sending him back to "tell [your friends] how much the Lord has done for you, and what mercy he has shown you" (Mark 5:19). Freire's greatest contribution is his lifting up of the role of the people and their voices, which the best grassroots Bible-study facilitators place at the forefront.

I have been deeply affected and educated by the perspectives of people both in my ministry among peasants in Honduras and with immigrants and inmates in North America. The people's voices often recount harrowing struggle and express deep pain. At the same time, these voices often communicate understandings of God that are deeply unsettling. In *The Academy of the Poor: Towards a Dialogical Reading of the Bible*, Gerald West warns that the Bible-study facilitator must be always aware that the voice that the people allow the facilitator to hear is often the voice that they think the facilitator wants to hear—expressing views that would be in compliance with the dominant ideology.[13]

West draws on James Scott to distinguish between the "official transcript," defined as the dominant interpretation of reality or ideology, and the "hidden transcript," consisting in people's true but self-censored views, which are hidden from representatives of the dominant culture. In order for people to venture their freest, uncensored understandings of God and reality they must trust the facilitator. This is certainly true in my experience of reading with marginalized people. West rightly cautions that people's theology may well be more positive and subversive than expressed in a public Bible study. However, while in South Africa positive images of God permitting resistance and liberation may lurk below theologies of compliance,[14] among unorganized people outside the church few have any positive views about God to hide.

My experience regarding street-level understandings of God is that the more marginalized and less organized the people are, the more the people will have internalized the dominant ideology of the official transcript. Many have not heard an alternative voice expressing good news that was convincing enough to win them over to a God on their side. Among the people with whom I minister, many exercise freedom vis-à-vis the mainstream and state that damns them.

The hidden transcript for the underclass in North America, as I experience its people, consists of an entire underground life involving illegal actions that often appear necessary, since the empire offers no legal way. Unfortunately, while they may or may not experience guilt for many of these activities, people often assume that their transgression is not only against the state and official theology of the church, but also against God. Since many are confused as to whether their illegal activities are transgressions against God, this ambiguity leads many to abandon any effort to consciously seek God. Rather, God is often viewed as to be avoided except in case of emergency. With little positive exposure to the Scriptures or guidance from the church, many people find themselves acting in increasingly criminal ways, dealing drugs, abusing alcohol and drugs, robbing car stereos, and acting unfaithfully to their partners in ways that lead to further alienation and often time in jail and prison.

It is essential for the Bible study facilitator to gain the people's trust in such a way that people become free to express this hidden transcript and bring it into conversation with the Scriptures and with other fellow strugglers. The good news is often as hidden in the Scriptures and in their stories as their hidden transcript is from the authorities. Once they begin to hear good news from a good God, they can hear themselves as addressed by God, forgiven for real guilt, released from false guilt, called to higher levels of freedom and responsibility. When people discover that God is a God of love and life, who is for them and with them in the midst of their struggles and even in their noncompliance with the official transcript, then they will begin to draw on the Scriptures for comfort and strength.

Scripture study must become a deliberate place for training in discernment of God's presence in history and in their own lives, revealing to them God's hidden work as one who has been and is presently with them. A Bible-study group can and should be a safe site where people can identify their experiences of peace in their noncompliance retrospectively as signs of God's presence with them. An important role for the facilitator includes helping people distinguish between the authentic voice of the Spirit at the core of their being and the external voice of the official transcript, which damns them.

The Bible-study leaders will often need to provide leadership in directly challenging common theological assumptions. This is especially important in jail and prison contexts, where people tend to read "in compliance" with God's perceived demands, fearful of offending the Deity and getting into still worse trouble.

Challenging Theological Assumptions

Directly challenge common assumptions. After determining the "idolatrous" image that is in the place of God (in the place of the Other), help the person question the legitimacy of this image by offering a counterimage from Scripture.

Challenge people's view of who God is. Jesus reveals the Father. You cannot know or even talk about the Father without the Son (John 1:14–18).

Welcome explanatory and creative interpretations. Invite people to freely
explore alternative ways of interpreting a biblical text. Modeling this
yourself will help people relax and explore their own risky readings.

*Challenge people's view of Christianity as "a moral/righteous lifestyle" and
the Bible as God's rule book.* Since most people open the Bible expecting to hear detailed instructions about what they are supposed to
do to be saved, the facilitator needs to deliberately and consistently
help people see that the Bible tells us of a God who saves us by
grace. Consciously ask the question: What does this Scripture passage tell us about who God is? What has God done for humans
according to this passage? What part do people play or not play?

Note the silences in the Scriptures. When you are reading the Bible, pay
attention to what God, Jesus, or a key character *does not* say,
require, or do as much as what he does say and do. The silences in
the text (what the text does not say) are sometimes as revelatory as
what the text does say.[15]

In addition to freeing people to read for life and liberation, people on
the margins are in desperate need of seeing the good news fleshed out
through respectful listening, advocacy, and/or acts of mercy or service.
John's Gospel reminds us that the physical incarnation of the Word is
God's preferential way of revealing love and grace.

And the Word became flesh and lived among us, and we have seen
his glory, the glory as of a father's only son, full of grace and truth.
(John 1:14)

In Jesus of Nazareth the Word became flesh in Bethlehem's stable, and
escaped as a refugee fleeing persecution, returning, resettling, traveling
on dusty roads, tempted in deserted places, teaching, healing, and serving
in Galilee's villages. In similar and new ways the Word must continue to
become flesh in every place and time, in every language and culture, gender, and age group. The best theology happens in the streets, jails, hospi-
tals, barrios, offices, homes, shelters, refugee camps—of this world,
among the people. And if this Word is the same Word we fully see in Jesus,
it will be filled with grace and truth.

Ministering in Jesus' name among people on the edge is a humbling
task. My many failures often make me wonder why I dare write a book like
this. While success and failure are often difficult to measure, I know I
often experience my limits, and find myself flailing my arms, sinking into

the sea in water that is way over my head. Reading Scripture and ministering to people at the margins is a refiner's fire for theology, which is put to the test and often found inadequate. Yet it is the very experience of absence, exile, and struggle that places believers throughout the ages in a posture of radical dependency and prayer, where we cry, "Come Lord Jesus, come Holy Spirit," and await our liberation with open hands.

Chapter Two

New Beginnings Require New Readings

Reading Genesis in and out of Jail

Genesis is a good place to begin reading with people who are opening the Bible for the first time. It makes sense to them to start a book at the beginning. The big, intimidating Bible becomes more approachable when it is read like any other book, beginning on page 1. It helps to point out to outsiders who consider themselves unworthy and unsaved that most of Genesis takes place outside the garden of Eden and outside the "Holy Land." Most scholars believe that much of Genesis was written by and for people who were exiles, uprooted from their homeland, living as indentured foreigners in the midst of an oppressive empire. Most of the stories have to do with struggles of migratory people who are rarely exemplary religious characters. The stories depict life situations that people on the margins easily identify with: falling to temptation, the tendency to show favoritism, jealousies between brothers, domestic violence, grief, natural catastrophes depicted as punishments from God, death in the family, sterility, wondering whether you are called by God, the vulnerability of being immigrants in foreign lands, hospitality, discrimination, sibling rivalry, fraud, running from the law, indentured servitude, oppressive working conditions, bribery, rape, incest, false accusations, unfair imprisonment, enmities within families, uprootedness due to famine, dependency on the privileged, and many more.

Genesis 1: Reading for Signs of God's Presence in the Darkness

For most Bible readers, Genesis 1 is a history of the creation of the world with no contemporary importance beyond combating those who argue for a godless beginning or that humans descend from apes.

11

"Not me, man," said a Chicano man once when inmates were discussing origins. "I didn't come from no monkey—God made people on the sixth day like it says in Genesis!"

For those trying to line up their thinking with the Bible in an attempt to get on the "right side" of God, Genesis 1 must be believed in a literal way. To reject a literal six-day creation account would be equal to rejecting God and the entire Christian tradition. This would be especially risky in jail, possibly bringing down God's wrath on you in the form of a harsher sentence. A literal reading of Genesis must be accepted, much as a released inmate wanting to stay out of trouble would need to follow the dictates of the court and the Probation Office.

Others who have given up on trying to please God, or who seek to distance themselves from the "holy rollers," note the contradictions and write it all off as untrue. Questions that often arise from inmates regarding Genesis 1–3 reveal how fruitless the dominant readings can be. An inmate's call from solitary confinement reveals this struggle. He tells me that since he has been seeking God others have been bombarding him with questions or directly mocking him. He tells me he will write me a list of the questions, the first of which is: "If Cain and Abel were the first to be born, where does Cain get his wife from, dude?" This question illustrates the frustrating impasse of literalism and historicism.

Reading Genesis as a story about God and humans then and now allows for liberating readings that go far beyond traditional pitfalls. A simple question to a group of inmates like "How's it going for you guys in here?" usually evokes responses like: "We're very sad, and there's nothing we can do about our situation." When people get more specific, they tell how they feel completely out of control and often feel desperate and discouraged. A timely reading of Genesis 1:1–2 with the intention of placing the biblical context in rapport with the people's reality can move discussion to new levels:

> In the beginning when God created the heavens and the earth, the earth was a formless void and darkness covered the face of the deep, while a wind from God swept over the face of the waters.[1]

"Here at the beginning, when God was creating the world, what were things like, according to this verse?" I ask a group of men.

People look down at their Bibles silently.

"It was chaotic. There was nothing," someone ventures.

"There was darkness over the deep," another man adds.

"Yes—this is talking about a place where everything is out of control, chaotic and dark," I say. "So do things ever seem that way now? Or has everything changed since then?" I probe.

"It's the same, man. Things are dark now too, really dark," someone ventures. Others nod their agreement.

"So, do you feel the darkness? When and where do you notice this?" I ask.

"Right now in this place," a man interjects.

"Outside too, things are bad. Chaos reigns. Drugs and shit, they're all over, man," someone else adds.

The men talk about their struggles with feelings of isolation, loneliness, and fear. Many are not able to call family members because of their refusal to accept expensive collect calls, or blocks on phones, no phones, or the sheer unaffordability of high phone bills for their spouses or parents making minimum wage. Some lament that their undocumented immigrant family members are afraid to visit them, as they do not want to run the risk of running into a Border Patrol agent at the jail. Others tell how they know nothing about their cases, since public defenders aren't visiting or in any way communicating with them. Many are estranged from spouses and other family members, after bridges were burned due to months or years of drug and alcohol abuse and tension and conflicts with family. Many are in the process of losing jobs and spouses. Some have had everything they own seized by the Drug Enforcement Administration (DEA) and the local drug task force. Many face unknown sentences, long stays in jail, years in prison, and/or deportation by the INS. I asked Juan, a 26-year-old Chicano man just released from nearly a year in jail, if and when he feels the darkness.

"Yea, like right now," he says. "I have no place to call home. I can't say: 'Hey, come over homes and let's watch TV.' I don't have a place. I feel deprived of something that someone else has. It might be jealousy or envy. I don't know what it is. I don't know if it's my fault, or my mother's fault. I don't want to point fingers at anyone. Like there is no light in my life, there's just been pure darkness. You want to know what darkness is? You have lots of little goals, and you can't achieve it. I want to pay my bills. How can I live if I don't even have a place to stay?"

It is easy for people on the streets or in the jail to talk about chaos, darkness, and the depths, and Genesis 1 suddenly seems like here and now.

"So what else do these first words of the Bible tell us about the beginning?" I ask, trying to move the study along in the direction of new hope.

"This says that 'In the beginning when God created . . . ,'" a man slowly reads.

"OK," I probe, "so right there in the chaos and dark God was creating something too?"

We talk about how, according to Genesis, God is at work creating, right there in the heart of chaos and darkness.

"So, how is God creating?" I ask. "What is God doing there in the darkness?"

"It says in my Bible the Spirit is hovering," someone says. "God is there, God is here," he continues.

"Then God says: 'Let there be light,' and there was light," another guy reads. "God speaks to us, and that brings light."

"So, what did the darkness have to do to experience the light? Did the chaos have to get its act together before God could come and speak?" I ask, trying to draw attention to the grace at the heart of this text. I find myself unable to resist pointing out narrative gaps that undermine the expected moralism.

The men look down at their Bibles.

"*Nada*, the darkness was just dark. God was there and spoke," someone says, looking intrigued.

"So do you think this can happen now? How might God be present and speak and bring light now in our darkness?" I ask.

The men answer quickly and confidently.

"God speaks now through this," a guy says, holding up his open Bible. "God can speak to us through someone like you."

"We come here to these studies. You help us understand. I feel peace when I leave," says another man.

I invite the men to be on the lookout for God to be present with them when they are back in their cells. If this story is still true now, then maybe God's Spirit is hovering over us, and God is ready to speak and bring light into our lives.[2]

I encourage them to use their time in jail to learn to identify God as with them and begin to listen for God's voice.

"While you are here in this jail, it is my hope that you will come to see for yourself that God is with you, that God is for you," I tell them. "While this is not all up to you, it helps to *learn to see* [another word for spiritual discernment].

"You already know how to see many things I cannot see," I tell them. "You can tell where crack cocaine or heroin is for sale. You know which cars are likely to have stereos worth breaking windows for. You know the telltale signs that alert you to someone from an enemy gang, or an undercover narcotics cop." People nod and laugh.

I tell them I am blind to many of these things. I have not learned to recognize. "But when it comes to identifying God's presence here with you, maybe I can help you. But reading the Bible can help you even more," I say. I encourage the people to use their time in their cells as if they were monks: calling out, seeking, and watching for God.

"You don't have to take this time in jail as a punishment. If you do, you are letting the system succeed in having power over you and making you unhappy. Use your time to learn about yourself and God. If you don't yet believe in God, cry out, search, and look for God. Be on the lookout. The first monks went to the desert to look for God. They lived in caves that they even called cells. They stayed in their cells, reading the Scriptures and praying. They watched and waited for God. If you want, you can try to see yourselves as monks here." In this way I introduce them to the spirituality of the desert.[3]

I offer to bring anyone a Spanish or English Bible of his own. I let them know that I am available for one-on-one visits if they want to talk. Nearly everyone asks for a Bible. Many want visits. The men are encouraged by this attention and care. They thank me and shake my hand. We stand, gather in a circle holding hands, and close with a prayer for light and the Lord's Prayer.

⚜⚜⚜⚜⚜⚜⚜

Julio is a moody but charismatic twenty-six-year-old man who I am immediately drawn to when I first meet him in a jail Bible study. He has dark eyes and a lean, handsome face, sporting a carefully groomed goatee, his raven-black hair slicked back from his forehead in classic Chicano style. He tells me he has already spent twelve years of his life in juvenile detention and prison. After Julio gets out of jail, I begin visiting him and his girlfriend, Laura, in a crowded low-income apartment unit where they stay with Laura's grandmother, aunt, and their children. Julio does start using drugs again, and occasionally sells crack cocaine. Customers arrive constantly as we read the Bible and talk together. Julio warmly invites them in to study with us. I know most everyone from the jail. Some of them stay and talk. Others move on, looking for *hale* (Spanish slang for crack or rock cocaine). One evening I show up for our weekly meeting. Julio greets me enthusiastically.

"What's up, pastor? Hey, Laura, it's Pastor Robert, get your ass down here," he yells up the stairs. I've come for our weekly Bible study.

Laura greets me with a smile. Her aunt was frying up breaded shrimp. Julio has me sit at their kitchen table, after we return from the corner store where we buy tartar sauce.

"I want a job like hers," Julio had said to the clerk, pointing to a store employee who stood casually chatting with another employee. He smiled, his gang lieutenant's star, tattooed over the outside of his left eyebrow, reminding me I am with one of East Stockton's gangster lieutenants.

Bibles are out. I have them turn to Genesis 1:1–4, and we read, "When God was creating the heavens and the earth, the earth was formless and void, and darkness was over the face of the deep."

We talk about chaos, about life when there is no order, no separations, a free-for-all. We talk about jail, when people feel remorse, hopelessness, darkness. Laura's aunt talks about her life. On her own at age fourteen, caring for her younger siblings beginning at age eleven. Being way too responsible. She shows me her Bible.

"A woman gave me this last time I was in jail," she says.

"Whenever you are in jail, I would be glad to visit you," I offer.

"Well, you can visit me," she said. "I'm going to Purdi [Washington State's women's prison in Gig Harbor] on Tuesday, to do thirty-six months."

She introduces me to her two oldest schoolkids as they return home from school. She looks proud, but sad. Her oldest son, known as Pukie, is doing seven years. We continue our reading.

"'The Spirit of God hovered over the face of the deep,'" she reads from Genesis 1:2.

God's Spirit is there, even when darkness and chaos seem to reign. When you're stoned on crack, in jail, or drunk, God's Spirit still can hover.

"Then what happens?" I ask.

"God said, 'Let there be light'; and there was light!"

God speaks. God's Word brings light where there was darkness. We notice that God does this. The darkness and chaos did nothing to deserve it. Next we read John 1:1–4, about how the Word that was with God and was God came into the world, to enlighten all people.

"Hey, Pastor Robert," says Julio. "Can't you just replace Word with Jesus' name here?"

"Well, yeah, you can. Jesus is God's Word, God's way of communicating, God's way of telling and showing us who God is."

Pukie's mom likes this.

"So what do you think it means here? The light that enlightens everyone?" I ask.

Kids are running to and fro. A three-year-old reaches for our Kool-Aid glasses and cries for water. Other hands reach up, pawing for munchies they cannot see on our table above them.

"Oh, I'm not getting this," says Julio, exasperated. "My head's full of snot and these kids are driving me crazy!"

Pukie's mom leaps to her feet.

"Bastard carbon Julio, you're wrecking the study. I'm gonna beat the shit out of you. I'm gonna . . ."

Julio jumps up and says he is getting out of there. He heads upstairs as Laura says:

"Pastor, now you see how he is when he's off drugs!"

After assuring her that it was OK, and hearing how they were being told they could no longer live in their grandmother's apartment, I leave to say good-bye to Julio. I climb the dark stairs and ask if I can enter his room. He is lying with his three kids around him, tears in his eyes.

"I want to go back to jail. I can't take this. Fucking don't have a fucking job. Fucking can't stand being in this fucking house, fucking can't stand Laura's fucking family. . . . She tells me to get money, but when I sell drugs I use them. Fuck man, I want to get the fuck out of here, go to Arizona. I want to fucking rob a fucking bank. I could do it. I wouldn't get caught." I pray for him, for God's peace and comfort. For the presence of the Holy Spirit over the chaos. I invite him to study with me the next night. He agrees.

And the Spirit of God was *Hovering over the Waters*

I talked with Juan at our Family Support Center several months after his release from nine months in jail. The Migrant Council has just decided to pay to do a work experience internship with us for two months.

"Yeah, it also says that the Spirit of God was hovering over the waters," notices Juan during a one-on-one conversation in our Family Support Center. "This means that God is all around us. If the human body is like 80 percent water, so he must be around us. We all have a little of him, if he's hovering over the water. We have to let him be in control of our lives. . . ."

"So what does this tell us about the way that God might be present? Is God forcing us, pressuring us?" I ask Juan.

"No," continues Juan, "he's around all of us. Not bothering nobody, just hovering. *It doesn't* say *andaba chingando* [messing/fucking around] over the water, making the water make bubbles and shit. He was letting the water be. The water is us. God is hovering around us. It's like you, homes; you've always accepted me for this brown crazy Mexican that I am. I think you'd accept me if I were pock-dotted. We just need to accept him."

I am struck by Juan's insight regarding the Spirit's respectful presence. A God who is creating a beginning in the midst of places where chaos and darkness reign is a consolation to people who feel hopelessly unworthy and alone. A Spirit of God who flutters rather than invades, is respectfully present and not busting doors down with search warrants or slapping on handcuffs, is unexpectedly good news to downtrodden people.

"So is it important to be able to notice that God's Spirit is present?" I ask Juan.

Is it important to become aware of the Spirit hovering over the water? Some people don't feel it. We were kicking back praying, before he went to help us get rent. Right when we said, "Amen," there was a phone call, and it was the bank. It rang right after we said "Amen." Maybe that's like: Let there be light.

It's a good analogy. There was not light until God spoke. Let there be light in Juan's life, and there was light. I really hope that this happens in my life.

More on the Spirit of God Hovering over the Waters

I am in the midst of preparing to teach graduate students a course on Genesis 1:1–3 when I receive a collect call from Manny, a Chicano man who had attended my Spanish Bible studies in the jail for two or three months while appealing one of his charges after a conviction and ten-year prison sentence. He claimed to be a Muslim, and let everyone know that he did not like all the rest of us. He believes in Allah and in the Koran, which he had been introduced to while doing time in the past. He listened carefully and participated thoughtfully in our discussions. Now, he is calling from the hole, a solitary confinement unit of Washington State Penitentiary in Walla Walla. He tells me how he's been sentenced to three years of solitary confinement for something he did in prison.

"To be honest with you, I'm not always doing that good," he says, as we begin our conversation.

I had also received a call a few days before from the Chicano man known as Pukie (Julio's girlfriend's cousin) from the same solitary-confinement unit. Pukie had been active in my Spanish Bible study for five months some four years before, when he was facing charges of armed robbery, negotiating pleas, and going through sentencing. Pukie's mother was imprisoned during most of his childhood. I remember Pukie in a group Bible-study setting as a scrappy eighteen-year-old gangster who was always whispering, cracking jokes, and provoking fights. In my one-on-one encounters I found him serious and respectful, desirous of quality personal attention and a different life. I had been worrying about Pukie since I had heard from his cousin that he had suffered rough times in the first four years of a nine-year sentence for armed robbery. He was encouraged to know that we pray for him every week. He told me that the Department of Corrections transferred him from prison to prison, punishing him repeatedly with time in the hole for hanging with the gangs. Now he is doing a year in the dreaded intensive management unit (IMU) solitary confinement unit, where he is lonely but "doing OK."

"I keep getting into trouble cuz I hang with the gang members," he told me. "I think I'm learning, trying to get my GED [General Equivalency Diploma], I'm doing OK, man."

He told me about Cruz, a guy from Mount Vernon, a nearby city, who is there too.

Now Manny Cruz is on the other end of the line. He stands alone at a pay phone, locked in a small recreation area to which the guards escort him handcuffed for an hour every other day. I have just been looking at a way of identifying characters, place, and movements in the Genesis 1:1–3 narrative as a basis for identifying contemporary equivalents. Manny agrees to let me read him Genesis 1:1–2:

> In the beginning when God was creating the heavens and the earth, the earth was formless and void, and darkness was over the face of the deep.

Manny tells me he has really been depressed lately. He has felt submerged in darkness. I read him again, "In the beginning when God was creating . . ." and point out that God is present in the darkness. God is creating. "Do you feel God's presence there with you, Manny?" I ask.

"Yeah, man, I do. Really, I feel like God is right here with me all the time," says Manny.

"Hey, listen to this, Manny," I say. "Let me read you the verse that follows the one I just read you. It says that the Spirit of God was hovering over the face of the deep. This is saying what you are experiencing," I affirm. "God is there in the midst of darkness. Before there is a light the Spirit is present." I ask Manny how and when he feels that God is present.

"Well, like today, man. Today I felt it," says Manny.

He tells me that he reads the Bible, and that he's been reading the psalms. Earlier in the day, before he called me, he read Psalm 23 to Pukie.

"You're kidding," I say, surprised. "How do you read to Pukie if you're there in the hole?" I ask.

"We have our ways," he says proudly. "You wouldn't believe all the things we learn while we're in here," he continues. "We've learned that if we both flush our toilets at the same time, we can empty the water from the pipes between our toilets. So we talk through the toilets!

"Just this morning I was reading to my brother Pukie. I read him the Twenty-third Psalm. That's my favorite," says Manny. "I read it to him through the toilet. It really touched him, man. And it really touched me that it touched my brother."

I nearly drop the phone, as I too am hearing the voice of God as Manny speaks.

"That is amazing," I tell him. "Do you know that in Genesis 1:2–3, the story continues: 'The Spirit of God was hovering over the waters . . . and then God said: "Let there be light."' The Spirit of God was hovering over the waters of your toilet bowls," I say, "and look, God spoke!"

Manny is blown away and I am too. I am caught off guard by an unexpected (and unorthodox) rereading of "And God said, let there be light." Over the waters between the toilets the Spirit hovers, and God speaks light to people alone in their cells. God speaks this word through Manny, condemned to solitude in his eight-by-eight-foot cinderblock cell. Yet it is precisely through men like Manny that God reveals. God comes with such humility that God is not ashamed to speak even through the soiled ceramic lips of toilet bowls.

I try to imagine the good news that they were hearing there in their narrow cells, alone. I try to imagine myself there in a solitary-confinement cell of a big prison. I imagine myself with my ear over a bare prison toilet, stripped of its toilet seat. What good news might they be hearing?

> The LORD *is my shepherd,* I shall not want.
>   He *makes me lie down* in green pastures;
> *he leads me* beside still waters;
>   *he restores* my soul.
> *He leads me* in right paths
>   for his name's sake.
> Even though I walk through the darkest valley,
>   I fear no evil;
> for *you are with me;*
>   your rod and your staff—
>   *they comfort me.*
> *You prepare a table* before me
>   in the presence of my enemies;

> *you anoint my head* with oil;
>   my cup overflows.
> Surely goodness and mercy shall follow me
>   all the days of my life,
> and I shall dwell in the house of the LORD
>   my whole life long.
> (Psalm 23, italics added)

I later reflect on this story in the light of John 10:22–30, where Jesus says "My sheep hear my voice." These sheep clearly include Manny and Pukie and so many others. Even and especially when they are straying or in dark places, finding faith difficult, God has them safe in God's tender but firm grip. "I know them, and they follow me," continues Jesus, the Good Shepherd. "I give them eternal life, and they will never perish. No one will snatch them out of my hand" (John 10:27, 28).

I am no longer convinced that Genesis 1 is first and foremost about the creation. I believe it speaks much more about God, and the particular ways in which God is present in the midst of our world. God's presence is real, even in the midst of darkness and chaos. God is creating, God's Spirit is hovering, and God's Word comes freely, bringing light into dark places.

Genesis 1:26–28: Made in the Image of God

At the beginning of jail Bible studies I often start by inviting people to actively share their ideas and feelings about the text. I begin by asking people how they think God speaks, and their two most common responses are "through the Bible" and "through pastors" like me. I then ask them whether they think God looks like a *gabacho* (white person), since they have just said God speaks through people like me.

"What do you think God looks like?" I ask. "Is God a Mexican with brown skin and black hair, or is God a white person? Is God man or a woman, mustached or without mustache, blue-eyed or brown, a baby or an old person? What language does God speak? Spanish, English, Hebrew, Chinese?" I continue.

Some say God is invisible. Others say God is everything and everywhere. Others nod their heads when I depict the standard white-bearded old Anglo on a throne. Then I ask someone to read Genesis 1:26–27.

> Then God said, "Let us make humankind in our image, according to our likeness. . . . So God created humankind in his image, in the image of God he created them; male and female he created them.[4]

I ask the men if this passage gives them any more ideas.

"So if God created humans in God's image, then what does God look like?" I ask.

The men usually look surprised at the obvious answer, but it often takes a while for someone to dare to say it.

"God looks like us?" someone asks, half expecting it to be the wrong answer.

"Well, it looks like this is what the passage is saying," I note.

I ask people what they thought it meant that God spoke of himself as a plural: "Let us create humans in our image" (Gen. 1:26). "Maybe that is why God says "Let us make the human in *our* image, after our likeness," I suggest, emphasizing the "our."

"So then if God is like us, which of us is God like? Is God then a Mexican and a *gabacho*?" I ask.

"No, God is like all of us, I think," says one of the Mexican men. "If God made us all in his image and likeness, then God looks like people of every race, old and young, man and woman. Look, it even says 'in the image of God he created them; male and female he created them,'" he said, looking surprised to be making such a discovery.

We agree that if we are all made in God's image, then God looks like each one of us: Mexicans, *gabachos*, mustached people, people without mustaches, fat people, skinny people, women,[5] children, and men.

I look around the group and spot someone that others might be least willing to associate with the way God looks, and suggest that God then looks like that person, and me, and the jail guards, and everyone.

"Might the 'us' in God include all of us together with people of every race and language?" I ask.

No one ventures an answer to this question, but I have the men's full attention. They have never heard anything like this. There are indigenous Mixteco-speaking farmworkers from Oaxaca present. The others are Spanish speakers and a few English-speaking Chicanos. Now that there is agreement about what God looks like, I ask them what language God speaks.

We quickly agree that if God is like us, God speaks every language—Spanish, Mixtec, English, Triqui, French, Chinese, Arabic, and the rest. At this point I return to the original question:

"So, how do you think God speaks today?" At first the men give the traditional responses. They mention the Scriptures, pastors, and priests. Someone asks whether I think God can speak through dreams. Perhaps they are too humble to say the obvious. So I say it.

"If God looks like all of us, and God speaks every language, if we are made in God's image, then could it be that God can speak through any one of us?"

People nod their heads and smile. They like this idea. I continue by telling them that I hope they will feel free to participate in our discussion.

"I believe that God can speak through each of you, through each of us. This is the way that God prefers to speak, through people like you and me. If you have a comment or a question during the Bible study, please speak. In my years visiting people here in the jail I have learned more from inmates than I ever learned in seminary," I say.

The men look encouraged. They appreciate the respect. It is Thursday and many have been over to superior court, where they have stood handcuffed in their red jail uniforms in the courtroom before the public. I know that what I am saying may seem unbelievable, so I continue.

"You may think that I am not serious, but it is true. Every time I come to the jail I learn things from you. If God speaks through all of us, then why should this be surprising? God looks and talks like you and me. God speaks through you and me. And Genesis goes even farther," I suggest. "But first let me ask you a question," I continue.

"Today when you went to court, how did you feel that the prosecutor, the judge, the guards, or any of the other people you encountered looked at you?"

"Like we were criminals," a man says.

"Like we are guilty, even before we have been convicted," says another.

"I felt like they had already decided, hey, this Mexican guy is guilty. They think we are guilty just because we are Mexican," says another man.

"So how did you feel with all those eyes on you?" I ask.

"Very bad. Like they think we are garbage," says another.

The men look miserable as they think back to their day in the courtroom. I suggest that God looks at them differently, and ask someone to read Genesis 1:31.

"'God saw everything that he had made, and indeed, it was *very good.*'"

"So after God finished making humans, male and female in God's image, on that sixth day, the text says that God saw that they were very good."

Before circling and holding hands for our closing prayer, I encourage the men to remember that in the eyes of God they are made in God's image.

"God sees you as very good.[6] God sees you as God created you. As you pray the Lord's Prayer, remember that when we call God 'Our Father,' we are speaking as God's children. We are brothers praying as children to our Father, who sees us and loves us."

We hold hands, and after I ask the men if they have anything they would like prayer for, we pray and end our study together by praying the Our Father in Spanish.

> Our Father who are in heaven, hallowed be your name,
> Your kingdom come, your will be done, on earth as it is in heaven.
> Give us this day our daily bread, and forgive us our sins,
> as we forgive those who sin against us.
> Lead us not into temptation, but deliver us from evil. Amen.

I hang around with the men, talking informally for a while after the study, before the guards come and escort them back to their cells. Individuals approach me and ask if I would visit them or bring them a Bible. Others tell me that their wife or parents do not know that they are in jail, or do not know how to visit them during their visiting hours. They are often visibly distraught, sometimes to the point of tears. They ask me if I would be willing to call or visit their families and tell them where or how they are, and how they can be visited. Others tell me that they have been in the jail several weeks and still have not been visited by their public defender. I take each name and call the Skagit County Public Defenders the next day to make contact with the court-appointed attorney. The men are very grateful for this support.

As the years go by and I converse with hundreds of individuals convicted of every possible crime, I find my view of people becoming increasingly positive. I am drawn to the anthropology of the Eastern, Greek Church fathers, which views humans as made in God's image and by nature very good. While St. Symeon the New Theologian speaks of "the faithful" in the following quote, I believe this category can be broadened to include all the people with whom I minister:

> We, the faithful, should look upon all the faithful as one single being, and should consider that Christ dwells in each of them. We should have such love for each of them that we are willing to lay down our lives for him. Nor should we ever think or say that anyone is evil: we should look on everyone as good, as I have already said. Even should you see someone overwhelmed by some passion, execrate, not him, but the passions that fight against him. And if he is mastered by desires and prepossessions, have even greater compassion for him; for you too may be tempted, subject as you are to the same fluctuations of beguiling materiality.[7]

Chapter Three

Getting Back into the Garden

A s I continued to lead Bible studies with people on the margins I ran repeatedly into what are probably the most debilitating images of God and self. God is seen as a strict, easily angered, punishing judge best kept at a distance to avoid more trouble.

One evening I met with Consuela, a twenty-three-year-old Salvadoran woman with three young children. She had told me that she needed to talk, and I assumed her difficulties were related to her boyfriend, Miguel, though he had urged our meeting. Both are active in a local Pentecostal-like church.

She said she feels pure pain.

"Do you know what is giving you so much pain? How are things going between you and Miguel?" I ask, assuming that her suffering is related in some way to struggles with him.

"No, my pain has nothing to do with Miguel. My hurt is related to God," she tells me.

She tells me that she believes that God is angry with her.

"I am afraid that I will never be able to succeed with God. I am always failing. I am really worried that when Jesus returns I will be left here during the tribulation," she said, beginning to cry.

She told me how she had felt at one point when she was making love with Miguel. "He suddenly said: 'This is not pleasing to God. What we are doing is wrong. You are married. We are committing adultery.' From that time on I felt horrible. When I got pregnant I felt especially bad, like I should abort the baby, or give it up for adoption. This baby was the fruit of sin. This baby is the fruit of adultery. When the baby was born and the doctor placed it on my chest, I looked at it and thought it looked like a worm. I despised it. Then I let it drink some of my milk.

"Later, after they had taken some blood and I saw her laying there with her Band-Aids, I thought, What did she do? I felt compassion for her. Now, she is the only one I feel good with. My daughter tells me: 'You are mine.' She strokes my hair and she kisses me."

"Well," I respond, "maybe this is God's way of showing you that God loves you. The fruit of your relationship is giving you comfort, not condemnation."

This was comforting to her. I ask her whether she would like to work on healing her relationship with God. She says yes, that was very important to her. I write down on a card a number of passages where Jesus relates with different women who felt condemned (John 4:7–54; 8:1–11; Luke 7:36–50; 8:42b-56), and we set a time to get together the following week. Like Consuela, many people are crushed to the point of despair by their perception that God views them as offenders.

Inmates are constantly under the close scrutiny of prosecutors and judges. They assume that God views them with even more rigor. Many therefore avoid God. They feel the need for refuge from the detective's inspecting eye. Many feel guilt for their offenses and fear that other, undetected crimes may at any time come to light, leading to new charges. Attorneys caution the accused that anything they say and do can be used against them in a court of law. Remaining silent or denying the truth is recommended as the safest course. Since God and the human judge tend to be collapsed together in many people's minds, hiding from the Deity or presenting one's "best" self appear the only options. Honestly coming to God with your real self is viewed as suicidal—much as it indeed would be before a human judge. I propose reading Genesis 2–3 viewing God as physician/spiritual director, the first transgression as distrust due to a negative image of God, and the law as medicinal. This interpretation runs into resistance from a dominant theology deeply rooted in people's memory.

The traditional read of Genesis 2–3, with its accompanying creation, fall, and redemption model, feeds many people's worst fears. Nearly everyone I work with is superficially familiar with the traditional interpretation, which usually goes something like this: God creates everything from the beginning in seven days, making it all originally good. God gives humans a perfect garden, and commands them not to eat of a particular tree. The evil serpent deceives the woman. Eve disobeys first, then Adam.[1] They eat the fruit and are no longer perfect, having committed the original sin. God curses everyone and casts them out of paradise. The first humans disobey God's command of their own free will, so they deserve God's punishments. Sins have consequences. God acts swiftly to punish wrongdoing. Criminals who get caught can thus expect to be swiftly punished. They deserve prison just as Adam and Eve deserved exile from the garden. It is thought that repentance (understood as being sorry for your sin and changing your behavior), submission to God's sentence, and obedience can save a person from being eternally punished. Everyone must submit to the moral order to be saved. If people cannot submit to God's decrees, they will be damned, and it's their own damned fault.

This traditional reading appears to have support from the Bible and provides an explanation for the current state of affairs. This explanation justifies God, presenting him as a cosmic law enforcer meting out a just sentence; the fair consequence he had warned of would come for lawbreaking. This story mobilizes some people by instilling fear, through reminding them of the consequences of disobedience. These interpretations are deeply ingrained in many people's minds, keeping them from a fresh reading of the first chapters of the Bible.

To set the context for a jail Bible study on Genesis 2–3, I ask the men whether they envision God as a judge, and what they think sin is. They look at me as if I have asked them the obvious. Everyone agrees that they see God as a judge and sin as disobedience.

"After all—that is why we are here?" someone says. "We are paying for our sins and crimes. God has us here."

"If sin is disobedience, what is it that we are disobeying when we are sinning?" I ask. "What do you think we are supposed to obey?"

"God," someone ventures. "The rules in the Bible," he specifies.

Most everyone in the group looks up, assuming this is the right answer.

"The laws of the country?" someone responds, wondering whether this is the answer I am seeking.

"Really, I am not sure," I say, in all honesty. "Let's look at a very famous passage to see if it helps us answer these questions. Let's see whether it supports the idea of God's being a judge and disobedience as being the worst offense."

I invite everyone to turn to Genesis 2:16–17, and one of the men reads it.

> And the LORD God commanded the man, "You may freely eat of every tree of the garden; but of the tree of the knowledge of good and evil you shall not eat, for in the day that you eat of it you shall die."

"Here we have one of the first commands that God ever gives humans. What is the first commandment that God commands?" I ask.

I encourage the group to look carefully at the text, noting exactly what is being said to whom, where, and when.[2]

"God said not to eat of the tree of the knowledge of good and evil or they would die," says someone.

I agree that this is one of God's commands. I ask the men if they see anything else in the text. After a long silence one of the participants says:

"It says here that they could eat of all the trees in the garden except that one."

In nearly every Bible study I lead on this passage, people pick up immediately on the negative command, interpreting it as a prohibition. This happens for two reasons: most interpreters assume Scripture is, first and foremost, information about how people are supposed to live so as to please God. Second, negative images of God as strict lawgiver and judge deeply affect their reading, causing them to gravitate toward supporting evidence for their worst fears.

The reigning image of God as judge and the Bible as God's laws crushes the hopes of most offenders from the start. The system's very labeling of people as "habitual offenders" accurately describes what men and women already feel about themselves. They do not have it in them to succeed at complying with the rigorous demands of the legal system and of its religious equivalents.

The rule of law in America is revered like a god by its law-enforcement agents, prosecutors, judges, probation officers. Its architects, the "lawmakers" in state houses of representatives and in the U.S. Congress, pride themselves on designing laws for the people and by the people for the preservation of life, liberty, and the pursuit of happiness. The public's demand that criminals pay for their crimes both through doing time in jail or prison and paying heavy fines has created a monster God whose demands are endless and desire for compliance insatiable.

The men who attend my jail Bible studies are there in jail to face the state's charges against them. They stand accused of many different offenses. Many have served time before, and are there on probation violations related to the same charges. The weight of the accusations and penalties is often heavier than they are able to carry. Consequently, they are either crushed to the point of suicidal despair or they refuse to take responsibility for their actions. They slide out from under the heavy weight of accusations by ignoring the gravity of their deeds and the resulting punishment or by denouncing the system as unjust, unworthy of their respect.

I know from direct experience with men and women released from jail that the system's efforts to hold people responsible for their actions can crush all hope. I see this with Julio, the twenty-six–year-old Chicano man from Stockton, California, in chapter 2. Julio ran with the gangs and dealt drugs, starting when he was ten. He tells me he's been in and out of confinement since he was twelve years old. He has two daughters with his twenty-two-year-old girlfriend Laura, who already has two other sons from a previous relationship. Julio's driver's license was taken away because of a previous drunk driving charge (DUI [driving under the influence]), so he cannot drive to work. In order to get his license back he must pay over ten thousand dollars to the courts in fines and restitution for past offenses. The courts have turned over all of Julio's fines to a collection agency, which has added its fees and compounded interest to the already impossible-to-pay-back debt. When Julio was doing his six months in jail, Laura had gone on welfare. Once released, Julio manages to find a good job constructing and setting up scaffolding. He comes into our Family Support Center one day, frustrated and angry.

"Look, pastor," says Julio in outrage, "they've garnished half of my wages. Look at this paycheck! The DSHS [Department of Social and Health Services] say that I have to pay back child support for my kids for the six months I've been in jail. Here I am, working to support Laura and my kids. But I can't support them now on half of my wages! I'm gonna quit and go back to selling drugs or something. What's the point of me working to pay back the fucking state?"

I see his point, and ask to look at the letter from DSHS. An 800 number, the name of a caseworker, and the extension number are written plainly in case there are any questions. I ask him if he has called the person, and he says it probably will not make any difference. I encourage him to try, and he says he is too mad. He asks if I will call.

I call the 800 number and reach a recorded greeting with a long list of complicated selections. I make a selection that requires a thoughtful, educated guess, and am routed to the voice mail of the caseworker. I am asked to leave my name and phone number. Julio, however, does not have a phone. For the time being he is living in a migrant labor camp. I leave my name and phone number. The caseworker calls me back the next day. I am able to negotiate the garnishing down to 15 percent of his weekly paycheck. The caseworker insists that Julio will have to pay back the full amount of child support that Laura had collected. Julio accepts this with great reluctance, and takes up his cross of a life of indentured servitude.

If I had not been there to bring him through this crisis, he would have been back dealing heroin within a few days. The courts and social system place weights of responsibility on men and women that give them almost no way out of being habitual offenders.

The First Commandment

Most of my habitual-offender attendees assume that God is even more rigorous than the system, since God sees and knows all. So it comes as a surprise to discover that God's first command is not what they expect.

We discuss how the first command is actually a positive command, to eat from every tree in the garden. Since most people are more used to hearing negative commands than positive, they miss this first, very positive command of God.[3] I observe that in Hebrew the text actually repeats the word "eat" twice, which is often translated as "freely eat" or "surely eat," and could be translated "eat, eat."

"So what does this first commandment tell us about who God is?" I ask, attempting to challenge the reigning negative theology right from the start.

I find that I often need to ask this question several times in different ways. Few people are accustomed to reading Scripture for what it teaches about God.

"If the only information we had about God was this first command, what would this call to 'eat of every tree in the garden' tell us?" I ask again.

The men are thrown off guard by the question, but soon are loosening up and offering answers. We talk about how God looks very generous and good based on this first command. God offers everything he has made to human beings. There are no advance requirements or charges for eating. Everything is a gift from a God who is gracious, wanting his creatures to freely share in the abundance.

"So how, then, are we to understand this second command?" I ask the men.

We talk about how this command reflects God's desire that people avoid dangers and death. This command can be heard as coming more from a physician or parent than from a judge. A doctor's orders to not eat something would be understood as preventive health advice, rather than as a legalistic prohibition. A parent's orders to a child to not cross a busy street show the parent's love and desire to protect. Trust in the parent or doctor is based on the belief that they care about our health and security and are working for our best interests. The fact that God does not say, "If you eat of the fruit I will kill you or punish you," supports reading this command as parental protection or a doctor's orders rather than as a legal requirement. The Hebrew text's ending, "for in the day that you eat of it you shall die," presents death as a natural consequence of eating rather than as a punishment.

Resisting the Serpent Theologian

Once we are off to a good start toward a new reading, I suggest that we read what the serpent has to say about God's command. The dialogue between the snake and the woman is the first theological discourse, where God is imaged in the third person. Before we read Genesis 3:1–3, I encourage people to listen carefully to both what the serpent says about God and the way the woman responds. Now that we know something about this first command, we can evaluate their perceptions of God.

> Now the serpent was more crafty than any other wild animal that the LORD God had made. He said to the woman, "Did God say, 'You shall not eat from any tree in the garden'?" The woman said to the serpent, "We may eat of the fruit of the trees in the garden; but God said, 'You shall not eat of the fruit of the tree that is in the middle of the garden, nor shall you touch it, or you shall die.'"

"According to the serpent, what was God's first command to the humans?" I ask.

"He says the opposite of what God said," responds a man enthusiastically. "He says that God said they were not to eat of any tree in the garden."

People are surprised to be able to spot so clearly a countertheology that is so different from God's original command.

"So, what do the serpent's words and depiction of the Lord's command tell us about the serpent's image of God?" I ask, hoping to draw out a summary of the first negative theology.

"The serpent presents God as prohibiting them from everything," someone says.

"A God of rules and laws, who doesn't let them enjoy the fruits of the garden," says another. "The serpent wants the woman to think that God is stingy, wanting everything for himself."

We talk about how unattractive God would be if the serpent were right. The image of a liberal, generous, good God who desires that humans enjoy life and who seeks to protect them from danger stands in stark contrast to the serpent's dark picture of an unlovable, miserly God of prohibitions.

The evil one draws people away from their first love by positing an idol in the place of God. This idol is a God of the serpent's making, a perverse God who is far less than the self-revealing God of Genesis 1:1–2:24. The serpent even refers to God using the generic title Elohim (literally, gods). He does not pronounce God's name LORD (YHWH), or refer to God using the personal name used throughout Genesis 2:4–24, YHWH Elohim.

"So what do you think of the woman's response?" I ask. "Did the woman answer the serpent rightly?"

At first everyone nods. They feel she has answered correctly. After a while someone mentions that the woman adds something to the command: "or touch it."

We talk about how the woman's addition of the second verb "nor shall you touch" shows that the woman is moving from seeing God as a liberal, loving, freely giving God to a God of rules and prohibition.[4]

I ask the group whether there is anything more the woman could have said about God to counter the serpent's theology. We talk at length about how the woman understates the positive "We may eat of the fruit of the trees in the garden" in a way that does not reflect an accurate, adequately positive image of God.

"The woman does not correct the serpent. The woman could have spoken much more forcefully about God. She could have said: 'No, you are wrong. It is not just any god who has commanded us. A personal God, the Lord God is a good God, rich in loving-kindness. The Lord God commanded us: 'Eat eat of *every* tree.' The Lord loves us so much that he warned us to be careful, because he does not want us to die. The Lord told us not to eat of *just one* of the trees,'" I comment. "But there is still much more that she could have said."

I invite the group to read Genesis 2:4b–9, 15. This section tells much about God that we as readers know is absent from the woman's response. I invite the men to keep an eye open for God's actions that reveal God's person as the text is read.

> In the day that the LORD God made the earth and the heavens, when no plant of the field was yet in the earth and no herb of the field had yet sprung up—for the LORD God had not caused it to rain upon the earth, and there was no one to till the ground; but a stream would rise from the earth, and water the whole face of the ground—then the LORD God formed man from the dust of the ground, and breathed into his nostrils the breath of life; and the man became a living being. And the LORD God planted a garden in Eden, in the east;

and there he put the man whom he had formed. Out of the ground the LORD God made to grow every tree that is pleasant to the sight and good for food, the tree of life also in the midst of the garden, and the tree of the knowledge of good and evil. . . .

The LORD God took the man and put him in the garden of Eden to till it and keep it.

I ask the men to consider how this story about God's actions for the first humans might have helped the woman respond more truly to the serpent. What does God do, according to this passage?

We discuss together how Genesis 2:4b–9 depicts God's actions using a number of positive verbs. The Lord God *made* the heavens and the earth (2:4b), *formed* man from the dust of the ground, and *breathed* into his nostrils the breath of life (2:7). We talk about the special and very personal attention that the Lord gives to the human, who is formed and given life completely by grace. The Lord takes the initiative throughout this story, *planting* a garden, *putting* there the human whom he had formed, and *causing to grow* "every tree that is pleasant to the sight and good for food" (2:9). To further highlight God's caretaking initiative and the human as passive beneficiary, the narrator even repeats that the Lord God *took* the man and *put him* in the garden (2:15). God's command must be read in the larger context of God's life-giving provision.

I suggest that a clearer remembering of God's past actions and goodness might have prevented the woman from being seduced by the serpent's bleak theology. The woman could have stressed to the serpent how different the Lord (YHWH) is from the God the serpent describes: This Lord has made the heavens and the earth. This God has personally formed the human, breathed into his nostrils, and given him life. This Lord has planted a garden for him, taken and placed the human there, and caused all the good and beautiful trees to grow for our food. Finally, this God gave me life through separating me from this human, giving me a special role before my husband, making us one flesh.

The woman says none of these things. Her theology is weak, vulnerable to the next assault of the serpent theologian.

"Let's look at how the serpent responds to the woman's theology," I suggest. A volunteer reads Genesis 3:4–5.

But the serpent said to the woman, "You will not die; for God knows that when you eat of it your eyes will be opened, and you will be like God, knowing good and evil."

The serpent goes even farther in its negative depiction of God. According to the serpent God is not only miserly, God is a controlling power-monger, who lies to protect his supremacy. The serpent succeeds in getting the woman to ponder a detestable God. This focus on a false image of God, the idol, pulls the woman away from gazing on the loving YHWH. Once the woman is no longer standing consciously before the true God of love, she becomes weak and vulnerable to being seduced by the image.

I constantly see that negative images of God are what most separate people from God. Distanced from love, we are vulnerable to seduction. People in revolt against God are often running from the God of deism, an imaginary God who is nothing more than a human-constructed idol. I ask the men why they think the serpent presents these negative images of God.

We talk together about how lies, gossip, and slander can be used to separate a lover from the beloved or a people from their leader. The serpent deliberately inspired distrust through suggesting that God is not good, but diabolical. Is the serpent jealous of the people's special relationship with God? we wonder. Maybe this creature represents the forces that covet and actively pursue the human's adoration and allegiance. We agree that the woman's listening to the malicious gossip affects her, distracting her away from the original command.

> So when the woman saw that the tree was good for food, and that it was a delight to the eyes, and that the tree was to be desired to make one wise, she took of its fruit and ate; and she also gave some to her husband, who was with her, and he ate. Then the eyes of both were opened, and they knew that they were naked; and they sewed fig leaves together and made loincloths for themselves. (Gen. 3:6–7)

After reading these final verses together that describe the "fall," I ask the group what they think finally leads to the first transgression. We agree that the woman's distrust of God as a result of envisioning God negatively led to her taking of the fruit. In addition, the men observe that the woman's seeing that the fruit was good and beautiful and her desire to be wise led her to take for herself. I point out that at the point that she takes for herself rather than receiving God's provision given by grace, she has separated herself from the garden, the place of total grace.

Discovering a Good God

Some of these ideas are difficult for people unaccustomed to Bible study and discussing ideas to fully absorb. Yet people are quick to make the connection between the woman's taking of the fruit and their own taking of drugs or having affairs. People often talk of how their use of cocaine and other drugs represents a similar action, taking care of their own anxiety through drinking, smoking crack, or having sex. Self-medicating takes the place of seeking and waiting for God's provision. Envisioning God negatively makes trust impossible, leading people to meet their own spiritual and physical needs rather than believing that God will provide.

I urge people to discover through a careful reading of the Scriptures that God is really good. A return to the original command would have kept the woman from being so easily swayed. Remembering the original word and contemplating it with care, as a word that reveals a good God, could have kept the woman strong. The image was more powerful than the word here, especially when the woman's bond with the Lord had been weakened by negative images. I decide to introduce an idea if people want to go deeper: the woman was not present when God commanded the man.

We speculate, like many of the ancient Jewish interpreters, that the woman could have known about the Lord's command only from her husband, who is standing beside her when the serpent speaks (Gen. 3:6). In a subsequent study we look in more detail at the relationship between man and woman in Genesis 1–3.

"What command had God given to the woman and the man together?" I ask, inviting the men to read Genesis 1:

> God blessed them, and God said to them, "Be fruitful and multiply, and fill the earth and subdue it; and have dominion over the fish of the sea and over the birds of the air and over every living thing that moves upon the earth." (v. 28)

"Did the woman fulfill this command?" I ask the men. "Did she exercise her dominion 'over every living thing that moves upon the earth?'" I ask.

Everyone can see that the roles are reversed in the rapport between the serpent and the woman. The woman did not exercise her dominion over the creeping thing. Rather, she even let the "living thing that moves upon the earth" define God for her. The men are surprised to discover how the Scriptures counter the dominant theology, which sees nature and history, anything that happens, as revealing God's will and person.

Humans' dominion over nature is not at all evident to most of the men and women with whom I work. Everything visible does not look as if it is really under the authority of finite, vulnerable humans. The New Testament affirmations—that in Jesus Christ's subjugation of death all things have been put under the feet of humans—are encouraging but not yet fully realized. The good news here is that humans are freed from a theology that subjugates them under the domination of the natural world (death, disease, ecosystems), identified as God's sovereign will. Accepting nature as God's will (hurricanes, sickness, death, crop failures, e.g.) fatalistically leads to identifying nature and God, creature and creator. Looking to nature, we encounter both a deterministic and a capricious God.

God sees the serpent as good, like all the other animals (Gen. 1:25). The problem lies in the woman's abdication of her role as image of God and crowning pinnacle of creation, with dominion over the serpent and the rest of creation. She gives up this role to the most cunning of beasts, which exercises dominion over her.[5] In stepping into a relationship with the creature, she lets the visible creation subjugate her by mediating God to her rather than hearing God's command through the invisible Word. This invisible Word would have come mediated to her through her husband, who also was the image of God. Rather than receiving and contemplating this Word as it is communicated to her through the human image of God, she heeds a false word from a creature. In so doing she exchanges the revelation of a good and loving God for an oppressive and unattractive God, in a way reminiscent of Romans 1:21–23:

> For though they knew God, they did not honor him as God or give thanks to him, but they became futile in their thinking, and their senseless minds were darkened. Claiming to be wise, they became fools; and they exchanged the glory of the immortal God for images resembling a mortal human being or birds or four-footed animals or reptiles.

We look at the minimal role of the man in this story, who appears to passively accept without questioning what his wife offers. We decide that the man's error is in his negligence and in his listening to his wife rather than to the Lord's original command to him. We close by reading Proverbs 3:17–18, an intertexual link to Genesis 2 through use of the same language for holding fast to wisdom as is used to describe the man's holding fast to his wife in Genesis 2:24:

> Her way are ways of *pleasantness*,
>   and all her paths are peace.
> She is a tree of life to those who lay hold of her;
>   those who hold her fast are called happy.

As inmates, Mexican farmworkers or Honduran campesinos begin to catch these distinctions between God and nature, Word and object, and between God's will and fate, a new, exciting theological world opens up to them. Many feel challenged to read more carefully, paying attention to what the text does and does not reveal about God.

Confronting God

After contemplating the good God visible in Genesis 1–2, people are ready to look at God's first words of confrontation with the transgressor humans anew.

Together we discuss the possibility that once the first humans have accepted and acted out of the serpent's negative image of God, it is only natural that they would fear God's presence. They have transgressed against a "bad god," and consequently fear a severe reaction. They hide their nakedness and shame, as if God were all-seeing. They seek to cover themselves in the same way they had taken and eaten for themselves, rather than depending on God to cover them: "They sewed fig leaves together and made loincloths for themselves" (Gen. 3:7).

God's presence walking in the garden and God's lack of omnipresence, as one who must ask them where they are, stand in stark contrast to their perceptions.

> They heard the sound of the LORD God walking in the garden at the time of the evening breeze, and the man and his wife hid themselves from the presence of the LORD God among the trees of the garden. (Gen. 3:8)

The first humans expect God to come as a punishing judge. If they had seen God as a parent and physician seeking to protect them, they might have come to God as a physician who can heal them, delivering them from impending death. God's call to the humans in verse 9 can be interpreted as the call of a concerned parent or physician coming to the rescue, rather than as a punisher to be feared.

> But the LORD God called to the man, and said to him, "Where are you?"

God's question to the man gives the man the opportunity to seek help after eating the deadly fruit. The man refuses to approach God as a parent, physician, or trustworthy confidant he can come to with his problem. He avoids speaking the truth as if he is hiding before an accusing judge. He says:

> "I heard the sound of you in the garden, and I was afraid, because I was naked; and I hid myself." (Gen. 3:10)

God's response invites the man to trust.

> "Who told you that you were naked? Have you eaten from the tree of which I commanded you not to eat?" (V. 11)

God's invitation to the man to trust his goodness and return to a relationship of confidence is once again rejected. The man and woman both seek protection through their own justifications, counteraccusations, and scapegoating.

> The man said, "The woman whom you gave to be with me, she gave me fruit from the tree, and I ate." Then the LORD God said to the woman, "What is this that you have done?" The woman said, "The serpent tricked me, and I ate." (Vv. 12–13)

Refusing God's help, the man and woman will now experience God's medicinal judgment. The Lord curses the serpent, placing it among the most humble, "upon [its] belly" (Gen. 3:14), making it an enemy of humans and assuring its final domination by the offspring of the woman ("he will strike your head, and you will strike his heel," v. 15).

Could the woman's pain in bearing/raising children be describing a condition that would lead the woman to depend on God? Could the judgment "yet your desire shall be for your husband, and he shall rule over you" (v. 16) be a way to focus the woman away from the creature, and back to the human, image of God and mediator of the Word? Finally the judgment for the man is related to his listening to her voice rather than the voice of God. The cursing of the ground means the man no longer lives naturally by grace, but by the sweat of his brow. God takes the humans' decision to "take and eat," or save themselves by their own work, seriously, placing them under the bondage of the ecosystem, seen not as revealing God but bringing them to a place of pain "all the days of your life" (v. 17). Rather than being passive beneficiaries of God's action for them, human life outside the garden of grace is marked by thorns and thistles (v. 18), sweat and death (v. 19). Exile from the garden means a life of "till[ing] the ground from which [he was] taken." The cherubim and flaming sword represent the impossibility of self-salvation by human action (eating of the tree of life). The humans are destined to live in a hostile world "east of Eden." The only sign of hope is God's willingness to continue in a protective role. "And the LORD God made garments of skins for the man and for his wife, and clothed them" (Gen. 3:21).

Who Gets Divine Favor? Understanding Cain and Abel

Immigrants with whom I work often complain about being discriminated against because of their nationality, race, language, or social class. Immigrant women complain that white people in grocery stores cling to their purses when they go by, and cashiers are often rude to them. Hispanic inmates regularly complain about how white defendants charged for the same crimes as they are get sentenced to less time. Hispanic people, whether Chicano or new immigrants, tell of harassment by the State Patrol and other law-enforcement agents, who look for any excuse to pull them over and question them about their legal status. Second- or third-generation Hispanics, known as Chicanos, often treat undocumented immigrants with respect, calling them "border brothers" and including them warmly in *la raza*. When a conflict arises, however, they are quick to label them "wetbacks" or "illegals." Chicano store owners and crew bosses often treat new immigrants harshly, pretending they do not understand their Spanish, pressuring them to do extra work, and even threatening to call the Border Patrol on them. Mixteco- and Triqui-speaking Oaxacan Indians are at the bottom of the immigrant pecking order in Skagit County. They are often given the hardest work and treated with the least respect.

I usually lead two separate studies on the Cain and Abel story, because of the tremendous richness and relevancy of this story. One evening in the jail I begin the discussion with an introduction and some questions.

"Right at the beginning of the Bible we have the first mention of sin and the story of murder. It does not take long to get to some bad crime. What is at the origin of violence and murder? How does God deal with this?" I ask, trying to spark interest.

People are silent, unable to enter into the discussion with such a theoretical question, and with too many questions. I try again.

"Have any of you ever seen someone around you get special treatment by someone in power, better treatment than was given to you? Was there someone in your family who was your mother's or father's favorite?"

"All of us have," one of the inmates responds. "At least, I have seen this in my family."

"In court the *gabachos* get better deals than we Mexicans. They get lighter sentences for the same crimes," said one Mexican man. Others nodded their heads in agreement.

"The police stop us just because we're Mexican," another guy said. "There is a lot of racism around here."

We talk on about beliefs in Mexico that if you're rich, it's probably a sign of God's favor, whereas if you're poor, it's seen as evidence that God is for some reason against you. Benefits are seen as divine blessings, and disadvantages or calamities are viewed as divine curses. Everyone agrees that it feels bad to not be favored, and that jealousy and anger are common responses.

"Let's check out this story about the first brothers and see if it helps us understands something new," I suggested. One of the men read Genesis 4:1–16, but I stopped him after verse 2.

> Now the man knew his wife Eve, and she conceived and bore Cain, saying, "I have produced a man with the help of the LORD." Next she bore his brother Abel. Now Abel was a keeper of sheep, and Cain a tiller of the ground.

"What do we know about these two brothers from this story?" I asked. The men looked down at their tattered jail Bibles, not yet convinced there was anything of particular importance to notice. Someone pointed out only that Abel was a shepherd and Cain was a farmer.

"Who appears to be more important, perhaps the most favored son of the man and Eve?" I asked, prodding them on to a closer read.

"Cain," said a man, "because he was the firstborn."

"Yes—in fact, he is the first human ever to be born," I add.

Interest grows as I point out that there was far more detailed description of Cain's birth, with mention of the man knowing his wife, Eve, and three motherly acts recorded: she *conceived*, *bore* Cain, and *spoke* ("saying"). Her words "I have produced a man [a full-grown man] with the help of the LORD," and her naming him Cain—"I have gotten"—show no sign of God's judgment that the woman would experience pain in childbirth. In fact, the woman's attitude sounds *machista*. Is she accepting the judgment as a challenge to be overcome through her strength and the vigor of her offspring? I wonder. Maybe the predicted pain will have more to do with what follows in the story, I suggest, inviting the men to take a close look at Eve's second-born, Abel.

We discover together that little attention is given to Abel in comparison to Cain. The mother is the subject of only one verb: "Next she *bore*," and the infant is referred to vis-à-vis Cain as "his brother Abel." I point out that the meaning of Abel's name (vapor/breath) and hardly noteworthy birth as second-born, in contrast to "I have gotten" and possibly "zeal," shows the special favor accorded to the privileged Cain.

"So according to this story, who is the preferred child? What would it feel like to be Abel compared to being Cain?" I ask.

"Cain is the preferred," someone says. "Abel is unimportant."

"Here there is discrimination right in the first family," someone observes. "Cain is the favorite child. He is the firstborn. He is stronger."

"So what happened next? Let's look at how God sees the two brothers," I suggest.

> In the course of time Cain brought to the LORD an offering of the fruit of the ground, and Abel for his part brought of the firstlings of his flock, their fat portions. And the LORD had regard for Abel and his offering, but for Cain and his offering he had no regard. (Gen. 4:3–5a)

"Why did God prefer Abel's offering over Cain's?"

The men gave answers I have grown to expect of people who know of no other way to gain divine favor than by successful religious posturing.

"Abel's offering was better," someone says. "It was from the firstlings of his flock, their fat portions. Cain's offering was just from the fruit of the ground."

"Maybe God prefers meat. God likes *barbacoa de borrego* [roasted lamb or sheep, a Mexican favorite] more than vegetable, fruit, or whatever Cain brought from the ground," commented a good-natured Mexican inmate.

We all laugh, and I feel sad for the men. The thought of their beloved food, salsas, and fiestas makes the jail fare of mashed potatoes and macaroni and cheese and sandwiches with no hot sauce that much more difficult to tolerate.

"Well, that is possible, and many people over the centuries have thought these things. Does God say why he chose Abel's offering over Cain's?" I ask.

"Abel brought his offering with a sincere heart," someone says.

"Cain was bad," another man mentions. "Later God says to him, 'If you do well, will you not be accepted? And if you do not do well, sin is lurking at the door'" (4:7). Cain must not have done well—for that reason he was not accepted.

"What do we know about Cain's vocation and his offering from Genesis 1–3?"

I point out that the first humans are still called to: "be fruitful and multiply, and fill the earth and subdue it" (1:28) and to: "cultivate and keep" (2:15) the garden. Problems arise, however, after the first humans lose their trust in God and disregard his later word to them. I invite the men to read Genesis 3:16–24. One of the men slowly reads verses 16–21 in Spanish as the others follow along in their Bibles.

> To the woman he said,
>
>> I will greatly increase your pangs in childbearing;
>>> in pain you shall bring forth children,
>> yet your desire shall be for your husband,
>>> and he shall rule over you.
>
> And to the man he said,
>
>> Because you have listened to the voice of your wife,
>>> and have eaten of the tree
>> about which I commanded you,
>>> "You shall not eat of it,"
>> cursed is the ground because of you;
>>> in toil you shall eat of it all the days of your life;
>> thorns and thistles it shall bring forth for you;
>>> and you shall eat the plants of the field.
>> By the sweat of your face
>>> you shall eat bread
>> until you return to the ground,
>>> for out of it you were taken;
>> you are dust,
>>> and to dust you shall return.
>
> The man named his wife Eve, because she was the mother of all living. And the LORD God made garments of skins for the man and for his wife, and clothed them.

The eventual conflict between the woman's two children and Cain's unsuccessful offering are best read with the earlier commands and divinely ordained negative consequences in mind.[6] I ask the men questions that point them back to Genesis 3:17–24 for information that might help us understand the nature of Cain's offering.

"What do we know about Cain and his vocation from this story?" I ask.

"Cain works the ground that God has cursed," someone observes.

"So what might the fruit of this cursed ground be, according to this passage?" I ask.

"It says the ground will produce thorns and thistles?" someone comments questioningly. He corrects himself and adds "plants of the field" when he realizes that Cain probably did not bring thorns and thistles to God.

This man's mention of thorns and thistles brings up an idea that could be helpful and needs to be pursued. I wonder why Cain brings this offering of the fruit of the ground in the first place. Before pursuing this question directly with the men, we discuss together that Cain is the first man mentioned who cultivates the cursed ground. I search for language to describe this scene that makes it easier for immigrants to see equivalents of this scene in their own lives.

"It looks to me as if God has deported the first humans from the garden and sentenced them to a lifetime bar to reentry," I suggest. "All-powerful Border Patrol angels are standing by." I invite someone to read Genesis 3:22–24:

> Then the LORD God said, "See, the man has become like one of us, knowing good and evil; and now, he might reach out his hand and take also from the tree of life, and eat, and live forever"—therefore the LORD God sent him forth from the garden of Eden, to till the ground from which he was taken. He drove out the man; and at the east of the garden of Eden he placed the cherubim, and a sword flaming and turning to guard the way to the tree of life.

"Cain is outside the garden of Eden, where he has to toil and survive by the sweat of his brow," I summarize. "Why do you think Cain brings an offering to God? Does God ask him to bring an offering?"

"No, God does not ask for anything," someone notes excitedly.

"Maybe Cain wants to win God over. Maybe he is trying to please God so God will let him back in the garden," someone comments.

This comment intrigues the whole group. We talk about how Cain's unsolicited sacrifice might provide a clue to understanding the origins of religion (in contrast to faith). Cain tries to win God's favor through a sacrifice, much as an inmate might try to win a judge's favor through

showing remorse, or a man might try to win over a woman through praising her or bringing her gifts. Cain's religion looks like an attempt to bribe
the Deity, to win God's favor through favors.

"Could God's rejection of Cain's offering be a rejection of religion?"
I ask.

The men are interested, but cautious to embrace this idea fully. They
are still far from convinced. The problem arises in part because God does
accept Abel's sacrifice.

"Why else might Abel's offering have been accepted?" I ask.

I remind the group that Abel is the second-born, the one with the name
that means "vapor," the one least regarded and the second to bring an
offering.[7] Could God's choice of Abel indicate God's choice of the underdog? I argue that God chooses "vapor" over "ardor," the second-born over
the firstborn, the weak one over the macho one as a way of showing that
divine favor comes freely by grace and not by the "sweat of your brow." I
invite the men to turn to 1 Corinthians 1, which appears to confirm this
interpretation, showing God's preference for the nobodies of this world
over the "somebodies."

> Consider your own call, brothers and sisters: not many of you were
> wise by human standards, not many were powerful, not many were
> of noble birth. But God chose what is foolish in the world to shame
> the wise; God chose what is weak in the world to shame the strong;
> God chose what is low and despised in the world, things that are not,
> to reduce to nothing things that are, so that no one might boast in
> the presence of God. He is the source of your life in Christ Jesus, who
> became for us wisdom from God, and righteousness and sanctifica-
> tion and redemption, in order that, as it is written, "Let the one who
> boasts, boast in the Lord." (1 Cor. 1:26–31)

Once the men hear this passage from 1 Corinthians 1, they are convinced
that God has chosen Abel because of God's preferential choice of the
underdog. This is unexpectedly good news for people who are accustomed
to thinking of God as being on the side of the powers and principalities
and the status quo.

I often end Bible studies on Genesis 4 at this point, unless people are especially interested and there is time to explore another issue regarding God's
choice. God's refusal of Cain's efforts to win his favor can be interpreted as
a divine "no" to human efforts to get back into Eden. Does the text suggest
any way back into the garden for people shut out of this place of grace?

Getting Back into Eden: By Efforts, or by Grace?

Cain's offering can be interpreted as designed to win God's favor, with the objective of lessening the curse on the ground or getting back into Eden. Cain attempts to save himself, but his efforts are not effective.

"Do you ever try to save yourself from a problem?" "How do you make yourself more secure when you feel insecure?" and "What are some ways that we try to save ourselves?" are different versions of a question I often ask people to get them to reflect on their lives during Bible studies.

This question leads to lots of individual sharing. New immigrants talk about poverty and lack of opportunity in their villages, which pushed them to leave their families in hopes of working in El Norte and sending money back home. Hope for high wages and the "American dream" draws people to take big risks, crossing the border illegally, wandering through scorching hot deserts with minimal water, toward an unknown destination in the United States. Others tell a far-too-common story, of turning to drug dealing in order to make quick money that they desperately need for a damage deposit and first and last months' rent to get their family into an apartment. Once they start making big money selling cocaine or heroin, it becomes increasingly difficult to go back to a minimum-wage job. Eventually they sell to an undercover drug task-force officer, are arrested and charged with delivery of a controlled substance. Still others confess that they energize themselves by smoking crack cocaine or using crystal meth, or blow away their anxieties drinking or shooting up heroin.

"Maybe we are all looking for what Cain was really looking for," I suggest. "Is what you are doing working? Are you finding the peace or the security that you seek? Are you realizing your dream for your life?" I ask.

Few people I read Scripture with would ever say they have found what they are looking for, have experienced success or security, or realized their dreams. Those outside the jail are submerged in the daily grind of hard physical labor. Many are estranged from their teenage children, who have often lacked the presence of their constantly working parents when they needed them. Now their children may have already dropped out of high school and be parenting their own children. Or they may be hanging with the gangs, stealing car stereos and using and dealing drugs, soon to join the masses in the jail and prison system. Many people lament the years they have spent away from their partners and children while they slaved away making money in the U.S.

Jail inmates are often in the process of losing their wives and children, who are estranged from them because of affairs and other drug- and alcohol-induced chaos preceding their arrest. Others face years in prison resulting from their decision to sell drugs or because of other crimes. Everything they have done has led to a big wall, a bottoming out before the "no" of the system, which is often reinforced by judgments from the church.

"How can we get to a place of peace and contentment? How can we get into Eden, where life is lived abundantly and by grace? How can we enter the kingdom of God?"

Cain's place outside the garden, his vocation to "till the ground from which he was taken," and his final destiny back to the ground reflect the consequences of living by the sweat of your brow or by "active righteousness" rather than by grace. God's no to Cain's offering is a "no" to reentry into Eden via pleasing God through your own efforts, whether they be vocational, political, or religious. Sacrifice, offerings, and bribery are all rejected as means to reenter the place of grace symbolized by the garden.

At the same time, the judgment "for out of it you were taken; you are dust, and to dust you shall return" gives a clue to the way back into the garden. The story of Cain and Abel begins at the same place as Genesis 2:4ff., in the dust outside the garden. The only way back into the garden, to the place of grace, is to return to the port of entry: the dust. In Genesis 4:1ff. humans end up where they began—a place of sterility, dust, and death. Yet this place is also a place of God's work.

"If we read how the first human entered the garden, what might it tell us about how we too can reenter?" I ask. I invite Bible-study participants to read aloud Genesis 2:4b–8, 15:

> In the day that the LORD God made the earth and the heavens, when no plant of the field was yet in the earth and no herb of the field had yet sprung up—for the LORD God had not caused it to rain upon the earth, and there was no one to till the ground; but a stream would rise from the earth, and water the whole face of the ground—then the LORD God formed man from the dust of the ground, and breathed into his nostrils the breath of life; and the man became a living being. And the LORD God planted a garden in Eden, in the east; and there he put the man whom he had formed. . . .
>
> The LORD God took the man and put him in the garden of Eden to till it and keep it.

Outside the garden is this place of dust. People can take up the plow and hoe and try to cultivate the ground out of which they were taken "by the sweat of [their] face." For many though, attempts to save themselves lead to disaster. They bottom out, coming to the place of brokenness and poverty symbolized by dust. Once people come to a place of powerlessness, there is a possibility of new life, of entry into the kingdom of God, of reentry into Eden. Failure or crisis shows that human life is radically dependent on someone who is there outside Eden with them, creating, hovering, speaking, forming, breathing, and ready to take and place them in the garden.

Two Scripture passages come to mind here that are directly related to Genesis 2–4 and often bring great hope to people when studying the Cain and Abel story and others. These passages are Lamentations 3 and Ezekiel 37. Both of them show possibilities for new beginnings. These passages suggest that the only way back into the garden is through the Spirit and the Lord's action of placing people. God alone can save. Just as the first humans were passive beneficiaries of God's forming, breathing, and placing them in the garden, people today can only reenter by grace. God's life-giving action forms life from the dust, benefiting those who have returned to the place of dust.

God's Call and Choice

On another occasion I lead a different Bible study on Cain, which focuses on the second half of the story, Genesis 4:6–16.[8] Though my original plan was to lead a discussion on God's call based on the Lord's call of Abram in Genesis 12, I shifted the study to Genesis 4 according to the need of the moment. Before reading the text I asked the guys an opening question:

"Do you think that God is calling you?"

Blank looks were their only response. I try again:

"Do you ever feel as if God may be calling you, trying to say something to you?"

Rickie, a mustached Chicano guy to my left, said: "No, I haven't felt anything, man. I haven't seen no vision or heard any voices or shit."

"Well, it's like there's an angel here," says Mario (motioning to right above him), "and a demon there" (he motions to his left). "The angel's telling me, 'don't do it,'" says Mario.

"There's something inside that I feel when I'm doing something I know is wrong. Maybe that's God," says Ernesto, an undocumented farmworker from Mexico.

"Maybe that is God," I agree, and then decide to abandon my plan to read Abram's call in Genesis 12 and to look instead at the Cain and Abel story.

When we were about to read the story of Cain and Abel in Genesis 4, one of the men said: "Aren't we going to pray?"

We stood and prayed, then a man read Genesis 4:1–16. We began by briefly reviewing the identity of the characters, what they did, and what happened in this story, before I asked a question designed to lead us in some yet unknown, new direction.

"Why was Cain angry?" I ask.

"He was jealous," responds Mario. "He didn't think it was fair that God preferred his brother's offering over his."

Some of the men want to speculate on why God chose Abel's offering over Cain's. I explain how Cain was the firstborn, and consequently had more rights in that cultural context. I also quickly note that more attention is given to Cain's birth. Eve's words, "I have produced a man with the help of the LORD," contrast with her silence after Abel's birth. Cain's name means "ardor, fervor, or eagerness" in contrast to Abel's, which means "vapor." Cain was the strong one, the brother with the power. Abel was the weak one, the powerless and insignificant man, with few or no rights.

We talk about how, when you are accustomed to seeing yourself as the special, strong, chosen one and firstborn, it is difficult when someone weak and less deserving gets favor, special treatment, or glory.

"Who are the people in our society that have no rights or special treatment?" I ask.

"Us," says Mario.

"No, man, we're not that bad off," says Juan.

"When you're in here, you've lost most of your rights," I add. "Maybe God chose Abel because he was the underdog, the weak one with fewer rights," I suggest. "God doesn't prefer someone with more power and rights. In fact, according to this, God chooses the weaker one. Jesus said: 'I haven't come to save the healthy, but the sick.'"

At this point Juan says: "Hey, did you do something bad in your life to make God punish you, putting you in here to work with us?"

"Well, maybe, but really I think this is a reward, not a punishment. I love working in here with you guys. I have learned more from all of you and others here in this jail than I learned from any of my teachers or nearly anyone," I respond. "This is a reward, not a punishment. The more I'm here, the more I've grown to respect you, often even more than people outside."

They all looked surprised.

"Hey, that's all right," said Johnny, a guy who has just been transferred to Skagit County Jail from Washington State Penitentiary in Walla Walla, for court.

"I actually think you guys are some of the most religious people I know. You're willing to take serious risks for what you believe, unlike most folks who are the supposedly 'good' people outside."

"Hey, now there is a way to look at it," says Johnny.

"So, getting back to the story: How did Cain respond?" I ask again.

"He got mad, he killed Abel."

"Why do you think Cain got so angry? What kind of things happen in your lives, say, right here in the jail even, that make you angry?" I ask.

"When someone disrespects me," says Johnny.

Johnny and others then talk about how white inmates make racist comments, and how some of the guards treat them disrespectfully.

"Jealousy, man, when I feel jealous, I often get angry," says Mario. "Like when I wonder what's happening outside with my lady."

Mario's comments are met with agreement from everyone.

"That's what makes me madder than hell, homes," says a Chicano man bitterly. "My *jaina* [gang slang for girl/chick] won't accept my calls no more, and she hasn't visited me for two weeks, man. One of my homeboys is messing around where he shouldn't be. I know who's going to pay when I get out. I'm gonna kick some ass!"

New inmates bring news and rumors from the street into the jail on a daily basis. People stand in line for the one pay phone in each pod. Often they cannot get through because of blocks for unpaid phone bills or disconnected numbers. The men often ask me to serve as messenger to their girlfriends or spouses, telling them that they are changing or that they love them. The most desperate people call me collect, coaxing me to let them do a three-way call so they can talk with their girlfriend. Powerlessness before a threatened relationship often leads to rage. The wrong look, an insulting comment, or the slightest sign of disrespect triggers fights in the jail, which land inmates in the hole, the solitary confinement cells where people are punished for days and even weeks for aggressive behavior.

"When I see injustices, when things are unfair, that's when I feel anger," says Juan.

The men once again are all in agreement. They mention how *la raza* gets targeted unfairly by the police and the courts. They talk about how their public defenders are not working for them, but are pressuring them to plead guilty rather than risk doing more time if they lose a trial.

"When there's a fight between the Mexican and a white guy, the guards listen to the white guy and throw the Mexican in the hole," says Johnny. "That's not fair, man, that's fucked up if you ask me!"

"Is it the injustice that offends you, or is it that you feel that you are being disregarded or made to look foolish and powerless in a way that makes you feel exposed and powerless?" I ask. "What exactly is happening here with Cain?" I ask, returning to the story.

I briefly present my interpretation that Cain is bringing an unsolicited offering to God to try to get God to lighten up on the sentence that he is serving outside the garden. This sentence includes having to painfully farm the cursed ground, full of thorns and thistles, by the sweat of his brow, a lifetime bar to reentering the garden, and an eventual return to dust in death.

"Could Cain's offering be seen as a gift to get God on his side, or even a bribe?" I ask. I explain how in Honduras, where I lived and worked, the police would often stop people for any little thing, confiscating a driver's license or an identity card, in hopes of getting a bribe. Almost everyone pays bribes to avoid hassles.

"Does this happen in Mexico?" I ask, already knowing the answer. "Have any of you bribed anyone?"

"Yes, all of us have," a man answers, smiling. Everyone in the room nods and smiles.

"How would it feel if the official refused, saying he would never do such a thing?" I ask.

"This would never happen, they always accept," someone says, eliciting lots of smiles and laughter.

"But if they didn't accept, how would you feel?

"Shame. Like a fool," says Mario.

"Have you ever tried to win over a woman by giving gifts and special treatment?"

"Yes, we all have," says Johnny, followed by hearty laughter from everyone.

"How do you feel if all your efforts fail, and then someone comes along and gets the woman with little effort?"

We talk about the feeling of exposure and shame that happens when you make an effort designed to effect change, to influence someone, that is seen and disregarded. The men agree that this may be happening with Cain, and that they have experienced this themselves. The feeling of powerlessness that comes after failing to win favor or achieve your objective can lead to anger, which appears to be the case with Cain.

"When do you get angry? Do you know when you are going to lose your temper?" I ask.

We agree that anger is usually something that builds, and that it can be related to a whole chain of events. At the same time, we observe, the moment when you "lose it" is hard to predict. I point out that in the Hebrew Bible, Cain did not get angry. Anger is described in the Bible as something that happens to people, not something people consciously do.[9] I stress that Cain was not bad, he was just taken over by anger. The Bible makes a distinction between the sin and the person. I state my growing conviction that people are not inherently bad, but are good, made in God's image.

Juan looks at Johnny and smirks. "Good?" They look at each other like I didn't know what I was talking about.

"People are weak," I say. "For this reason we fall to temptations: to anger, lust, pride, envy. . . ." I was trying out my newfound anthropology, gleaned from reading the early Greek church fathers. I tell them how hard-core gangsters who had done time for murder and all kinds of hard crimes had told me, sobbing: "I look scary with my build and all my tattoos and shit, but down deep I'm soft and tender."

"All of us are the same down deep," I conclude.

Juan and Johnny look a little more in agreement, but are not convinced.

We return to the story. "How did God respond to Cain?" I ask.

We talk about how, when anger came upon him, God was present. God wanted to help Cain, to be reconciled to him. God said: "Sin is crouching at the door, but you can dominate it." This distinction between sin and the person appears to encourage the men. God's presence at the moment of Cain's anger, though, is especially surprising. That God would come to Cain in the first place challenges people's view of God as someone whom we have to approach and initiate contact with. God's coming when Cain is angry further challenges an image of God who would only show up if your life is together, or when you are piously praying during Sunday Mass.

"Have any of you experienced anything like this? Has God come to you when you were about to beat up on your wife, fight someone, or something?"

No one can remember ever being visited the way God visited Cain. I phrase the question differently, in hopes that people can think back over their own experiences freshly.

"Do any of you remember ever being interrupted in some way right when you were about to lose your temper, say something out of anger, or get in a fight?" I ask.

Nearly everyone could think of times when they were right on the edge of hitting their partner or fighting somebody. A momentary reflection on the consequences and decision to draw back kept them from being overcome by anger. I suggest that this may have been what happened to Cain. Maybe God comes to us, but we do not recognize God. This is in fact what happened to Cain. I invite the men to reflect on how God spoke to Cain: "Why are you angry? Why has your face fallen?"

"What is God like, according to this passage?" I ask, engaging the men in a theological discussion.

"God does not seem to know why Cain is angry? It's like he doesn't know everything," says Juan.

"Maybe God is trying to get Cain to think about the deeper reasons for his anger. Thinking and understanding himself might have kept him from just reacting," I suggest. "Does God seem like a judge or more like a doctor here?" I ask.

The men can clearly see that God appears more like a doctor or counselor here than like a prosecutor or judge. God is not criticizing Cain, but asking Cain to describe what is wrong with him. If Cain had talked about his jealousy, feelings of powerlessness, and exposure the story would likely have been different. God does in fact offer advice that could also be interpreted as coming from a physician wanting to ensure Cain's success and protection:

> If you do well, will you not be accepted? And if you do not do well, sin is lurking at the door; its desire is for you, but you must master it. (Gen. 4:7)

God shows respect for Cain and confidence that he can overcome this lurking power called "sin." "You must master it!" sounds like the earlier call to the first humans to "fill the earth and subdue it; and have dominion over the fish of the sea and over the birds of the air and over every living thing that moves upon the earth" (Gen. 1:28). God does not give a command like a judge that includes a threat of punishment. God's word to Cain is more like a physician's prescription or preventive health advice. Cain is silent before God's question and disregards God's prescription.

"So what happens if we fail to pay attention to God's call to us?" I ask. "Let's see what happens to Cain." One of the men rereads Genesis 4:8:

> Cain said to his brother Abel, "Let us go out to the field." And when they were in the field, Cain rose up against his brother Abel, and killed him.

Cain's planned killing of his brother Abel looks more like premeditated first-degree murder that could lead to the death penalty in most states, than a crime of passion in the heat of anger. Abel is presented as not only innocent, but even righteous, adding to Cain's offense. These details make the story better news than ever for offenders. The text offers no information justifying Cain's action. Sin is still depicted as separate from Cain, in spite of his planned assassination of his own innocent brother. All the same, God comes to Cain again and again, pursuing him even as he continues to avoid God.

I suggest to the men that even after Cain kills his brother, God does not come as all-knowing judge. God's question to Cain, "Where is your brother Abel?" gives Cain the opportunity to tell God what he has done. God gives Cain every opportunity to approach him for help, much as God had done after his parents' first offense in the garden. Cain shows no remorse and refuses God's advances, responding with a lie and a cold question to the Lord: "I do not know; am I my brother's keeper?"

"As this murderous action becomes worse and worse, it appears that God is more and more present," I say. "What does God finally do?"

> And the LORD said, "What have you done? Listen; your brother's blood is crying out to me from the ground! And now you are cursed from the ground, which has opened its mouth to receive your brother's blood from your hand. When you till the ground, it will no longer yield to you its strength; you will be a fugitive and a wanderer on the earth." (Gen. 4:10–12)

God's questions to Cain must not be read as showing God's ignorance. The fact that God knows is evident when God declares that Abel's blood is crying out to God from the ground. God does not disregard violence, but responds by allowing the violent to suffer the consequences of their actions.

"What finally gets Cain's attention?" I ask, inviting someone to read the next few verses.

> Cain said to the LORD, "My punishment is greater than I can bear! Today you have driven me away from the soil, and I shall be hidden from your face; I shall be a fugitive and a wanderer on the earth, and anyone who meets me may kill me." (Gen. 4:13–14)

"What gets Cain's attention is when God gave him his sentence," says Johnny. "That's when Cain woke up. That's what happens to lots of us," he continues. "At least, speaking for myself, that's what's happening to me, I hope anyway."

"Does this passage mention that God punished Cain?" I ask the group.

We observe that while Cain blames God, God does not take responsibility for punishing Cain. The exile is described as a natural consequence of Cain's action.

We conclude by discussing how Cain starts out as a religious person bringing an offering to a God with whom he has no relationship. The story takes a turn when Cain becomes angry. At that moment God intervenes, taking the initiative to visit and talk with Cain before, and ever more frequently after, he murders his innocent brother. Finally the Lord promises protection, putting a mark on Cain so that no one will kill him.

> Then the LORD said to him, "Not so! Whoever kills Cain will suffer a sevenfold vengeance." And the LORD put a mark on Cain, so that no one who came upon him would kill him. Then Cain went away from the presence of the LORD, and settled in the land of Nod, east of Eden. (Gen. 4:15–16)

Though God approves of Abel's offering, God relates far more with the guilty offender than with the righteous. The righteous even dies, while the offender receives protection. God's grace and protection are freely given, regardless of Cain's actions. God's grace does not force the offender back to God and is not conditional upon Cain's repentance. In fact, the story ends with Cain's going away from the presence of the Lord.

A mark is placed on Cain that assures God's protection. Cain belongs to God in spite of his distancing. The story becomes a parable of Paul's later words: "Where sin increased, grace abounded all the more."

God as Forgiver, Savior, Liberator, or Healer: Which Image?

The images in Genesis 1–4 of God as caring therapist or parent, who shows up when humans are most in trouble, are new for inmates, and recent for me as well. Through my friendship with Daniel Bourguet, membership in the "Fraternité Spirituelle Les Veilleurs" in France, and my reading of the Desert Fathers and early Greek fathers I am exploring some helpful new ways of thinking about God and spirituality. I have been experiencing a growing dissatisfaction with my previous models, which do not appear to bring about healing and liberation for those most in need.

Viewing sin as spiritual malady and God as therapist or physician is giving me a new perspective on the Bible and salvation.[10] For most of my life I have understood sin primarily as willful disobedience or transgression, and salvation as the result of God's forgiveness. The God who forgives is a God envisioned as judge. Liberation theology and my experience in Honduras broadened my perspective, revealing to me the biblical images of sin as economic injustice and oppression, and salvation as justice and liberation by a God viewed as liberator of the poor and oppressed. These models are clearly present in the Scriptures and must be understood and embraced. Alongside them, however, are other ways of imaging God that may be more pastorally fruitful in my new context.

The confession of sin and declaration of forgiveness model operating in Presbyterian, Lutheran, and other mainline churches I frequent is at times of tremendous value. In the jail context, however, it often feels hollow and nearly empty of relevance and any effective power. When I declared to the men and women I counseled that their sins were forgiven, I often felt as if I was using a shotgun approach to proclamation. There are, indeed, those who need this particular word. But when the guards come and take the men through the three steel doors into their confining cells, I feel I have set them up for frustration. The forgiveness I declare has no teeth. The redemption part of the creation, fall, redemption model is relevant only for the other world. The church's forgiveness makes no difference to their physical bodies, which remain in jail to face accusations and possible convictions before the judge, who really has the power. The forgiveness I declare does not correspond to Jesus' forgiveness, which was accompanied by acts of actual deliverance from maladies and demons. Forgiveness meant healing or deliverance for the people Jesus forgave[11] (though Jesus did not expressly forgive many of the people he healed). Since sin was seen as resulting in physical maladies, healing was a concrete sign. What corresponding concrete sign accompanied my proclamation of forgiveness? Absolutely nothing!

The message of forgiveness of sin must continue to be proclaimed when appropriate, but this message, together with salvation by grace alone, must be used with more discernment and precision. When I declare to inmates that they are saved by grace, am I considering the thousands of dollars of court fines, restitution, back child support, and months of probation that await them? Offenders and ex-offenders are immersed in a system that emphasizes to the extreme salvation by works. Salvation by grace alone assumes an image of God as judge or celestial sovereign that is present, thankfully, in the Scriptures, but in precise contexts and accompanied by palpable signs. If this message does not correspond with actual debt forgiveness and relief from painstaking accountability to progress-measuring probation officers and judges, then either God's salvation is invisible and merely "spiritual" or the state is really the more powerful force/God.

I run up against the limitations of the liberation paradigm on a regular basis, as well. There is clearly a place for advocacy among immigrants and inmates, who often lack a voice, adequate legal representation, and knowledge of their rights, and experience exploitation by employers and discrimination from the larger society. Sometimes posting bail is a possible and appropriate sign of redemption. I am often powerless, however, to actually physically liberate someone from INS detention, or from jail or prison. Even when I am able to bail someone out or advocate for someone's actual release, many ex-offenders for whom I advocate go straight back to drugs and violence in spite of their (and my) best intentions to change their lives. They commit crimes that land them back in jail, where the message of concrete, physical liberation cannot be fleshed out in their lives. Neither forgiveness of sin nor liberation from oppression is always the appropriate message or action. They may sound like good news, but they are of no consequence and little more than pie in the sky when it comes down to real possibilities.

The more I read the Bible with people on the margins, the more I see the poverty of the church's proclamation, which is often irrelevant to people on the streets. I am seeing the Scriptures like a doctor's bag with a vast array of remedies. The church's proclamation is too often so limited in scope and depth that it fails to bring people (especially the damned) the needed liberation. With our message of forgiveness of sins or even salvation by grace, too often we treat hurting people like physicians who only know how to prescribe one drug for every illness. To someone with a headache, "Here, take this tetracycline." To someone with a broken leg, "Tetracycline will make you better!" To one suffering from insomnia or depression: "Tetracycline!" God the judge is ushered in to pronounce pardon—a spiritual acquittal with no immediate bodily repercussions. While in our own society we have every manner of expert ready to respond to a wide diversity of needs, we too often fail to see the vast diversity of ways God shows up, speaks, and acts in the diverse circumstances in which God's people find themselves.

The notion of sin as sickness and God as spiritual healer is profoundly biblical. In Isaiah 6:9–10, lack of understanding, spiritual blindness, and deafness are depicted as maladies that result from being turned away from God. Returning to the Lord leads to healing.

And he said, "Go and say to this people:

'Keep listening, but do not comprehend;
keep looking, but do not understand.'
Make the mind of this people dull,
   and stop their ears,
   and shut their eyes,
so that they may not look with their eyes,
   and listen with their ears,
and comprehend with their minds,
   and turn and be healed."
(Isa. 6:9–10)

In Jeremiah 3:22, God says: "I will heal your faithlessness," depicting unfaithfulness as something to be healed, not punished or forgiven. Psalm 103 describes God as healing all of the soul's diseases:

Bless the LORD, O my soul,
   and all that is within me,
   bless his holy name.
Bless the LORD, O my soul,
   and do not forget all his benefits—
who forgives all your iniquity,
who heals all your diseases.
(Ps. 103:1–3)

In Psalm 41:4 the psalmist cries: "O LORD, . . . heal my soul" (NASB). God is the one who heals the soul. According to Scripture, God is the only one who heals[12] and forgives. Envisioning God as a healer of sin, understood as sickness and spiritual troubles, can lead to a whole new comfort level before God. Before a God envisioned as condemning judge, we are more likely to hide our sin, understood as crime—like the first transgressing humans—or deny the problem, like Cain. Before a God envisioned as physician, we are more likely to talk about our sickness or reveal the problem, hoping to find relief from our illnesses.

Discerning as Diagnosis

My new readings of Genesis 1–4 have provided some new direction for my reading of Scripture with people on the margins. People on the margins and those in crisis are often desperate for help they do not see as available to them. Yet if God's Spirit is indeed with us, accompanying us in our struggles, coming to our aid when we call, healing us of our maladies, then awareness of this presence must be cultivated. Learning to identify, in the diverse stories of Scripture, the way God comes can provide training in discernment regarding the ways that God is present in the varied circumstances of our lives. Discerning God's presence also requires learning to identify and respond to the many voices and temptations that are not God. This requires watchfulness, an active posture that best permits welcoming God's word and presence or resisting false images of God or distractions that lead us away from the narrow path.

Knowing that God is creating at the beginning in a place of chaos and emptiness encourages an attitude of watchfulness for this creative presence. Learning of the Spirit's respectful hovering over the waters before God's pronouncing light from darkness helps me watch and wait with more hope. Awareness that the serpent's distorted image of God differed radically from God's positive commands reminds me and those I read with to carefully differentiate the life-giving words of Scripture from those coming out of a malevolent image of God. Mindfulness that these negative images of God come from outside the human heart into human consciousness alerts me that this could happen again and again, inviting spiritual vigilance. Remembrance that God initiated a respectful dialogue with the transgressors in Genesis 3–4, either after their offense or in the midst of the temptation, inspires me and my reading companions to be watchful in our own lives for signs of God's respectful questioning. Prior knowledge that passions attack like foreign aggressors that we can master (Gen. 4:7) can help people anticipate and effectively resist destructive passions. Genesis 4 invites an understanding of sin as external aggressor, a spiritual malady or passion, and God as the one who offers healing.

A vast corpus of early monastic literature emphasizes watchfulness. I make use of teachings on watchfulness and spiritual combat from the Hesychast tradition, which calls attention to both the diagnosis of spiritual maladies and the welcoming of God's healing presence.

> Watchfulness is a continual fixing and halting of thought at the entrance to the heart. In this way predatory and murderous thoughts are marked down as they approach and what they say and do is noted; and we can see in what specious and delusive form the demons are trying to deceive the intellect. If we are conscientious in this, we can gain much experience and knowledge of spiritual warfare.[13]

St. Hesychios the Priest and many other writers of the Philokalia urge people to cultivate attentiveness to the activity of their inner life. John Cassian writes:

> For everything lies at the innermost recess of the soul. When the devil has been chased away from it and when sin is no longer in charge of it, then the kingdom of God is established there. This is what the evangelist conveys to us when he says, "The kingdom of God will not come as something to be observed nor will people cry 'Here it is! There it is!' Amen, I tell you the kingdom of God is within you" (Lk 17:20–21).[14]

The human soul must be watched over both to identify and to respond to harmful temptations and other threats that might lead a person unawares toward destructive action or inaction. At the same time spiritual awareness helps us identify God's work and presence in our lives, or maintain the ever-assaulted fruits of the Spirit.

> It is impossible for the mind to remain undisturbed by thoughts, but anyone serious about the matter can certainly permit them entry or drive them away, and although their origin does not lie entirely under our control we can choose to approve of them and to adopt them.[15]

This attitude of awareness includes diagnosis and treatment in a way that is close to a medical model of spiritual healing.

> We must therefore keep a close eye on this threefold scheme of our thoughts and we must exercise a wise discretion concerning them as they surface in our hearts. Right from the beginning we will scrutinize their origins, their causes, their originators, deciding our necessary reaction to them in the light of who it is that suggests them.[16]

Discernment is necessary in order to be able to diagnose the threats to our well-being (salvation) and to welcome God's presence and call. While discernment is a gift of the Holy Spirit, it can also be learned through observation, study, and prayer. It can be learned, too, with the help of groups like Alcoholics Anonymous, who train addicts and alcoholics to be alert to the subtle ways in which addictions can lead them to use addictive substances. I work with many inmates addicted to drugs and alcohol, helping them learn to watch for and identify the slightest triggers for their reactive, addiction-driven behaviors. However, since many addicts are unaware of a spiritual presence or "higher power" that they can go to to help them face their often intolerable anxiety, I focus first on discerning and welcoming the presence of God in their lives. Later, the work of identifying the destructive passions and dealing constructively with temptation can be pursued.

Chapter Four

God Empowers the Down and Out

Nonheroic Reading of the Patriarchal Narratives

Most people on the margins are not expecting God to show up in their lives in any positive way. Since they do not expect God's help, comfort, presence, or call they are usually not looking for it either. They assume that God calls exemplary people: the saints, who are righteous, martyrs, and heroes. They consequently come to the Bible with the assumption that those God addresses in a positive way must deserve God's special attention. They must be good, having measured up to God's high standards before God would ever speak to them. Some have tried and failed miserably. Many others are failing at their efforts to succeed in realizing their dreams apart from God. I often study different call texts in the Bible, seeking to help people make connections between the biblical characters and their own lives, so as to minimize the distance caused by exemplarism. God's call of Abram in Genesis 12 is a good place to start. In these Bible studies I sometimes ask one of the following questions to help people reflect on their own experience before we read the biblical text.

"Have you ever come to the point of having all your plans/dreams threatened or completely stopped? Have you ever perceived yourself to be in a no-exit situation? If yes, what was that like?"

People are usually quick to respond to this question in the jail, where everyone knows that he is in a crisis.

"I left my wife and four children in Mexico, hoping to find work and wire money back to them. Now I have problems. I don't know what will happen. Everything has gone bad," laments Omar, a man facing thirty-six months in prison for drug dealing.

There is always someone in a group who is the oldest son in his family, and whose parents expectantly await checks. Such men fear telling their mother that they are in jail—the family's hopes would be dashed. Others have sold properties in order to pay the smuggler to cross them from Mexico into the United States. Now they are facing deportation after having barely started making money to pay off their debt. Everyone complains about being locked in a small cell with another cellmate or two eighteen hours a day. Many inmates feel completely cut off: often nobody will accept their collect calls and often nobody visits them during their limited visiting hours. Parents and girlfriends often want nothing more to do with them after they've abused their relationships by crazy drug- and alcohol-induced behaviors.

"What are the forces that hold you back from [have kept you from] realizing your dreams or doing what you deeply desire?"

"The doors of this jail," says someone.

"*La policia* and the *migra*," says someone else, referring to the Immigration and Naturalization Service (INS).

"Drugs," and more precisely, beer, marijuana, and cocaine all get mentioned.

God's Call of Abram and Sarai

I invite people to look at the story of Abram to see if they see any connections between Abram's obstacles and their own. I usually do not invite a volunteer to read Genesis 11:27–32, but read it myself. There are too many difficult-to-pronounce names that would slow down the reading, frustrating the reader and the group.

> Now these are the descendants of Terah. Terah was the father of Abram, Nahor, and Haran; and Haran was the father of Lot. Haran died before his father Terah in the land of his birth, in Ur of the Chaldeans. Abram and Nahor took wives; the name of Abram's wife was Sarai, and the name of Nahor's wife was Milcah. She was the daughter of Haran the father of Milcah and Iscah. Now Sarai was barren; she had no child.
>
> Terah took his son Abram and his grandson Lot son of Haran, and his daughter-in-law Sarai, his son Abram's wife, and they went out together from Ur of the Chaldeans to go into the land of Canaan; but when they came to Haran, they settled there. The days of Terah were two hundred five years; and Terah died in Haran.

"What do we know about Abram from this story so far?" I ask the group. "What does this story tell us about Abram and the rest of his family?"

"Terah had three children—Abram was the firstborn. Then there was Nahor and Haran. Haran had a son named Lot. Then Haran died," answers Ernesto, a confident Mexican man in his mid-twenties who has been coming to my Bible studies for over two months and is now actively participating.

"They left their country," says another young Mexican man, who was facing deportation. "Terah, Abram's father, had taken them."

"Yes, that's right. So they were immigrants, right?" I suggest. "Do we know why they left or where they were going?" I ask.

"It does not say why they left," says someone. "Maybe because the harvests were bad, or there wasn't enough work. Who knows? We know one of Terah's sons, Haran, died. Maybe that tells us that life was hard there in Ur, like in Mexico," he continues.

"Here it says they were going to Canaan," another man volunteers, a finger pointing to the verse in his tattered, coverless jail library Bible.

"OK, let's say that this immigrant family had left Mexico City, and they were heading for El Norte—even though Terah and his family were all going to Canaan. What happened next?" I ask. "Were they successful?"

The men all look down at their Bibles for the answer. Several of them are reading softly aloud, like many campesinos in Honduras, moving their finger from word to word.

"No, it looks like they didn't make it," a young immigrant who had not yet participated noted. "Here it says that they settled in Haran. There in Haran, Abram's father died."

"So, we can say that this Mexican family only made it as far as Tijuana, and then the father dies."

"Or maybe it was worse than that," a man suggests. "There are worse places in the desert in the north of Mexico before Tijuana," he continues.

I briefly explain that in ancient Mesopotamia people felt obligated to stay permanently where they had buried their dead. While Terah had not done that himself with his son Haran, Abram may have felt that out of respect for his father he must not migrate.

"What else do we know about Abram?" I ask.

"He had a wife, Sarai," someone answers. "She was sterile."

I ask the men why they think this detail is mentioned. When no one is able to respond, I invite them to look briefly at the genealogy earlier in Genesis 11. I tell the group that if Sarai is sterile, then the genealogy would stop, since he does not have a son to continue his family's lineage into the future. The whole family, which began with Adam, is threatened here by Sarai's sterility. This meant that the command "Be fruitful and multiply, and fill the earth and subdue it" in Genesis 1:28 and 9:1, 7 could not be realized.

I point out that usually only the firstborn sons are mentioned through-out the genealogy (11:10ff.). Our story includes three sons, which hap-pened once before, when Noah's three sons are mentioned (5:32). After Noah had three sons, there was a flood. Maybe three sons here means something disastrous is about to happen, or at least something unexpected.

"So what do you think Abram was thinking and feeling?" I ask the group.

"He was probably very sad," someone says. "Everything had gone wrong."

Everyone agrees that Abram was stuck in a hopeless situation. After this introduction, I invite a volunteer to read Genesis 12:1–4.

> Now the LORD said to Abram, "Go from your country and your kin-dred and your father's house to the land that I will show you. I will make of you a great nation, and I will bless you, and make your name great, so that you will be a blessing. I will bless those who bless you, and the one who curses you I will curse; and in you all the families of the earth shall be blessed."
>
> So Abram went, as the LORD had told him; and Lot went with him. Abram was seventy-five years old when he departed from Haran.

"So what happened to Abram?" I ask. "What happened in this story?"

"The Lord told him to go," says Ernesto. "God called him to leave his country, his race, and his father's house."

"OK, that's true," I say. "What did God say that God would do?" I ask the group.

People looked down at their Bibles until one of them reread part of the passage that had just been read.

> "I will make of you a great nation, and I will bless you, and make your name great, so that you will be a blessing. I will bless those who bless you, and the one who curses you I will curse; and in you all the fam-ilies of the earth shall be blessed."

I talk about how God promises to bless Abram: making him a great nation, making his name great, blessing him, protecting him, and even blessing all the families of the earth through him. I then ask a question that I find often most excites people who do this study.

"Why did God call Abram? Was there something special about Abram that made God call him? What was Abram doing when the Lord called him?"

The men all look down at their Bibles. I suggest that Abram was probably praying when God called him. I suggest that he must have been a really religious person.

"No, he was not praying," says one of the men. "According to this he wasn't doing anything," he continued, pleased by this discovery.

"Really?" I prod. "Are you sure?" I ask. "He must have at least been a righteous person," I continue. "My Bible says that Abram was in mass, when the Lord said: 'Go . . .'"

The men all search the passage in their open Bibles on their laps. They look up at me confused, shaking their heads.

"It doesn't say that in my Bible. He was in Haran, his father had died. He was not in a church, he was not at mass," someone notes triumphantly.

I point out that what the passage *does not* say is sometimes as important as what it *does* say. Narrative gaps show details that were not considered important to the narrator.

"What were the requirements that God gave Abram before he could be called?" I ask, to drive home my point. "Did God say 'Abram, I want you to stop smoking marijuana, stealing car stereos, and selling drugs. I want to see a change. I would like to see you stop swearing and sleeping around with lots of women. I want you studying your Bible and praying every day, and going to mass! I am going to go away for a few months and come back. If I find that you have done all these things, then be ready. I will call you'?"

The men laugh. They seem delighted that this story does not support the gospel of bondage they were expecting. Gradually the good news is sinking in that Abram's call had no preconditions. The details that are absent from the text are the expected religious requirements that most demobilize irreligious or criminal types. People are pleasantly surprised to discover that the Bible does not here elevate heroic religious figures, like the saints they have grown up revering and to whom some have lit candles or prayed. We note together that there is no mention of God checking out Abram's criminal record. The text tells us nothing about whether Abram even knew God or prayed to him before this story. God does not call Abram because he is a righteous person, even though one man points out that Abram must have been righteous, since he went. The men are surprised and excited that God calls Abram out of his problems, right when everything was the darkest. Suddenly Abram is unexpectedly not so different from them. Like them, Abram and Sarai are up against a wall, facing a crisis.

"But Abram obeyed," a man ventures, thinking that he has discovered the expected bad news or a laudable, exemplary characteristic explaining God's otherwise haphazard choice.

"Some people think that God called Abram because God knew he was righteous," I say. "They assume that God knew he would obey, and that is why God called him. Let's look at another time when God speaks in Genesis that is kind of like this. Let's see if this helps us answer this difficulty." I invite the men to turn to Genesis 1:1–3.

> In the beginning when God created the heavens and the earth, the earth was a formless void and darkness covered the face of the deep, while a wind from God swept over the face of the waters. Then God said, "Let there be light"; and there was light.

"In this story, God speaks. What happens when God speaks?" I ask.

"God said, 'Let there be light,'" responds Ernesto. "And there was light."

"What did the light do? Did the light obey?" I ask. "Maybe God's word gave Abram the faith or made him move, just the way God's word brought light into darkness. Let's look at another text, in Acts 7:2–4," I suggest, inviting people to first read Joshua 24:2–3.

> And Joshua said to all the people, "Thus says the LORD, the God of Israel: Long ago your ancestors—Terah and his sons Abraham and Nahor—lived beyond the Euphrates and served other gods. *Then I took*[1] your father Abraham from beyond the River and led him through all the land of Canaan." (Josh. 24:2–3, italics added)

I also invite people to turn to Stephen's speech in Acts 7:2–4, regarding Abram:

> And Stephen replied:
> "Brothers and fathers, listen to me. The God of glory appeared to our ancestor Abraham when he was in Mesopotamia, before he lived in Haran, and said to him, 'Leave your country and your relatives and go to the land that I will show you.' Then he left the country of the Chaldeans, and settled in Haran. After his father died, God had him move ["removed him," NASB] from there to this country in which you are now living."

I point out that after Abram's father died, God *removed* him ("had him move") from there to Canaan.

At this the men are all smiling. God's call looks amazingly easy and maybe even fun. People would be more than happy to be removed from the jail instead of deported by the Border Patrol.

To be fair to the broader tradition, I point out that rabbinic interpreters often interpreted Genesis 12 in the light of the Lord's promise of blessing to Isaac in Genesis 26:4–5, which reads:

> I will make your offspring as numerous as the stars of heaven, and will give to your offspring all these lands; and all the nations of the earth shall gain blessing for themselves through your offspring, *because Abraham obeyed* my voice and kept my charge, my commandments, my statutes, and my laws." (Gen. 26:4–5, italics added)

This nearly undoes much of the grace that people were beginning to hear, until I point out that the word translated "obeyed" in Hebrew is actually the word "hear." Abram heard God's voice, and then later observed the charge, commandments and all.

Abram did in fact go in response to the Lord's word. He heard the voice, and this voice made a difference in his life.

"So how do you think God spoke to Abram?" I ask. "Do you think it was a loud voice or a soft voice?"

People look down at their Bibles, searching in vain for an answer.

"Here it does not tell us. It could have been a loud voice. We do not know," a man responds.

"OK, so how do you think you would know if God was calling you?" I ask.

Nobody can think of an answer.

"Do any of you sense that God is with you in any way? Do you hear God's voice to you here in the jail?" I ask.

Most of the people look down humbly. Some are shaking their heads back and forth. "*Nada*," one of the men says. "No, I don't hear God's voice," he continues.

I sympathize with the great difficulty involved in hearing or perceiving this apparently silent and invisible God. On the other hand, I remind them that this story emphasizes God's action. In Abram's life God took the initiative. This places the burden of the call on God. In scrutinizing Abram and Sarai's life situation for signs of any possible precondition for God's call, one thing can indeed be said. Lives or situations marked by chaos, emptiness, and darkness as in Genesis 1, or by failure, exile, and sterility as in Genesis 11:27–12:4, are the kinds of places where God shows up, speaking a word that brings light and movement out of darkness and paralysis. God calls people out of places of stagnation and death, initiating movement and new life.[2] God's call can bring liberation and meaning, which is consistent with the work of a God envisioned as therapist or empowering liberator.

Not all the people in the jail have hit bottom. Many are not yet facing the gravity of their situation. The younger men and women, between eighteen and twenty-two, are less likely to bottom out to the point of being truly open to any real alternative to the crazy life. Many remain in denial of their addictions and distracted by ongoing temptations. The undocumented Mexicans are usually the most receptive. Most have made great sacrifices and taken harrowing personal risks to venture to the United States. Time in prison, eventual deportation, and the humiliation of a return to their villages, neighborhoods, and families often breaks them to the point of Abram and Sarai. They await a call, day after day, week after week. They freely tell me any progress or lack of progress.

"Not yet. God has not spoken to me yet. I still haven't felt anything."

I remind everyone that God's call is very personal: "The Lord said to Abram." We talk about what it might be like to be addressed. I tell them how in the Hebrew the Lord says, word-for-word: "You go for you," or "go to/toward yourself." Might this not mean that God's call is an invitation to show the utmost respect to our own deepest self? I suggest that God's call might feel as if someone is respecting us more completely than we have ever been respected. Since many of us have not experienced such loving care, we may find it difficult to fully recognize it when it happens. I ask the people questions to help them reflect on what they truly desire.

"What are the things that keep you from what you most truly desire?" I ask.

People always appreciate this question, regularly mentioning lists of substances like pot, cocaine, heroin, beer, and institutions like the Border Patrol, the courts, the law, the police, and other temptations like desire for money, sex, respect, friends, their homeboys, and so on. The Bible-study participants themselves make the connections between many of these things that keep them from their deepest desires and the trappings that Abram was called to "go to/for yourself *from.*"

"But where exactly did God tell Abram to go?" I ask, steering the conversation in a new direction.

"Canaan," someone says.

"No, God does not say where!" someone corrects. "It says here, 'Go . . . to the land that I will show you.'"

"Yes, the text does say 'go to the land that I will show you,' or even 'to a place that I will cause you to see.' Where do you think that is?" I ask.

We talk at length about how God takes responsibility for Abram's direction and for the entire fulfillment of his call. If Abram asks, "How am I to be a great nation as Sarai is sterile?" God's word already includes the response: "I will make of you a great nation." God's word to Abram answers many of his questions. God will bless Abram, make his name great so that he will be a blessing, and protect Abram. All of this is done with God's final objective in mind: "In you all the families of the earth shall be blessed." The destination of Abram's call is consistent with the call. It is a place that "I will cause you to see."

I invite people to read further in Genesis 12 to look for clues as to Abram's own journey. I suggest there may be signs both in this very chapter and in the eleven chapters in the Abraham and Sarah narrative that follow. We read together Genesis 12:7–9, and I point out a clue. I tell them that the word "appear" is best translated "was seen."

> Then the LORD *appeared to* Abram, and said, "To your offspring I will give this land." So he built there an altar to the LORD, who had *appeared to* him. From there he moved on to the hill country on the east of Bethel, and pitched his tent, with Bethel on the west and Ai on the east; and there he built an altar to the LORD and invoked the name of the LORD. And Abram journeyed on by stages toward the Negeb.

Might Abram's final destination be the Lord himself? The Lord causes Abram to see God's very self, calling Abram to a spiritual journey that leads to seeing God. This reading finds additional support when we read together Hebrews 11:38–12:2, which describes both the journey, the laying aside of encumbrances, and the destination that is looked to, Jesus.

> They wandered in deserts and mountains, and in caves and holes in the ground.
>
> Yet all these, though they were commended for their faith, did not receive what was promised, since God had provided something better so that they would not, apart from us, be made perfect.
>
> Therefore, since we are surrounded by so great a cloud of witnesses, let us also lay aside every weight and the sin that clings so closely, and let us run with perseverance the race that is set before us, *looking to Jesus* the pioneer and perfecter of our faith, who for the sake of the joy that was set before him endured the cross, disregarding its shame, and has taken his seat at the right hand of the throne of God.

We talk about the struggle to find this place, and Genesis 12:1's ongoing response: "I will cause you to see" (au. trans.). The people appear challenged by the high adventure of God's call to faith, and enjoy talking about watchfulness. They like the idea of being constantly on the lookout, seeking to discern the voice of a God who totally respects them. Could this be true?

Week after week I continue my studies and one-on-one visits. I keep asking the individuals who are on the journey whether they are sensing God's presence with them. In the Bible studies I regularly ask if people are hearing anything in their reading of Scripture that seems to be coming to them from God.

"Not yet. I still have not heard anything. I don't feel anything," some keep saying. "But it's not a problem. Who knows when it will happen?" one of them tells me with an air of confidence.

Then one day it happens. Someone tells of sensing God's presence. God has answered a prayer. This person has been touched in some way. I watch faith grow, and often get letters from people who have long since gone to prison, describing their conversion, their having been met by Jesus. Willie writes me from Washington State Penitentiary, witness of God's presence:

> Brother, As Shadrach, Meshac and Abednego were in the fire, it gives me joy to know that the patience and mercy God gives us makes us strong in order to be in the fire and pass through the flames and not get burned, nor feel those flames that rip apart steel and the biggest rocks in the world.
>
> And after having suffered a little, he will set us at his side like victors and will give us lots of strength and power for that which lies ahead and for the plans of the tricky devil.
>
> I live by the pure mercy of Jesus Christ that Lucifer wanted to take from me; and he tried to many times, but because of the immense love of Christ, nothing is impossible; that from this dark life, Christ gave me life and light; and from death itself and a jail sentence he gave me life, joy and hope of getting out in a few years; my tears are tears of thanks to him for which nothing is impossible, nothing.
>
> He is the one that brings hope to the guys that are at the lowest possible point any human being can be at in this world; that was me.[3]

Oppression and Liberation in Hagar's Story and Ours

In a recent contextual Bible study on Abram and Sarai's conflict with Hagar in Genesis 16:1–16, I began a study with 15 Mexican inmates in a local jail with the following questions: "Do you ever feel like other people or forces are acting upon you and have power over you? When have you seen this happening? What does this feel like?"

The men are quick to respond to the first two questions.

"All the time," insisted an undocumented Mexican man accused of dealing drugs. "The guards tell us when to eat, when to sleep. They lock us in our cells. They handcuff us and take us down to court."

"Once the harvest is over, the INS agents pick us up and deport us back to Mexico. We are treated like objects."

Heads nod in agreement and others give examples.

"So how does that make you feel?" I ask.

"Humiliated," one man says, looking down.

"Powerless . . . very small," says another. "I feel lots of anger," says someone else.

After listening to people's feelings of powerlessness and anger in these situations, I invite them to read Genesis 16:1–6, suggesting that this story may or may not offer helpful parallels to their lives.

I begin by inviting a volunteer to read a short section of the text, in this case Genesis 16:1–6, which describes Hagar's condition as slave of Sarai and Abram. I ask the people to identify the characters in the text and to say whatever they can based on the information the text provides. Here in my role of biblical scholar I invite them to discover more about these characters from the larger narrative context.

Since the education gap between myself as Bible scholar and pastor and the untrained reader can so easily disempower the untrained, great caution must be used in offering "behind the text" knowledge inaccessible to the majority. Narrative approaches to the text that focus on characters, place, plot, together with literary approaches that show literary genre, structure, delimitation of the pericope are all skills that people with a Bible can and should be taught. While scientific exegesis is important to highlight its foreignness and otherness before those who have domesticated it, these methods can further remove it from the masses. The best intercultural exegesis will be informed by the latest biblical studies research, illuminated by detailed knowledge of the current reading context and a pastoral sensitivity to individual readers.

To minimize the knowledge gap I invite people to turn and read a few sections beginning in Genesis 11:27.

"What do we know about Abram and Sarai from these verses?" I ask.

The men observe that according to Genesis 11:27ff. Abram and Sarai were migrants who had faced difficulties. Abram's father had died and Sarai was sterile (Gen. 11:30). I ask a volunteer to read Genesis 12:1–4 and people note that YHWH called Abram to a mission and promised to bless all the families of the earth through him (Gen. 12:3). I point out that Abram and Sarai were wealthy (Gen. 13:2ff.) and that Abram was considered righteous because he believed God. In this story they represent "insiders"—those who have faith, blessing, God's favor, wealth, and in this case power over outsiders—like Hagar, their Egyptian slave.

I briefly point out that God had not called Hagar. She was a foreigner, an Egyptian, a woman, and a slave of Sarai. As an Egyptian I note that she reminds the reader of Abram's unbelief, when he deceived Pharaoh by claiming Sarai was his sister. Pharaoh gives Abram slaves and animals. Possibly Hagar came into Sarai's possession then. From here I move quickly to other questions that the group can easily answer, providing them with more opportunity to talk about their views of God and their lives.

"What view of God (theology) do Sarai/Abram have?" I ask.

Someone notes that Sarai thinks that God has kept her from having children (Gen. 16:2). I ask whether they know people who believe God is to blame when they cannot have children or experience other difficulties. People nod and talk about how in Mexico this is common. I ask the people what God is like if Sarai is right.

"A God who gives and takes according to what he wants," someone ventures.

"A God who is in control of everything," another says.

"So, how did Sarai and Abram treat Hagar?" I ask.

The men note the obvious. "Like an object," said one inmate, "with no respect."

"Sarai gave her to Abram to get a child for herself that she herself couldn't have," said another man.

The men note that Hagar was never asked permission or in any way consulted, never called by her name, never directly addressed. She is treated like their possession. Abram uses her, and immediately she is pregnant. After Hagar looks down upon her owner, momentarily empowered by her fertility, Sarai is humiliated and treats her violently. Abram does not protect his wife Hagar, but lets Sarai abuse her.

At this point I ask the group if they see any parallels between this story and their own lives. At first the men are silent, reluctant to identify with Hagar because she is a woman and abused slave.

"No," someone says, "not us."

Another corrects him, "all the time here in the jail. Here we're a number, or maybe a last name."

Soon everyone is talking, making connections between Sarai and Abram and the jail guards, the police, the courts, INS, and exploitive employers. In a study of the same text outside the jail farmworkers are quick to equate Sarai and Abram with an abusive husband, employer, landlord, and always the police and INS.

Here I move the discussion to a new level of theological reflection by reminding the people that God had called Abram and said that through him all the nations of the world (including Hagar) would be blessed. I ask the men a question that would make explicit the negative theology reflected by these bearers of the promise:

"If Sarai and Abram are bearers of the blessing and represent God to Hagar, what image of God would Hagar have after this experience?"

The men are quick to respond, noting that Hagar would see God as a distant, impersonal, uncaring dictator, who makes use of people for his purposes, treating them like objects. This would be a god on the side of the powerful and unsympathetic to the poor and weak. Nobody notices that Sarai and Abram's treatment of Hagar is similar to the way Sarai thinks God is treating her, but I make a note to myself and move on.

"So how does Hagar respond to this situation, to this theology?" I ask.

"She flees, running away into the desert," someone says.

"Maybe this is a healthy response to this kind of abuse," I note. "If God is in fact the way God's representatives here portray him through their behavior, running away is a good alternative. Let's read the part of the story to see whether Abram and Sarai are representing God correctly."

As Bible-study facilitator one of my most important roles is to help people identify parallels between their stories and the place, characters, and happenings in the text. Since most texts express within themselves opposing theologies, my role is to help clarify the oppositions in such a way that people can more easily hear the liberating Word in the narrative. The bad news in the text must be drawn out and looked at for the theology that it reflects so that any countertheology that may be present can appear in the clearest form possible. I seek to deliberately subvert the oppressive dominant theology with a fresh new Word that I encourage people to discover for themselves. In contrast to "scientific exegesis," which claims to be objective and unbiased theologically, the socially engaged biblical scholar must both encourage people to directly question and challenge assumptions about God that most oppress them and invite them to consider a liberating alternative way of reading.

At this point in the Bible study I invite a volunteer to read Genesis 16:7–16 and ask the group to identify the characters and describe what happens in this story.

"Where is Hagar and what is she doing when the messenger of the Lord meets her?" I ask. "Was she seeking God?"

These questions highlight a surprising absence in the narrative of the expected holy, religious place and pious behaviors. Drawing attention to the narrative gap subverts pietism and moralism, wherein the reader's attempt to hear good news is subverted from the start by the three questions: "What do I have to do to be saved?" "Where do I have to go?"—the assumed answer being "to church or mass"; and "What do I have to know?"

The people are surprised and even excited as they answer that Hagar is running away, is in the wilderness, and has no prior knowledge of God when God finds her.

"What kind of God does the messenger of YHWH reveal by means of his words and actions?" "What does the messenger of YHWH do for Hagar?" I ask, and continue.

"How is this God different than the god Hagar would know of through Sarai and Abram's treatment of her?"

"The messenger calls her by her name," someone says.

"But he calls her Hagar, slave of Sarai," observes another.

I note that maybe God comes as "the messenger of the Lord" to the "servant/slave of Sarai" as a way of meeting her as an equal—a hypothesis that pleases the inmates.

"He asks her where she is coming from and where she is going," notes someone, and continues: "The Lord's messenger treats Hagar with respect and not like an object."

"Maybe that is like asking her: 'tell me about your life, where have you come from, what have you done? What do you desire? What are you hopes and plans for the future?'" I suggest. "This God cares about her, and even gives her a special blessing."

This reading must not be imposed on people in any way, which would reinforce people's past experience of the teacher or religious expert as dispenser of "the truth" to the "ignorant." Rather I seek to carefully and repeatedly invite participants to venture other interpretations through asking questions that draw people to respectfully examine the detail of the text. And the discussion gets quite animated as people discuss how this new view of God is completely different from the image of God Hagar might have gotten from her owners.

The God who meets Hagar in the desert is human, close, and personal. This God takes the initiative, looking for her and finding her. This God is gracious, blessing her without any conditions. This God is personal and attentive, naming her unborn son Ishmael, "God hears," even though God knows he will be a "wild ass of a man" who will experience continual conflict.

"Do any of you know any wild-asses-of-men?" I ask.

Everyone laughs, especially two, muscular, tattooed white guys who tower over the rest of us.

"God hears even the wild asses of men who've got troubles, and God here promises that Ishmael will one day break free," I say. In response to this human God who calls her by her name, Hagar feels free to name God El Roi, the "God who sees." She has met a God who is not oblivious to abuse and suffering but sees and does something about it. I point out that this Egyptian slave woman is the first person in the Scriptures to name God.

The greatest difficulty for people is that the messenger addressed Hagar as "Hagar, slave of Sarai" and sends her back to submit to her abuser Sarai. And yet one inmate in his late 50s who has been in and out of jail repeatedly for alcohol-related offenses and has a history of noncooperation with the courts said matter-of-factly: "This tells me that God wants me to directly face my problems instead of always running."

Perhaps what is most liberating about this narrative is the clear differentiation between Sarai/Abram and God. God is separate from the system and the dominant theology. Through the messenger of YHWH God looks for, finds, addresses, respects, cares, blesses, and promises life and liberation. This makes a big difference for Hagar and a big difference for the immigrant women and men with whom I work. Their only hope of employment is stoop labor for minimum wage from employers who are often exploitive. Law enforcement agents continue to practice racial targeting, and the Border Patrol is strictly enforcing increasingly rigid immigration laws. The good news for Hagar is that God is a respectful, personal, and very human presence who promises blessing and liberation in spite of her current experience of marginalization. This gives hope to the immigrant, the outsider, and anyone experiencing oppression.

Resisting Rejection by the "Elect" in Genesis 25–27

People who are truly on the margins do not expect to receive benefits legitimately. Accustomed to being rejected by the powerful, they learn to survive by hook or by crook. If Scripture is to be relevant to today's "damned," it must be freed from the dominant theological paradigm, which assumes that blessing in this world is a reward for good behavior and exclusion a punishment for bad.

In my Bible studies and one-on-one conversations I engage people in theological reflection by helping them see themselves in the stories of struggle and liberation in the Scriptures. I seek to formulate questions that draw people out about issues that directly affect them. Most often I begin with a question about people's lives, and then introduce a biblical story and ask questions that help uncover the deeper truths of the text. Other times I begin with the text, as in the following description of a Bible study on the birth of Jacob and Esau and their subsequent power struggle.

Jail guards usher me through two thick steel doors along tan cinder-block corridors into the jail's multipurpose room. Tattered, coverless books lie strewn about on the table. I collect the ones I recognize as Bibles, and arrange blue plastic chairs in a circle as guards usher red-uniformed inmates from their cells and pods into the room. After an opening prayer calling on God's Holy Spirit to show us the deeper meaning of the story, I invite a volunteer to read Genesis 25:19–22, which introduces the larger narrative.

> These are the descendants of Isaac, Abraham's son: Abraham was the father of Isaac, and Isaac was forty years old when he married Rebekah, daughter of Bethuel the Aramean of Paddan-aram, sister of Laban the Aramean. Isaac prayed to the LORD for his wife, because she was barren; and the LORD granted his prayer, and his wife Rebekah conceived. The children struggled together within her; and she said, "If it is to be this way, why do I live?" So she went to inquire of the LORD.

"Who are the characters in this story so far?" I ask, to get people looking into their Bibles.

"Abraham," someone says.

"No, man, it's Isaac, Abraham's son," another guy corrects. "Then there are the twins—the Lord and finally Rebekah are mentioned."

"Who has power in this story and who doesn't?" I continue.

"The Lord has the power," someone responds, assuming this to be the right answer. "The Lord answers prayers, and Rebekah gets pregnant." A few heads nod. Everyone looks to me for my reaction.

I agree with them that Isaac and later Rebekah both pray to the Lord, and the Lord grants their prayers. Since God is in the story, we assume that God has all the power. I suggest, though, that we look closely at the story again to see what it is about. "Who has power among the other characters?" I ask.

"These are the descendants of Isaac," someone reads. "Isaac has power."

"OK, that's true. He alone is certainly getting the credit for descendants. Why doesn't the story begin 'These are the descendants of Isaac and Rebekah'?" I ask, trying hard to free up the men to question the power relations in the narrative rather than assuming they are God-ordained.

We observe together that between Isaac and Rebekah, Isaac clearly has the power. Isaac *takes* Rebekah, praying to the Lord for *his* wife because she was barren. We observe together that Isaac's name is mentioned five times, while Rebekah is mentioned only twice in Genesis 25:19–26. Rebekah is a weak, even powerless, figure, defined in terms of her relationship with men (Isaac takes her, she is referred to as "his wife," Bethuel's daughter, and Laban's sister) and in terms of her inability to conceive. The Lord's answering Isaac's prayer shows that God stands behind him.[4] When Rebekah finally conceives as a result of Isaac's prayer she is once again acted upon, experiencing her future "descendants of Isaac" struggling in her womb to such an extent that she does not want to continue living.

"Who are the Rebekahs in our society?" I ask.

"*Nosotros* [we are]," says José, an undocumented man facing kidnapping and assault charges.

"The Mexicans, immigrants," says another.

"Who are the people who have power over you in your life?" I ask the men.

"The judge," someone immediately replies. "And the prosecutor."

The guards, the *migra* (the INS), and drugs are all subsequently mentioned.

We look together at Rebekah's problem. An internal struggle between two children in her womb is making her life difficult. She asks God about the nature of this struggle, which does not seem natural. José Luis reads Genesis 25:23 to see how the Lord responds.

And the L ORD said to her,

> "Two nations are in your womb,
>   and two peoples born of you shall be divided;
> the one shall be stronger than the other,
>   the elder shall serve the younger."

We talk about how the Lord tells only Rebekah, the one who is powerless in the story, a special word that only she and we the readers know. The stronger, older son, who normally would have the power, will serve the weaker, younger son, who normally would be powerless.

"So God told Rebekah some information about Isaac's descendants that only she knows. Let's read on to see how that surprising word actually gets realized in real life." I say.

The man who has been reading continues by reading Genesis 25:24–28.

> When her time to give birth was at hand, there were twins in her womb. The first came out red, all his body like a hairy mantle; so they named him Esau. Afterward his brother came out, with his hand gripping Esau's heel; so he was named Jacob. Isaac was sixty years old when she bore them.
>   When the boys grew up, Esau was a skillful hunter, a man of the field, while Jacob was a quiet man, living in tents. Isaac loved Esau, because he was fond of game; but Rebekah loved Jacob.

After the remaining verses of this story are read, I ask the men what we now know about each of Isaac and Rebekah's sons.

"What do we know about Esau?" I ask.

"He was the firstborn," someone said.

I talk briefly about how in the Mesopotamian cultures of that period, the firstborn son had all the rights. Esau, being the firstborn, had the birthright.

"He was red, and covered with hair, a man of the country, a very macho man," says someone else. "He hunted animals for his father."

"Esau was his father's favorite. His father liked to eat meat," says another.

In contrast, Jacob is the second-born. He grasps Esau's heel. He is a smooth man, who lives in tents. Most importantly, he is the preferred of his mother, the one who has no power. Compared with his brother, Esau, Jacob has no rights.

I talk briefly about how Jacob, the second-born, is not favored by his father, who has the power.

Since Isaac does have the power that Jacob needs, he is like God to Jacob. "If Isaac reflected who God really is, what would God be like?" I ask the men.

"Unfair—a God who loves the stronger and ignores the weaker," says José Luis.

"Powerful, old, and wealthy," says another. "A God who shows favorites, who blesses only some."

"Isaac likes only the strong, the skilled. He discriminates, preferring Esau because of his race, his skin color," says another.

We talk at length how if Isaac reveals God, this is a God who is distant and hard, even impossible to please. Isaac reveals a God who has his favorites and loves because of what is brought him (i.e., meat). This image of God as sustainer of the status quo is all too familiar to the underclass in North America and in Mexico and Central America.

"What does Jacob lack that Esau has that would bring him his father Isaac's favor?" I ask.

The men repeat the list of Esau's distinguishing attributes: red color, hair, being a skillful hunter, a man of the field who gets game. Jacob also lacks being the firstborn and, most importantly, his father's love.

"What do you lack to have the power to do what you most want?" I ask the men, hoping people now will talk about their own lives.

"In Mexico, it would help to be the son of a politician or rich person," says Armando, a Mexican man in his mid-twenties.

"Lots of money so I would not have to work," says another man.

"What nationality would be ideal? What race or skin color?" I ask.

"It would be better to be an American, a U.S. citizen," says José Luis.

"If we were white, we would definitely have more opportunities," says Armando.

"Not necessarily," insists Dominic. "I'm white, and I don't have any power. To be white and to have money is to have power."

"No, there are still more benefits to being white," counters Armando. "White people get paid more than we Mexicans. Mexican children are made to work when they are very young. We are used to hard labor and are hired to do jobs that white people would never do. And we are paid less."

Dominic sees his point and nods in agreement.

Clearly the closest example there in our jail Bible study of a modern equivalent of an Esau (one who has favor, power, and the like) would be me: a white male, American.[5]

"So, who are you in this story?" I asked, inviting people to look back at the text. While people were slightly embarrassed to be associated with the tent-dwelling, cooking, mama's boy Jacob, they readily stated that they most closely resembled Jacob in the story.

"So, was there any way for Jacob to win favor? Would there be any way for you to be white Americans?" I ask.

"No, Jacob is trapped. The only thing he can do is take advantage of his brother. He stole his birthright by taking advantage of Esau's hunger," one of the men notes.

"There is nothing we can do either. We are brown-skinned. We are Mexican. Unless the laws change we will always be illegal. We are screwed."[6]

"But you have to do something. What do you do to get what you want?" I ask.

"Rob, break into homes, sell drugs," says Dominic matter-of-factly.

"Not me, man," responds José, insulted.

"Yeah, but you steal jobs from Americans," says Dominic, getting a rise from the Mexicans. He smiles, and says he's just kidding.

"What other kinds of things do you do?" I ask.

"We cross over the border without papers," says Felipe. "We walk over the hills, paying coyotes, risking our lives so we can come here to work."

"We use false papers that say we are legal," says José Luis.

"I do that too, man," says Dominic.

"Really?" I ask, wondering if there is some rivalry going on about being the baddest dude.

"Yeah, I have to work under a false name. Otherwise my wages would all be garnished to pay child support, fines, and shit," continues Dominic.

"Some of us sell drugs, steal car stereos, and do other illegal things to make more money," says another man.

Everyone laughs at this blunt assessment of each of their lives. They, like countless other undocumented and other underclass people, find themselves in legally impossible situations.

"Do you ever feel guilty before God when you have to do these things?" I ask the men at this moment of honesty and vulnerability. "Tell me honestly, do you sometimes think that God might punish you, that God might someday make you pay for all this?"

We talk about the Mexican mother's oft-repeated threats: "Behave yourself, my son, otherwise the good God will punish you."[7]

"Do any of you see God as punishing you now through this experience in jail?" I ask.

At least half the men are nodding and saying, "*Sí*."

"Yes, whatever our mother (*jefita*) says, has to be fulfilled," says José.

Most of the men and women with whom I work view God as siding with the moral and punishing the "bad guys." When they open their Bibles they assume that any characters that God in any way favors must be chosen because of their goodness. Jacob, though he is the youngest, they assume is good and deserving—even a moral hero. Esau, in contrast, they assume must have been rejected because he is evil.

Moralism and heroism are characteristics of the dominant theology in which contemporary underdogs are immersed. Yet this theology is ancient, as can be seen in the following quotes from early Jewish sources.

And . . . Rebekah bore to Isaac two sons, Jacob and Esau, and Jacob was a smooth and upright man, and Esau was fierce, a man of the field, and hairy; and Jacob dwelt in tents. And the youths grew, and Jacob *learned to write*; but Esau did not learn, for he was a man of the field, and a hunter, and he learned war, and all his deeds were fierce. And Abraham loved Jacob, but Isaac loved Esau. (*Jubilees* 19:13–15; italics added)

And the two boys grew up, and Esau was a skilled hunter, a man who went out to the fields, and Jacob was a perfect man who frequented the schoolhouse. (*Targum Onqelos* Gen. 25:27)

The righteous Jacob, who observed the entire Torah, as it is said, "And Jacob was a perfect man, dwelling in tents." (*Sifrei Deuteronomy* 336)

When she passed by houses of idol-worship, Esau would squirm about, trying to get out, as it says, "The wicked turn astray [*zoru*] from the womb" (Ps. 58:4); when she would pass synagogues or study-houses, Jacob would squirm to get out, as it says, "Before I formed you in the womb, I knew you" (Jer. 1:5) (*Genesis Rabbah* 63:6)

Assumptions of Jacob's worthiness in these commentaries and within today's dominant reading community rob this story of its relevant meaning for those most in need of its message. A careful read of the text with the dominant theology in mind can help take the text back from its usurpers and return it to its rightful contemporary beneficiaries.

There are clear connections between people on the margins and Jacob, who exhibits the ethics of survival. I invite the men to look at how Jacob, and then Rebekah and Jacob, deal with their powerlessness.

> Once when Jacob was cooking a stew, Esau came in from the field, and he was famished. Esau said to Jacob, "Let me eat some of that red stuff, for I am famished!" (Therefore he was called Edom.) Jacob said, "First sell me your birthright." Esau said, "I am about to die; of what use is a birthright to me?" Jacob said, "Swear to me first." So he swore to him, and sold his birthright to Jacob. Then Jacob gave Esau bread and lentil stew, and he ate and drank, and rose and went his way. Thus Esau despised his birthright. (Gen. 25:29–34)

The men are quick to label Jacob an opportunist, who takes advantage of Esau's desperation for food to get the birthright. I remind them that Jacob's name means heel grabber, deceiver, or even trickster.[8] But he still lacked the most important thing that would guarantee success for him and his descendants: his father's blessing.

"Where is God in this story?" I ask the men. We observe that God is absent, or at least silent. God does not stop Jacob from his scheme.

I remind the men that the Lord had given Rebekah the secret—that the stronger, older one would serve the weaker, younger one. Yet in the story this looks like an impossibility.

"Let's see how Rebekah and Jacob deal with these obstacles." I invite the men to turn to Genesis 27, and ask someone to read the entire chapter.

As Armando reads the story, the other men follow closely. They appear surprised by Rebekah's bold scheme to deceive her husband.

As we read we overhear with Rebekah Isaac's special arrangement with his favored son, Esau, that he is to hunt for wild game, make him a meal, and come for the blessing before Isaac dies (27:1–4). The men are intrigued that Rebekah is listening in and acts with such bold cunning, ordering and coaching Jacob to disguise his identity, imitating Esau before their blind father to deceptively steal the blessing (vv. 5–10). The inmates are amazed that Rebekah helps Jacob so much (v. 9), even to the extent of taking any curse upon herself should Jacob be discovered (v. 13). The details of Jacob's counterfeit identity—the skins of the kids on his hands and neck (v. 16), the savory food that his father loved (v. 17), and Jacob's bold-faced lies about his identity (v. 19) and even about God's helping him get the game quickly (v. 20)—shock the men. They are expecting failure, and grow increasingly sure that powerful Isaac, though blind, will discover the trickery.

The men I am reading with have all been caught for their crimes in varying degrees. Their very presence in jail, impending court appearances, or sentencing are constant reminders. Yet many have succeeded numerous times. They can see that Jacob's crime was no easy feat. Isaac's command that he come near so he can feel whether or not he is really Esau reminds Armando of a time when the police pulled him over, running a background check on a false name he gave at the spur of the moment, hoping to escape arrest for a warrant he knew he had. The trick worked that time, as Jacob's ruse succeeded.[9] Would Jacob's next moment with his blind but intelligent father lead to detection? Suspense grew among the men, perplexed as Jacob's success is achieved step by agonizing step. These are men who know firsthand Jacob's stress, as Isaac notices the voice of his lying son is Jacob's, not Esau's (v. 22); and he asks him one more time: "Are you really my son Esau?" (v. 24), before his final request: "Come near and kiss me, my son" (v. 26).

"Is this *mica* [permanent residency card] really good?" I ask, pretending to be an employer or a Border Patrol agent. Everyone laughs.

To sum up our findings so far, I ask the men how the powerless, discriminated-against people in the story, Jacob and Rebekah, get the power and favor they lack: How do you get favor if you are damned by the one with power? What means did Jacob and Rebekah use that allowed them to succeed?

Together we made up a list with ease, as criminal minds are quick to see the survival wisdom of the Bible's underclass. Trickery, lies, using false identities, counterfeiting, fraud are all mentioned as part of Jacob and Rebekah's arsenal. I remind the men that Jacob's name actually means trickster or deceiver. They smile uneasily, looking surprised to encounter a character they can so easily identify with, and such a real-life story, in the Bible. I remind the men that Rebekah was driven to help her son Jacob by a word from God in a dream that the stronger and older would serve the younger. We still do not know how God feels about Jacob and Rebekah's criminal behavior, though they have clearly succeeded in the world of power-struggling humans.

"So, how do you think God looks at these kinds of actions? How do you think God will respond to Jacob and Rebekah?" I ask.

"Probably God was not in agreement," says Armando.

"God will probably punish them later," says José Luis.

God's Presence with the Rejected, Genesis 28

After briefly telling the story of Esau's angry discovery of Jacob's crime, his plot to kill his brother, and Jacob's escape to a foreign country, I invite someone to read the story of the Lord's first encounter with fugitive Jacob after this incident. One of the men reads the story of Jacob's dream at Bethel in Genesis 28:11–16:

> He came to a certain place and stayed there for the night, because the sun had set. Taking one of the stones of the place, he put it under his head and lay down in that place. And he dreamed that there was a ladder set up on the earth, the top of it reaching to heaven; and the angels of God were ascending and descending on it. And the LORD stood beside him and said, "I am the LORD, the God of Abraham your father and the God of Isaac; the land on which you lie I will give to you and to your offspring; and your offspring shall be like the dust of the earth, and you shall spread abroad to the west and to the east and to the north and to the south; and all the families of the earth shall be blessed in you and in your offspring. Know that I am with you and will keep you wherever you go, and will bring you back to this land; for I will not leave you until I have done what I have promised you."

After reading the story of the Lord's encounter, I ask the men again how God responds to Jacob's crime.

"God doesn't say anything. It's like it didn't matter," says one of the men.

"God blessed Jacob, promising that he would be with him," says another man in amazement.

"God is different than we expect here," I comment. "If we were to look at Jacob's life, what does Jacob do that makes him worthy of God's presence with him and promise of blessing?" I ask. "Was Jacob a religious person? Was he a person who prayed, went to church, read his Bible?"

The men look down at their Bibles. Hesitantly they begin to comment:

"He wasn't a religious man. He didn't do anything good," says Armando. "He took advantage of his brother, stealing his birthright. He had just lied to his father and stolen his brother's blessing."

"He wasn't seeking God when God came to him. He was escaping his brother," says José Luis. "He committed a crime and fled."

"He was sleeping when God visited him," says another man, stirring everyone to laughter.

"So, is this story telling us that it is OK with God if we commit crimes?" I ask.

"Maybe God is not worried about every crime. Some crimes are OK," someone says. "Maybe this story is telling us that even when we commit crimes, God can still come to us and bless us."

"I don't know, man. This don't feel like a total blessing to me," says Dominic. "Jacob has to flee. He has the birthright and the blessing, and God is with him and shit, but he's on the run, he's separated from his mom and dad, his brother, and his country. This looks like a hard road."

I sit with the men in a big circle, Bibles open on their red, jail-issue pants, plastic thongs planted on the brown cement floor of the jail's multipurpose room. I encourage them to take the story of God's appearance to and blessing of fugitive Jacob as a clear announcement of God's love for and willingness to bless the underdog—the ones who have no legal rights to benefits, who often feel paralyzed by the restrictions and enforcement imposed by the principalities and powers. I suggest that we look together at Jacob's reaction to God's appearance to him. We read together Genesis 28:16–18, 20–22:

> Then Jacob woke from his sleep and said, "Surely the LORD is in this place—and I did not know it!" And he was afraid, and said, "How awesome is this place! This is none other than the house of God, and this is the gate of heaven."
>
> So Jacob rose early in the morning, and he took the stone that he had put under his head and set it up for a pillar and poured oil on the top of it. . . . Then Jacob made a vow, saying, "If God will be with me, and will keep me in this way that I go, and will give me bread to eat and clothing to wear, so that I come again to my father's house in peace, then the LORD shall be my God, and this stone, which I have set up for a pillar, shall be God's house; and of all that you give me I will surely give one-tenth to you."

We end the study by talking about how Jacob recognizes after his dream that God was there with him even though he did not know it—a reminder to all of us that God's presence is perhaps hard to discern and unexpected. The men notice the unbelief of Jacob too, and his vow full of conditions: "*If* God will be with me and protect me, and feed me and bring me back home in peace, *then* the Lord will be my God." The men are delighted. They feel as if there is room for them and their unbelief. I encourage them to not believe too quickly, but to look for signs of God's presence with them and not be afraid to ask God to demonstrate God's presence and care for them.

"So who is God, according to this story? What is God like?" I ask, wrapping things up before our closing prayers.

"God is with us and cares for us even when we are doing bad things, like committing crimes," someone says.

"God comes to people and blesses them, even when we are not looking for him. God came to Jacob when he was running away."

We talk about how God works through other people, like Rebekah. Rebekah had a special word from the Lord that the younger, undeserving son is the chosen one. Her response to this word represents her becoming a separate subject, one acting in her own and another's liberation. God's word to her freed her to break allegiance with the dominant theology/culture and help her son, taking risks by serving as an accomplice in Jacob's crime.

The men appear to be encouraged as we gather in a circle and hold hands. We pray the Lord's Prayer as brothers. I feel some peace and can see that the men are more hopeful. Armando approaches me with a smile, and says he is really excited and needs to talk right away. I press the buzzer for the guards, and ask them to bring Armando up to the front of the jail, where I wait for him in a small visiting cell.

Discerning God's Voice to Us

After the guard locks us into the privacy of our cell, Armando excitedly tells me his plan.

"This study was incredible. I feel free to do something now and want to know what you think," he began. "The narco detectives [drug task force police] visited me this week and want to make a deal with me. You see, I was very active dealing drugs here, and I know lots of people who sell drugs—big dealers, who they would like to catch. They told me that if I point out and help them arrest seven to nine people, they will let me return to Mexico. Otherwise, they want to give me thirty-six to forty-eight months in prison. I can't go to prison, Roberto. I have a wife and three kids back in Mexico. They need me. I want to go back to be with them. After this study, I feel like I am free to cooperate with the narcos. What do you think?"

I sit there stunned, feeling my friend's predicament, but at the same time resisting his interpretation. I have little sympathy for the destruction wrought by drug abuse, but I see no wisdom in the state's strategies of incarcerating offenders in its unsuccessful war on drugs. I ask Armando some careful questions about the risks involved in telling on other drug dealers. He responds in a way that surprises me all the more, pushing the ethical implications of our Bible study to new levels of complexity.

"No, Roberto, don't get me wrong," continues Armando. "I couldn't tell on my brothers. I'm not a *rata*, and never would actually do what they want. What I want to talk with you about is this: I need your help. You see, the name I am using here is not my real name. I am wondering whether you think it would work if my family sent you my real Mexican ID, with my real name. With this, do you think I could buy a plane ticket and fly to Mexico?" he asks.

"Yes, I do not see any problem with this. If you have any kind of identification with your photo that says you are a Mexican citizen, you can get a plane ticket and fly," I responded, still not clear about what Armando wanted from me.

"OK, good. What I want is your help. I do not have an address in Skagit County. Could my family send you my papers? Would you then be willing to do me the favor of buying me a plane ticket to Mexico for the day that I get out? I need to know whether you would be willing to pick me up and drive me to the airport, so I can get away from here. Maybe you cannot, but I have to ask you anyway," he said in a calm but urgent voice.

What should I do? The story of Rebekah and Jacob played back in my brain. Armando had interpreted this story well, seeing implications that went far beyond my vision for this story's relevancy. Armando saw himself as Jacob, and me as Rebekah. Indeed, I had received the Word from God over and over that God sides with the weak, advocates for the least, and gives his life for the sheep. Was I willing to serve as a Rebekah for Armando?

I thought about the cost of Rebekah's advocacy for herself. She had told her son, "Let your curse be on me, my son" (Gen. 27:13).[10] Rebekah's success meant enmity between the two brothers and permanent separation from her beloved son. I pointed this out to Armando, and told him that I would need to think about the risk and potential cost, for myself and my family, of this sort of aiding and abetting an escape. I told him that if we were caught, I would face time in prison and separation from my wife and children. I told him that I opposed my government's treatment of drug dealers with long prison sentences and wished I could help him rejoin his wife and children, but that I was not ready to take the risk that helping him would involve. I warned him that if he were caught, he could face as much as six additional years for escape. I offered to look more into the consequences and the probabilities of his being apprehended, so he would have a clear idea about the risks. I prayed with him and left, amazed and deeply unsettled by yet another night in the jail.

I think back to the man who visited me at our first farm in Honduras, where my wife and I worked with peasants for six years, beginning in the early '80s. He had asked me for money to take a bus to the capitol, then for a shirt, so he would look more presentable for a job. I had freely given him these things, only to be hit up for a pair of pants and finally my own shoes. I am deeply aware of the limits of my love, both then in Honduras and here in El Norte. I am both inspired and unsettled by my encounters with people like Armando and by the Scriptures, which together push my faith and understanding to places I would rather not go. I recently came upon one of the sayings of the Desert Fathers that speaks to one of my ongoing questions. I now quote it in full:

> Going to town one day to sell some small articles, Abba Agathon met a cripple on the roadside, paralysed in his legs, who asked him where he was going. Abba Agathon replied, "To town, to sell some things." The other said, "Do me the favor of carrying me there." So he carried him to the town. The cripple said to him, "Put me down where you sell your wares." He did so. When he had sold an article, the cripple asked, "What did you sell it for?" and he told him the price. The other said, "Buy me a cake," and he bought it. When Abba Agathon had sold a second article, the sick man asked, "How much did you sell it for?" And he told him the price of it. Then the other said, "Buy me this," and he bought it. When Agathon, having sold all his wares, wanted to go, he said to him, "Are you going back?" and he replied, "Yes." Then said he, "Do me the favor of carrying me back to the place where you found me." Once more picking him up, he carried him back to that place. Then the cripple said, "Agathon, you are filled with divine blessings, in heaven and on earth." Raising his eyes, Agathon saw no man; it was an angel of the Lord, come to try him.[11]

I feel continually tested through my encounters with people on the margins. I, like Rebekah, have heard the word: the older will serve the younger, the last shall be first, by grace you have been saved. I am continually seeing that "God chose what is foolish in the world to shame the wise; God chose what is weak in the world to shame the strong; God chose what is low and despised in the world, things that are not, to reduce to nothing things that are, so that no one might boast in the presence of God" (1 Cor. 1:27–29). Am I willing to follow Rebekah's bold path of resistance, breaking allegiance with the dominant religion and mainstream culture in my solidarity with the underdog? I have no sense of having passed the many tests that come my way. Rather, I am humbled by my limitations and pushed to pray and discern more clearly God's voice and presence to me as I am met and challenged by people on the margins.

Isaac's unwitting and unwilling part in Jacob's blessing, in spite of his role as representative of the dominant theology and mainstream, comes strangely as a word of grace to me. Maybe his violent trembling when he discovers he's been tricked represents a sort of conversion (27:33). Finally, this story assures me that God's will can be done on behalf of others both when I am a willing accomplice like Rebekah and when I am a blind and unwilling actor in people's liberation like Isaac. My faith and my lack of faith can both serve God's purposes. This is good news for the damned and good news for me.

Unexpected Encounters in the Bible
An Illiterate's Penetrating Interpretation of a Humble Story

During our four-week summer visits to Minas de Oro, Honduras, our neighbors and Tierra Nueva promoters come to our home nearly every night for Bible studies. Maria, an illiterate woman in her forties, comes occasionally with her two daughters, Choncita and Miriam. Over the nearly twenty years that we have known this family, Maria has become one of my wife Gracie's closest friends. They live below us in an adobe house surrounded by a pine slat fence and enormous granite boulders. Maria often roasts green coffee beans, the rich aroma drifting up the steep barrio to our house. She has been a washerwoman all her life, and regularly hikes barefoot high into the mountains to hoe her family's corn and bean plot and carry back firewood on her head. She's known to carry a loaded revolver in her skirt, to keep abusive men at bay.

"I know nothing," insists Maria, her rubber thongs stretched across swollen feet planted firmly on the floor. "I come because I want to study the word of God in the Bible. I know nothing about the Bible, and very little about God. I hardly ever go to church. People say I need to be born again. I don't know. I will just listen," she says, looking down.

The evening's study is on the mysterious encounter between Jacob and the enigmatic aggressor at the River Jabbok in Genesis 32:22–32. Two months before, I had presented an academic paper in Montpellier on this narrative, so I am familiar with the latest research.

After an opening prayer and a few songs accompanied by an out-of-tune guitar, I briefly talk of the related events that precede this story: Jacob's stealing of the birthright and blessing from his brother Esau; Jacob's escape from his raging brother; God's meeting him, and his conditional "If God will be with me . . . and I come again to my father's house in peace, then the LORD shall be my God" (Gen. 28:20–21); Jacob's twenty-one years of labor for Laban and flight; Laban's pursuit of Jacob; Jacob's worried preparations to meet his estranged brother, Esau; his prayer of last resort (32:9–12), and final attempts to appease Esau through elaborate gifts. Ramiro reads aloud the story of the wrestling. After asking the group what happened in the story and getting minimal responses, I ask Ramiro to read it a second time, slower.

People begin to get into the story, and comments begin to flow. People laugh at how faithless and lacking in courage Jacob appears.

"What a man! This Jacob sends his wives and children ahead toward Esau, while he remains behind, alone," says Elia with a smirk.

"The men these days! They make us do all the work, while they lay back and sleep," says Maria, eliciting smiles and laughs from everyone.

"But in spite of all his efforts, a man is there who wrestles with him all night," notes Ramiro.

We talk about how the man could not beat Jacob, and cripples him by striking his hip. The man says he has to go before daybreak, but Jacob will not let him get away until this mysterious man blesses him.

"What do you think of this man? Who might he be?" I ask the group.

Everyone is silent, looking down at their Bibles, except Maria, who looks up and tentatively begins to talk.

"I know nothing, because I never went to school. I cannot read or write. I am an ignorant person. But it seems to me that this man may have been a spirit of the river or an angel, because he appears and says he has to go before it gets light. Or it could have been Esau. But the Bible says he was a man, and he did not give his name."

I sit amazed as Maria presents and dismisses three theories I had recently read by German exegetes. Yet this is not the end of Maria's interpretation.

"I do not know anything, but it seems to me that this is a man, but also God, like our Lord Jesus Christ. The man says, 'You have striven with God and with humans, and have won.' Then Jacob says, 'I have seen God face to face, and yet I did not die'?"

"Yes, Jacob names the place Peniel, 'the face of God,'" I respond. "The man does say, 'I have seen God face to face, and yet my life is preserved.' So, if this man is God, what does this tell us about God?" I ask.

"God comes as a man. This is a God who is full of mercy. God could have destroyed Jacob. God lets Jacob beat him. This is just like our Lord Jesus Christ, who lets us crucify him," continues Maria. "This is a good God."

This gets the group talking, as others begin to make connections. We talk about the grace of God, how God meets and blesses Jacob even though he does not have faith and is doing everything he can to save himself. We talk about how God shows strength by being merciful, and this looks like weakness. We notice that God is humble, not telling his name or overpowering Jacob.

"It is like Jacob met Jesus Christ here, but he had not yet been born, so he did not tell him his name," says Elia, offering a contemporary version of Martin Luther's reading of this text.

"So what happens after this wrestling? What will happen when Jacob finally meets Esau?" I ask, inviting someone to read Genesis 33:1–11.

Eda reads the eleven verses haltingly. The group notices that Jacob is limping, and several make comments.

"Jacob is not the same man after this," says Maria. "Before, he sent everyone ahead to face his problems. Now he goes ahead of his wives and children, limping. He is humble. He bows seven times to his brother."

"What happened to Jacob?" I ask. "Why is he so different?"

"He had just wrestled with God, and God did not punish him but blessed him. So he has nothing to fear," says Ramiro.

"I am probably mistaken," adds Maria, "but it seems to me that Jacob's meeting with God makes it so things work out with his brother. Look, Jacob says to Esau: 'Seeing your face is like seeing the face of God.'"

Once again, I sit amazed, hearing some of Wilhelm Vischer's finest exegesis expressed freshly by illiterate and semiliterate people, who have all gone far beyond most modern interpreters.

We talk about how, when the mysterious man/God lets Jacob win when he should have lost, God is showing Jacob that even though he deserved to be beaten by Esau, he is shown mercy. We talk about the parallels with the father in the prodigal son story in Luke 15. There, the father comes running and kisses his younger son, representing Jesus' welcoming of the sinners with whom he eats (Luke 15:1–2). We end the Bible study by reading Ephesians 2:13–16, which reinforce Maria's interpretation:

> But now in Christ Jesus you who once were far off have been brought near by the blood of Christ. For he is our peace; in his flesh he has made both groups into one and has broken down the dividing wall, that is, the hostility between us. He has abolished the law with its commandments and ordinances, that he might create in himself one new humanity in place of the two, thus making peace, and might reconcile both groups to God in one body through the cross, thus putting to death that hostility through it.

That night, over the rumble of our portable generator, I witness what I now have come to anticipate. In an uncontrollable moment, in and through what is included and excluded from the text, a strange, unexpected identification emerges. God becomes visible, identifying with the weakest character in the story. God reveals himself as one who meets Jacob at his point of weakness and accompanies him. Printed words on a page, words read aloud in a Bible study and remembered, become a medium for communicating a Word from outside the page. Revelation appears to happen precisely when we see that this weak one, this one wrapped in the swaddling clothes of the text, is God's very self. Through the weak, powerless word and its feeble mediators, the Word becomes flesh and lives among us. The apparently distant God draws close. In this case through Maria, an impoverished, uneducated campesina woman—an outsider to the church and an outcast in her community.

Chapter Five

Encountering God in Exodus
and at Today's Margins

One night in the jail, five men showed up for Bible study—three Mexicans and two Anglos. We did a bilingual study on Exodus 1–2. I ask volunteers to read the text in Spanish. I ask the men to describe in their own words what was happening in the story.

I introduce the Bible study on Exodus 1–2 by briefly providing the men with background information on the Israelites up to Exodus 1:7. I tell the story of how Jacob and his twelve sons were immigrants. Famine threatened the food supply of Jacob and his family, pushing them to Egypt, an affluent empire. There the family settled, much the way many immigrants from Latin America put down roots in El Norte. We look carefully at Pharaoh's response to the growing, teeming masses. The powers were threatened by the growing number of foreigners. They responded with increasingly oppressive measures.

"Let's read this story slowly, trying to figure out what happened," I suggest. "Let's think about our own reality here too. Maybe there is a relationship between this story and our own lives. Could someone read for us Exodus 1:8–14?" I ask.

> Now a new king arose over Egypt, who did not know Joseph. He said to his people, "Look, the Israelite people are more numerous and more powerful than we. Come, let us deal shrewdly with them, or they will increase and, in the event of war, join our enemies and fight against us and escape from the land." Therefore they set taskmasters over them to oppress them with forced labor. They built supply cities, Pithom and Rameses, for Pharaoh. But the more they were oppressed, the more they multiplied and spread, so that the Egyptians came to

dread the Israelites. The Egyptians became ruthless in imposing tasks on the Israelites, and made their lives bitter with hard service in mortar and brick and in every kind of field labor. They were ruthless in all the tasks that they imposed on them.

At first Pharaoh oppressed them as a labor force, putting taskmasters over them to drive them to build his cities. However, the more he oppressed them, the more they multiplied.

"Does this sort of thing happen today?" I ask.

Donald, a man in his late twenties who is half Italian and half Upper Skagit Native American, responds: "You're not kidding. The state gets less money because of initiative 695.[1] Now they take it out on us. They make us pay to come to jail and then cut back on everything. When we're in prison they take a bit part of any money that is sent to us. Then outside, they're cutting back on help for single moms, taking away people's food stamps, welfare, and shit. That's not making them have less kids. They're still having babies, it's just harder now."

I mention a few things about how the laws are getting harsher, and ask others what they think. Jay nods and says things are definitely getting harder.

"So is this tendency of the state to clamp down on people working?" I ask.

"No way, man. There are more of us than ever. They're putting away all kinds of people. The jails and prisons are full."

Donald goes on to tell me about how he's just been released from prison.

"While in prison I got my GED, a certificate in welding, and other things. But since I've been out no one has wanted to hire me. They want me to be seven years out before they'll give me a job. So what am I supposed to do? I went and did what I'm good at. I sold drugs. I'm not here for that, but for assault. Now I'm heading back to the joint where I'll get some more diplomas. But for what?"

We moved on to Pharaoh's next strategy for dealing with the masses: ordering the Hebrew midwives to kill the male babies.

> The king of Egypt said to the Hebrew midwives, one of whom was named Shiphrah and the other Puah, "When you act as midwives to the Hebrew women, and see them on the birthstool, if it is a boy, kill him; but if it is a girl, she shall live." (Exod. 1:15–16)

"Why was Pharaoh so threatened by baby boys?" I ask. "Why wouldn't Pharaoh have the baby girls killed? Or both the baby boys and the baby girls?" I continue.

At first the men are silent. They cannot figure out why anyone would be threatened by a baby boy. I invite them to turn to Exodus 1:9–10 to read what Pharaoh said to his people. "Maybe if we read this, we will discover why the Egyptians felt threatened by their immigrant neighbors," I suggest.

> He said to his people, "Look, the Israelite people are more numer-ous and more powerful than we. Come, let us deal shrewdly with them, or they will increase and, in the event of war, join our enemies and fight against us and escape from the land."

Clarity came with the reading of these verses.

"Pharaoh was worried that the people would outnumber them," says Chris.

I point out that Hispanics are quickly becoming the number-one minority group in California, and that in twenty years Mexico's popula-tion will catch up with the United States—except that the majority will be under age fifteen.

"Why would baby boys be targeted?" I ask again.

"They were worried that the boys would grow up and turn against the state," someone says. "For that reason they decided to try to kill them before they became a problem."

"Do you see this happening in any way today?" I ask.

People are thinking silently for a while, unable to come up with any-thing. I mention that in many wars that are being fought around the world young boys are doing the fighting. Someone mentions abortion.

"I don't like that, man," says Johnny. "It's not right to take out a life when it's growing in there," he continues, gently caressing his own heav-ily tattooed stomach.

I mention that many mainstream people are afraid of young Hispanic men like them. "Prisons and jails all across America are filled with young men of color," I say.

"It's true," says Juan, who recently did time in the Washington State prison system. "Most of the inmates are black, Hispanic, or Indians."

"Yeah, man, they must be afraid of us. The police stop us for nothing, only because we're brown-skinned," says Jesse.

"Here it says that the Pharaoh was also worried they would lose their workers," someone adds.

He rereads the verse where this is stated: "They will increase and, in the event of war, join our enemies and fight against us and escape from the land."

"The Egyptians needed the people because they themselves didn't want to do the work. Here it's the same. The *gabachos* don't want to do the work picking fruit, the work in the fields. Only the Mexicans do this. Yet the *migra* still deports us," he continues.

"So how do the Hebrew midwives respond to Pharaoh's order?" I ask. "Let's check it out by reading the passage again," I suggest. Someone reads Exodus 1:17–21:

> But the midwives feared God; they did not do as the king of Egypt commanded them, but they let the boys live. So the king of Egypt summoned the midwives and said to them, "Why have you done this, and allowed the boys to live?" The midwives said to Pharaoh, "Because the Hebrew women are not like the Egyptian women; for they are vigorous and give birth before the midwife comes to them." So God dealt well with the midwives; and the people multiplied and became very strong. And because the midwives feared God, he gave them families.

"They didn't obey. They feared God," someone says.

"They lied to the Pharaoh when he asked them why they weren't obeying," says someone else.

"And how did God respond?" I ask.

"He blessed them. He gave them families," someone said. "So what did Pharaoh do next?" I ask. "He told the people to throw the male babies in the river."

At this point I ask the men to list the people in the story, from the most powerful to the least powerful. It took awhile to get them to list everyone in order: Pharaoh, the taskmasters, the Egyptians, the Hebrew midwives Puah and Shiphrah, the Israelites, the Israelite women, the babies.

"So who's at the top?" I ask.

"The Egyptians," says one.

"Pharaoh," says another.

"Who are at the bottom?" I ask.

"The women," someone says.

"The babies," says another.

"So whose side is God on?" I ask. "He's with the babies. He's with the women."

This excites the guys. Then God is not on the side of the state, which is oppressive. God is with the weak people, the babies, people in jail. . . . "How did God work to save the weak people?" I ask.

"Through the midwives, the women."

We briefly discussed how God brings salvation through people, and through people who don't have the power. No matter what the Pharaoh did, he couldn't win. The forces of darkness and death kept looking for a way to destroy the people. But God is for life. The forces of life consistently won over the forces of death.

Exodus 2–3: Journeying with Moses Toward True Solidarity
Shifting Social and Narrative Locations

I often read the story of Moses' awakening and call with incarcerated Latino immigrants attending my weekly bilingual Spanish-English Bible studies in Skagit County Jail, in Washington State. People in our reading circle immediately identify with characters in the narrative of Exodus 2:11–3:12, and appear to feel excluded from other roles in the story. Participants' first-glance assumptions about each biblical character's social location and their own place in the world lead to a prejudiced reading of the story. These biased interpretations of biblical stories are often alienating, reinforcing people's feelings of powerlessness or exclusion. I am convinced that oppressive interpretations can be subverted by careful reading of the narrative itself. This is most likely to happen when guided by facilitation that directly questions assumptions and invites unexpected identifications.

Moses Goes Out to the People

The story in Exodus 2:11ff. opens with Moses, adopted son of Pharaoh's daughter, now grown up, going out to his people. Privileged Moses, going out from Pharaoh's household to see the people's forced labor and seeing the Egyptian beating a Hebrew, at first glance does not resemble anyone except maybe me—the white, middle-class, educated professional's presence there in the jail to "help" the inmates. Their first impressions are of my eyes meeting each of theirs as guards usher them into the jail's multi-purpose room, where we sit together for an hour or two in a circle.

The oppressed Israelites resemble the people I read Scripture with: Mexican, Chicano, white, or Native American male inmates between eighteen and forty-five years old. The most visible equivalents to Israelite forced labor and beatings at the hands of Egyptians include the jail or prison sentences, court-ordered fines and probation, addictions to drugs or alcohol, or minimum-wage jobs harvesting crops or processing fish or poultry. The taskmaster invites identification with everyone from me, as representative of taskmaster religion, to judges, jail guards, probation officers, girlfriends, or the DSHS social workers, who require child-support payments. Other nonhuman forces, such as cocaine, anger, and jealousy, are occasionally brought up as equivalents of taskmasters. Pharaoh represents the domination system or the status quo.

The story's first impressions of abused Israelites' fighting with each other and distrusting their prospective liberator elicit contemporary versions of the same. Would-be liberator Moses' impulsive killing of the abusive taskmaster, denounced presumably by the very slaves whom he sought to defend, leads to his having to flee to a foreign country—a failed, paternalistic savior who is now completely absent from the scene. The Israelite slaves and their Latino immigrant equivalents remain passive objects of Pharaoh's, and now our, perpetual domination system. God is absent from the scene in the story, and too often in people's lives, failing to intervene to keep things from messing up.

A first read might leave these characters' and their readers' social roles intact were it not for the story's surprising turns. As the narrative unfolds, and people take note of the text's rich detail, discussion deepens. New identifications, increasingly challenging to both inmates and myself, become possible as Moses journeys deeper into marginality. Can a trained reader from the domination system move from being identified and rejected as an Egyptian taskmaster or paternalistic Moses to a new place as effective agent of call, empowerment, and liberation? How can inmates and immigrants move from identifying themselves with subjected Israelite slaves to hearing the call of Moses to advocate for their people before the powers? The journey toward empowering solidarity requires great care on my part, as the trained reader who seeks to facilitate this reading process without getting in the way.

Egyptian Taskmaster or Privileged Moses—My Status?

My own social location among Latino immigrant inmates more closely parallels Egyptian taskmaster status than privileged Moses stature before the Israelite slaves. My race, gender, language, nationality, and education mark me as a representative of the dominant mainstream American culture to my mostly undocumented, brown-skinned, Spanish-speaking, immigrant, jailed Bible-study participants. My racial profile looks similar to the characteristics of most employers who hire people for minimum-wage stoop-labor fieldwork or other physically demanding, low-paid jobs. Apart from the uniform, I resemble the jail guards, police agents, prosecutors, and judges that arrest, detain, judge, and sentence the people. Guards usher me into and out of the jail's multipurpose room, making me appear like an officially authorized benefit afforded to inmates by the powers. Yet, since I am not one of the people who has power over them (like an attorney, judge, or prosecutor), I am viewed as someone neutral, or even positively. Still, since I am Caucasian, a pastor, and known to them as the director of Tierra Nueva, I am viewed as clearly having more power than they do.

My status as pastor and expounder of the Bible also associates me with religious taskmasters of the dominant theology. As pastor, I am automatically associated with God's social location, which in the minds of most inmates is far removed from theirs in the privileged, luxury utopia of heaven. Most view God as hyper-sovereign—a distant judge whose powerful will has predetermined everything. While many confess that their troubles are of their own making, they simultaneously insist that God has their lives all mapped out in advance. They tend to consciously or unconsciously attribute all the negative things that happen to them as God's will. Since their theology assumes that God is just and good, people logically figure they must be bad and deserving of all the calamities that have befallen them. In Skagit County Jail, inmates often tell me, "God has me in jail—I was going down a bad road." Others say that they are there because of their own mistakes. They see God as both unwilling and maybe even unable to help them out. They expect no redemption, unless bail can be posted by a fellow drug dealer or a sympathetic family member.

People's perception of me as religious taskmaster unconsciously comes into play the moment people begin attending my Bible studies. Some of the people come to the gathering with an attitude of indifference, with no visible expectation of hearing any good news. They come for a combination of reasons, from socializing with friends from other pods to escaping the boredom of the correctional facility's repetitive, predictable, military-like structure. Many people I work with, both inside and outside of jail, have given up on Christianity after finding that "accepting Christ as their Savior" with the evangelicals, or attending mass for a while on a regular basis, did not solve all their problems as the pastor promised. Addictions to drugs and alcohol and failures to change in other areas often beat people back into submission to the powers. The voice of the Satan, accuser and tempter, too often sounds louder and more powerfully than that of the Paraclete—advocate and comforter.

Other people's attendance may at first be motivated by duty before a probation-officer-like God, who they consciously or unconsciously think might look at their "religious" efforts favorably, rewarding them with a lighter sentence or bringing them back into favor with an estranged spouse. This view of God is visible in people's tendency to interpret every biblical text as calling them to behave in an obedient, morally righteous way. Inmates often reveal their assumptions about what pleases God when they apologize after a swear word slips naturally from their mouths in an uncensored moment, or berate themselves as hypocrites who seek God only when they are in trouble, but avoid anything religious once on the street. New inmates who do not yet know me are guarded with their language and self-disclosures. Others are looking for my affirmation regarding their efforts to approach God through Bible reading, pious talk, and even fasting. I believe that, underlying the most negative motivations, people are thirsty for an authentic encounter. In most people there remains a buried hope that something real may yet happen between them and God. The trained reader of Scripture who facilitates Bible studies in settings such as a jail or prison must be clear about his or her role and means in engaging people in liberating, transformational reading of Scripture.

My role involves deliberately subverting as many of the barriers to hope and empowerment as possible, while at the same time inviting life-giving interpretation that replaces the old, paralyzing theology. I seek to help people directly identify and confront the dominant negative theology, even before it appears in their interpretations. Identifying and countering evidence that appears to reinforce the dominant theology in the biblical stories is critical if the Bible is to be salvaged as the medium of an empowering word. Salvaging apparently irrelevant or oppressive biblical stories must include helping people come to see themselves in the stories in ways that maximize the possibility of their hearing a liberating word addressed to them. Salvaging the story includes broadening the possibilities of Bible-study participants' actual identification with appropriate characters in the story. This broadening of identifications is occasioned in part by means of careful examination both of the biblical characters' narrative social location and of the participants' own actual social location. As this is accomplished, a shift in social locations up or down the hierarchical power ladder in the text and in the group can be revealed that makes room for people to take on new roles. Privileged, pretentious, Moses-like would-be liberators can become humble, wandering fugitives awaiting new calls. Oppressed slaves and their contemporary equivalents can move toward new roles as Moses-like liberators of their people. So how can I, as facilitator, negotiate the barriers afforded me by my own privileged social location?

Shifting the Facilitator's Perceived Social Location

My own awareness that my social location associates me with the Egyptian taskmasters has led me to seek to distance myself from taskmasters in a number of ways. Firstly, I try to help people identify contemporary manifestations of both social and religious taskmasters. Before launching into our study of Exodus 2:11–3:12, I first briefly present Genesis background that shows Jacob and his sons in Canaan being pushed to migrate to Egypt because of a famine. I then continue with a brief review of Exodus 1—a separate Bible study, which I have often done at the previous weekly gathering. I describe how God's people were hammered by a powerful Pharaoh, who sought to crush them through forced labor, physical abuse, and death penalties. The Pharaoh's fear-based repression against the multiplying Israelite immigrant community provides fertile ground for Latino immigrants' contemporary comparisons. The Egyptian leadership's oppression of Israelites through hard labor looks a lot like U.S. government lack of enforcement of labor laws set up to protect workers from abuse. The harsh targeting of male children for extermination invites comparisons ranging from racial profiling of immigrant men by law enforcement, and mass incarceration for minor drug-dealing offenses, to deportations and permanent bar to reentry to undocumented immigrant men—most of whom are fathers to U.S.-citizen children residing in the United States. I emphasize that close study of the text shows how God's promise of life cannot be stopped, but even increases with every death-blow. My facilitation style invites people to make associations that gradually lead them to see me as on *their* side. This establishes a gap between my identity as trained Bible reader and the Egyptian Pharaoh, Egyptian people, and taskmasters.

Continuing in my efforts to show the Exodus writer (and myself) as on the side of the oppressed, I remind people how the Israelites resisted, refusing to comply with Pharaoh's laws. Moses was a slave baby who was saved because his family hid him, finally placing him in a basket and hiding him in the reeds by the river. There Pharaoh's daughter found him and had compassion on him. After unknowingly hiring Moses' very mother as Moses' nanny, Pharaoh's daughter adopted Moses, raising him with all the royal privileges. He was an Israelite, but he may well have been sheltered from the realities of his people's lives.

To help people shift in their perceptions regarding God's social location, I point out that God is not siding with oppressor Pharaoh. Rather, the story shows God visibly standing with the weakest, most vulnerable ones in the story—the baby boys targeted for extermination. God blesses those who resist the forces of death through refusing to carry out Pharaoh's order and lying to him when confronted: the Hebrew midwives. Exodus depicts God as sovereign—but in a completely unexpected way. God's sovereignty is exercised, not through the males identified by Pharaoh to be the greatest threat, but through mothers, a young girl, and even the foreign princess. Their resistance takes the forms of covert disobedience, lying and hiding and noncompliant adoption of the victim. The legal system cannot stop the fulfillment of God's covenant.

Yet everyone there in the jail is all too aware that the forces of death crush human lives. The principalities and powers wreak havoc on humans and on creation. In spite of God's movement in the world, people suffer: "The Israelites groaned under their slavery, and cried out" (Exod. 2:23). This cry did not fall on the deaf ears of an impersonal deity who wills the oppression as some kind of punishment. The text tells us:

> Out of the slavery their cry for help rose up to God. God heard their groaning, and God remembered his covenant with Abraham, Isaac, and Jacob. God looked upon the Israelites, and God took notice of them. (2:23b–25)

People in my Bible studies are taken by surprise when they realize how God works in this story. Could this really be the way God works in our world today? Interest is sparked. The men are open to reading on. I recognize that it is not enough for them to know that, according to the Bible, God sees people's suffering. While this is encouraging, people want to know how God actually responds to oppression if God is in fact good and acts. My visible agreement with and excitement about God's strategy partially confounds people's assumptions about my theology as one apparently associated with a sovereign punishing and/or Pharaoh and his taskmasters. Yet the narrative offers no clear character equivalents to myself as facilitator other than Pharaoh's daughter. None of these first mediators of liberation in Exodus 1–2:10 are male, nor are they required to gain trust. Most importantly, the Israelites remain slaves.

At this point in the story, Moses once again enters the scene, and the Bible study is about to begin. I invite people to pay close attention to the story of Moses we're about to read. I invite them to look for tips about what this might mean for us. God is about to call a human being to a special task. The way God calls and the qualifications of the savior figure tell us a lot about God—and open up possibilities for us as well.

I remind the men that we know from the story that Moses had been given a special break. He'd escaped death thanks to his mother, sister, and Pharaoh's daughter. He was adopted into Pharaoh's household, benefited from special opportunities, and escaped the grueling slavery of his people.

Seeing the Misery through Going Out: Me and Moses

The brief telling of my own story at this point invites a comparison with emerging Moses, instead of with the oppressive taskmasters, that can be helpful as part of the process but potentially harmful if left there. I tell people how I too am from immigrant ancestors—though the comparisons are of limited value. My parents were both born in the United States. My grandfather on my father's side migrated from Sweden at the beginning of the twentieth century, while on my mother's side my forebears trace back to some of the first English settlers in the eighteenth century. Unlike Moses, a child of slaves once immigrants, I grew up as a privileged member of the dominant U.S. ethnicity, and benefited from many opportunities, including an undergraduate and graduate education. I now am an ordained Presbyterian pastor, jail chaplain, and director of an ecumenical ministry to immigrants called Tierra Nueva (New Earth).

When leading this Bible study, I often share my story of "going out to see" the people that began over twenty-four years ago with life-changing trips to Europe, Israel, Mexico, and Central America. This process has continued, including six years of work teaching sustainable farming and leading Bible studies among poor Honduran peasants during the 1980s. "Going out" now includes regular visits to farmworkers in migrant labor camps and other immigrant workers in ghettolike apartment complexes, and weekly Spanish Bible studies in Skagit County Jail. I use great care to not express my going out in ministry in heroic or victorious ways. If anything, I err on the side of confessing my weakness and ignorance in knowing how to effectively help people to find healing and liberation from the most insidious forms of oppression (addictions to heroin, crack, methamphetamines), and my need for God's direct help in my work with people. In addition, my going out to see the inmates is brought about through the agency of uniformed jail guards, who usher me through the thick steel doors into the jail's multipurpose room. The guards' releasing of the red-uniformed inmates who want to attend my study from their individual cells and pods and the corralling of these inmates through two steel doors to take their places in the circle of blue plastic chairs reminds us all who actually is in the power position.

The men with whom I read more closely resemble Israelite slaves in Egypt than I embody Moses. Many are originally peasants from impoverished rural villages in Mexico. Pushed away by landlessness, drought, unemployment, government neglect, and global market forces, they, like Jacob's family, were drawn to the bounty of El Norte (the U.S.A.)— modern-day Egypt. Once in the United States, they find work as farm laborers or minimum-wage workers. Their willingness to work hard for low wages has made them invaluable to farmers, meatpacking plants, and countless other employers. Most of the people I read with have entered the United States illegally, and live on the margins of American society. Many do not have valid driver's licenses or even identification, and make use of counterfeit residency and Social Security cards. Most have partners and children to support, sometimes both in Mexico and in the U.S.A. This is a near-impossible feat when making minimum wage. Some are tempted by and succumb to small- and larger-scale drug dealing for extra cash. Theirs is a life of constant insecurity. If ever arrested for anything, they can be assured they will be deported back to Mexico by the Department of Homeland Security immediately after doing their jail time.

Trusting God does not come naturally. People learn to lean, rather, on their own survival strategies, the "weapons of the weak." I continually struggle to determine how I, a trained reader of Scripture and professional religious worker, can best function as an agent of call or liberation. I propose reading the story of Moses' origins and first encounter with the oppressed in Exodus 2 and 3 with this question in mind: Who does God call as agents of liberation, and how? How do would-be liberators gain trust?

Moses' journey toward solidarity appears to begin when he goes out and sees the oppression of his people. When I lead a Bible study with inmates, I often launch the actual study with the questions. The following dialogue is actually a composite of several Bible studies, but is reflective of the way I lead this study, and the ways inmates often answer.

"The first thing we know about the adult Moses is a description of his awakening to the pain and struggle of the people. Let's see what happened to Moses," I suggest, inviting someone to read Exodus 2 in Spanish and then in English:

> One day, after Moses had grown up, he went out to his people and *saw* their forced labor. He *saw* an Egyptian beating a Hebrew, one of his kinsfolk. (v. 11; italics added)

"What did Moses see when he went out?" I ask the group.

"He saw the hard work they were doing," says Chris, a Chicano man in his early thirties fresh from ten years in a Texas prison.

"He saw an Egyptian beating one of his people," says Vicente, an undocumented Mexican immigrant man in his mid-twenties.

"This has happened to me too in many ways," I continue. "I came from a middle-class family, where I had lots of privileges. I was sheltered from the struggles of immigrants, poor people, people in prison. If I, or someone like me or Moses, came into your lives, your families, or your villages in Mexico, what would they see?" I ask.

"A lot of poverty," says Vicente. "In Mexico one makes in one day what one makes in an hour here."

"Discrimination," says Chris. "Last week in court there were five of us Mexicans and twelve, maybe even fourteen *gabachos* [white people]. Every one of the white guys was released. All of us Mexicans are still here."

"Lots of struggles," someone else adds. "In my home growing up, there was lots of fighting between my old man and old lady. Lots of drinking too."

"Drugs, addictions," says Jesse.

"So what sorts of ways do we react to injustices or hardships in our lives?" I ask the men.

"We use violence. We take out our frustration on someone," says someone.

"Some of us use drugs to blow it all away, to escape the pain," says someone else.

"Let's see how Moses responds," I suggest, inviting someone to read the next verse, Exodus 2:12. A volunteer reads:

> He looked this way and that, and seeing no one he killed the Egyptian and hid him in the sand.

"Whoa, I thought Moses was a righteous dude," says Chris. "But he killed a man. He broke the commandments."

We talk about how Moses' *going out* and *seeing* change his life forever. Direct exposure to poverty, injustice, or oppression—of whatever sort—can lead us to react with violence. Moses' seeing clearly impacts him—as encounters with oppression always do. The next day he returns, trying his hand at conflict resolution between two Hebrew slaves.

"How did the Hebrew slaves react to Moses when he tried to break up their fight? Did he prove himself in their eyes by taking a courageous stand against the bad guys?" I ask.

"They didn't respect him," insists Julio, a confident Chicano man in his late twenties. "They saw him as a violent man, acting the same as the Egyptians."

"I thought that being a bad-ass dude, defending yourself when you're dissed, doing a drive-by on a rival gang, got you respect. Isn't that true?" I ask, half teasing.

"Well, it does in a way, but not real respect that lasts," someone responds.

"What about being a tough, strict parent. Isn't that a good thing? How many of you were harshly punished by your parents when you were children?" I ask. Over half the group raise their hands immediately.

"So did it make you respect your parents more or less?" I continue.

"Way less—punishment didn't work," someone blurts out.

"It just made me more angry," says another man.

"And how about the police or the court system. Do the harsh sentences to enforce the laws make you respect them more?"

Heads are all shaking no.

"Yeah, like George Bush beating up on the Iraqis. He just used his power. That didn't gain him no respect," adds Roberto, a thin Chicano guy who hadn't said anything until now.

"So what would he [Moses] have had to do to win their respect?" I ask, trying to get the men to place themselves in the Hebrew slaves' shoes.

"He'd have to show respect, and be more humble," says Julio.

We talk together about how seeing can lead us to reflect and act in many different ways. I point out that Moses' mother saw that Moses was a beautiful baby boy, and she hid him. When Pharaoh's daughter saw baby Moses crying, she had compassion on him, adopting him as her own even though she knew he was a condemned Hebrew baby (Exod. 2:6).

We wonder together how people think Pharaoh found out that Moses was the killer. Did the Hebrew slaves need to denounce him in order to avoid being blamed for the crime? Did the slaves feel more secure with the known system the taskmaster represented than they did with the unknown Moses? What would it take for the Hebrew slaves to trust Moses as their liberator? The text is silent regarding all these questions, leaving the reader surmising that Moses' heroic act likely was inadequate to earn him the allegiance of the Hebrew slaves, who had to act in their own security interests.

One thing is certain. Moses' murder of the taskmaster forces him to become a fugitive. Rejected by his people, his crime exposed, Moses is now on the other side of the law. His lawbreaking in solidarity with the oppressed has made him an enemy of the Egyptian state. His adoptive mother's father, Pharaoh, now pursues him in order to kill him—showing that dominators cannot be trusted. With a warrant issued by Pharaoh himself, Moses flees for his life (a reactive move—like many offenders).

Now he's in exile, wanted for murder, a failed liberator/reactionary—unappreciated by his people, a sojourner in a foreign land, shepherding for a living. At the same time, Moses' crime, exile, and location in the desert significantly broaden the possibilities for others to identify with this character.

"When people in Mexico commit a crime and are being hunted by the police, where do they go?" I ask the group.

"*Al Norte* [to North—to U.S.A.]," they responded. I have met many men who came to the Skagit Valley precisely to escape troubles at home.

Many end up in jail or prison for new crimes committed in North America. Others work in the fields, picking strawberries, raspberries, blueberries, cucumbers, or working in meatpacking plants. Some sell drugs.

"So where was Moses when God met him?" I ask the guys in my study. "Was he in mass or in some church? What was he doing? Was he praying, studying the Bible, looking for God?"

The men look surprised and slightly uncomfortable with the obvious answer. They're not used to looking at narrative gaps—at what the text doesn't say. Might there be good news there too?

"Moses was in the desert. He was working, shepherding his sheep," they observe.

"But he must have done something good, he must have been a holy person, he must have known God, otherwise God would not have met him," I insist, inviting them to look closer at the text. "What do we know about Moses?"

Occasionally people have stated here that Moses was chosen because he grew up in Pharaoh's court and had the knowledge and social-class background to be a liberator. This assumption is visible in ancient Jewish and Christian exegesis too, which seeks to make sense of God's choice of Moses for such a key leadership role and to respond to the contradiction, and even offense, of Moses' claims about himself in Exodus 4:10: "But I am slow of speech and slow of tongue." For example, see Acts 7:21–22. While these readings make room for people like me and other trained readers to find their place in the popular liberation struggles, the absence of any signs of Moses' having benefited by his life with Pharaoh's daughter makes room for people on the margins to identify with Moses.

The guys look in their Bibles. Someone dares to answer: "He was a murderer. It wasn't even an accident. He looked this way and that. He hid the body in the sand."

Moses, indeed, became an immigrant and a fugitive, working a minimum-wage job in the wilderness. His life did not yet have a place in God's project of liberation and life. Moses needed to do more than just "go out to see" oppression. Another kind of seeing was necessary for Moses to discover his new vocation. But this second "seeing" was not his own doing.

Encounter with God in the Desert

I point out to the men that the place of God's encounter supports seeing this as God's initiative. The desert is the place where the rejected were cast (Hagar, Ishmael). It is also a place of revelation, of being set apart or finding your identity as God's people (and not just as Pharaoh's slaves).[2] Moses drives his flock "beyond" the wilderness—a place of utter desolation? It's in this no-man's-land that he comes to the mountain of God.

It is here that the angel of YHWH appears to/is seen by him. He sees a flame in a bush, a curious sight. The flame is approachable—it does not burn up the bush. He's drawn to contemplate. God calls him by name: "Moses, Moses!"

"So what does this mean for us?" I ask the guys in my jail Bible study.

"It's like God shows up where we work, man. He comes to the field, he comes to the factory. He appears right there," someone says. Another guy adds: "The desert is right here. This jail is the wilderness where we've been led. God appears to us here, when we've come to the end of our rope."

When Moses is told he's in God's presence, a holy place, he hides his face in fear. "Why do you think he was afraid?" I ask the inmates.

"He felt dirty. He felt ashamed to be in God's presence. Like he wasn't good enough," says one guy.

"He knew he was guilty of murder. He thought God would punish him, or take him in to Pharaoh," says someone else.

"So what *does* God do? Does he slap on the handcuffs and take him away? What does God say? Let's read the next verse," I suggest.

> I have observed ["seen"] the misery of my people who are in Egypt;
> I have heard their cry on account of their taskmasters. Indeed, I know
> their sufferings, and I have come down to deliver them from the
> Egyptians, and to bring them up out of that land to a good and broad
> land, a land flowing with milk and honey. (Exod. 3:7–8)

The inmates can hardly believe it when they hear these words. It's like they're waiting for the hammer to fall, the bad news to be announced. But it just gets better and better. When I ask them what the people did in order for God to come down and save them, they smile with delight at the absence of religious-looking behaviors.

"They did nothing! They were in misery, they groaned, they cried out," someone says.

It surprises people that God says nothing to Moses about his murderous act—and someone else even observed that it was this same Moses who later was given the tablets of stone where God wrote with his very finger: "You shall not murder" (or: kill; NRSV note). God shows surprising solidarity with Moses' first "seeing." God too sees the oppression, and God has come down to do something about it. I ask the men at this point if God's knowledge of the people's condition differs from Moses'.

We look together at a detail that speaks clearly to any would-be liberator. Moses does go out, and sees the burdens and an Egyptian beating one of his people. In the Hebrew text, YHWH speaks in the first person, using the emphatic doubling of the verb "to see" that echoes Moses' seeing. God's seeing of the misery of his people is followed by two other verbs that suggest a deeper solidarity, not yet experienced by Moses. YHWH continues:

"I have heard their cry on account of their taskmasters. Indeed, I know their sufferings."

YHWH's words to Moses are suggestive to any would-be liberator that a deeper solidarity is required, which implies a descent into the condition of the oppressed. Hearing people's cries related to their taskmasters and knowing their suffering imply a shift in social location.

In addition, God's response differs markedly from Moses' murderous act. YHWH speaks in the first person about coming down to deliver the people from the Egyptians, and to bring them up out of that land to a good and broad land, a land flowing with milk and honey. This coming down, delivering, and bringing the people out implies a commitment to a liberation process on behalf of the entire people, rather than a violent removal of a single perpetrator on behalf of one victim. The reader is left wondering at this point how God will accomplish such an ambitious project. A volunteer reads the next verse, which clearly states God's surprising choice for the task.

> The cry of the Israelites has now come to me; I have also seen how the Egyptians oppress them. So come, I will send you to Pharaoh to bring my people, the Israelites, out of Egypt. (Exod. 3:9–10)

God calls Moses and sends him back. This time armed with a staff and the word of YHWH. God uses Moses, the failed liberator, the reluctant savior. In response to Moses' repeated protests: "Who am I that I should go?" God says: "I will be with you." God assures Moses of his very presence along the way.

Moses is no hero figure, and his task is not easy. He presents excuse after excuse to not go. "What if they don't believe that you appeared to me?" (4:1). "But I don't know how to speak" (4:10), and finally "O my Lord, please send someone else" (4:13). Moses' reluctance makes room for our excuses and fleeing. God's persistence and final victory over Moses shows us God's unwavering commitment to liberation—in spite of our resistance.

God is recruiting, calling people to lead others out of slavery and misery and into the promised land of freedom and abundance: a land flowing with milk and honey. God recruits unexpected people, common people. So how is this good news? Roger, a fellow-American white male and codirector of Tierra Nueva's Family Support Center, sums up by saying:

"Moses, he's so unsure of himself. He's so human. This makes me realize, hey, I'm not alone. There's another really important guy in Israel's history who didn't feel cut out for this. Look, God used him. God can use me too."

Israel, a Mexican man serving two years in prison, sums it up this way:

"This makes me very emotional, because Moses was a sinful person. So God can use people like us. Yes, God is calling us. This jail is a desert, there is nothing that we can do. But God gives us a mission. Even though Moses is a sinner, God continues to call him, even though he was very rebellious."

José too says it in his own way: "God works through humble people, people who are rejected, people with vices, and he uses us to announce his kingdom and the good news to the world."

Toward the end of the Bible study I invite the men to read 1 Corinthians 1:26–29:

> Consider your own call, brothers and sisters: not many of you were wise by human standards, not many were powerful, not many were of noble birth. But God chose what is foolish in the world to shame the wise; God chose what is weak in the world to shame the strong; God chose what is low and despised in the world, things that are not, to reduce to nothing things that are, so that no one might boast in the presence of God.

People are nearly always visibly delighted by God's surprising choice of the nobodies as God's mediators. To conclude this study, I often ask people to try to summarize how their image of God has shifted, or more specifically who they now perceive God to be according to our reading of this story.

Chapter Six

God's Empowering Call to the People

Reading Isaiah with Exiles

The story of Moses' rescue, adoption by Pharaoh's daughter, and coming to awareness provides entry points for mainstream people and others of relative privilege to identify with Moses as one called to a prophetic vocation. Moses' reactive beginning as a murderous would-be liberator and God's call to him in spite of his status as a fugitive, immigrant shepherd broaden possible identifications to include criminals, immigrants, and others at the margins. In the same way, the prophets offer many entry points for people of different social locations to hear a distinct message and call that are tailored to their circumstances.

Undocumented immigrants, inmates, and ex-offenders who find themselves pursued and persecuted by the state find it encouraging to learn that prophecy began as an intentional divine check to the power of the king. Samuel preceded Saul, and anointed him. Each of the prophets took up the cause of the poor and the oppressed of their time before the authorities: denouncing injustice, defending the weak, and promoting faithfulness to God's agenda of life and liberation. Prophets themselves were often called from what would have been the mainstream of their time, or were raised up from among the exiles themselves. In Isaiah's sixty-six chapters, a diversity of prophetic vocations are visible, which challenge people differently.

A look at prophetic literature clearly shows us the importance of linking specific messages to specific addressees. Careful attention must be paid to the literary and historical context before determining the contemporary application of the text.

Isaiah Denounces Oppression and Privilege

Before reading from Isaiah 1–39 with people in the jail, a Honduran village, or anywhere for that matter, I inform people that the prophet Isaiah was living in a time when great divisions existed in Judah between the rich and the poor, and corruption and idolatry were rampant. I ask them whether they see divisions like that today, and if they have personally experienced or witnessed oppression.

People have no trouble coming up with many examples of what they see as oppression, including employers' underpaying immigrant workers, rich landowners' exploiting peasants in Mexico and Central America, drug dealers' taking advantage of desperate addicts, America's bombing of Afghanistan and Iraq, discrimination and racial profiling by local law enforcement, and unreasonably harsh sentencing and fines by the courts.

People are surprised by the harsh critique leveled against the powerful ones of Isaiah's time, since they naturally assume that God has sanctioned governing authorities, the entire status quo, and anything apparently religious. The following texts comfort them as they discover that God is not the invisible hand upholding the unjust system but rather, through the prophets, denounces injustice and commands oppressors to change.

> Trample my courts no more;
> bringing offerings is futile;
> > incense is an abomination to me.
> > > (Isa. 1:12b–13a)

> Cease to do evil,
> > learn to do good;
> seek justice,
> > rescue the oppressed,
> defend the orphan,
> > plead for the widow.
> > > (Isa. 1:16b–17)

God's exposure of the crimes of the governing authorities shocks people who assume that the state is always sanctioned by God to accomplish divine will.

> Your princes are rebels
> > and companions of thieves.

Everyone loves a bribe
   and runs after gifts.
They do not defend the orphan,
   and the widow's cause does not come before them.
(Isa. 1:23)

The LORD enters into judgment
   with the elders and princes of his people:
It is you who have devoured the vineyard;
   the spoil of the poor is in your houses.
What do you mean by crushing my people,
   by grinding the face of the poor? says the Lord GOD of hosts.
(Isa. 3:14–15)

People can hardly believe how graphically the prophet Isaiah denounces the arrogance of the privileged in Isaiah 3:16ff.

The LORD said:
Because the daughters of Zion are haughty
   and walk with outstretched necks,
   glancing wantonly with their eyes,
mincing along as they go,
   tinkling with their feet;
the Lord will afflict with scabs
   the heads of the daughters of Zion,
   and the LORD will lay bare their secret parts.

In that day the Lord will take away the finery of the anklets, the head-bands, and the crescents. . . .

Instead of perfume there will be a stench;
   and instead of a sash, a rope;
   and instead of well-set hair, baldness;
   and instead of a rich robe, a binding of sackcloth;
   instead of beauty, shame.

These Scripture passages and their equivalents from Amos, Hosea, Jeremiah, and other preexilic prophets show a God who unexpectedly sides with the powerless and condemns the powers to destruction.

In the light of Isaiah 1–5, the call of the prophet Isaiah must be presented as an exemplary conversion and call story regarding a religious insider from the dominant society, and not a model conversion of a notorious sinner. This story gives hope to shame-filled bad guys as it brings about equal footing, permitting real solidarity between the powerful and the powerless as the privileged one breaks allegiance with the status quo as the result of a transformational encounter.

Readers who are marginalized to the extent that they would consider themselves "unclean," and therefore unworthy of entrance into a house of worship, are given a privileged, insider's glimpse into an encounter between a "clean and worthy" Isaiah and unexpectedly different God in the temple. They need to be helped to see that Isaiah's vision of God subverts his and their theology, revealing the Lord to be enthroned, and not the unjust ruler. According to some of the Lord's hosts, the seraphim, this Lord is far different from what Isaiah and they could ever have imagined, offering good news to them and highly disturbing news to Isaiah.

> Holy, holy, holy [read "different," "foreign," "separate," or "strange"
>   for holy] is the LORD of hosts;
> the whole earth is full of his glory.
>
> (Isa. 6:3)

Inmates are delighted to see the impact of a real encounter with God on religious insider Isaiah, who goes from seeing God as with him and his clean, blameless class to God as exposing him as an unclean one among the unclean:

> Woe is me! I am lost, for I am a man of unclean lips, and I live among a people of unclean lips; yet my eyes have seen the King, the LORD of hosts! (Isa. 6:5)

The prophet sees himself as radically distant from the Lord and unworthy, at a time when people from Judah's privileged class viewed the Lord with relative indifference as a God who was domesticated, silent, and compliant with their worship in a way they took to signify agreement with their agenda.

The poor, the widows, and those experiencing injustice in the courts are already living under the shadow of bad news. The good news for them is that God is not providing a divine blessing legitimating the status quo and defending the oppressors. God is calling them to repentance, breaking down the clean-unclean barrier that keeps insider "haves" apart from the outsider "have-nots." God is willing to let it all come crashing down if necessary for the new reign of God to emerge. This is good news only to those who have nothing to lose or who are dissatisfied with normal existence. "Blessed are the poor in spirit, for theirs is the kingdom of heaven."

This good news includes a call to speak God's word where it is least welcome—right into the hearts of the people going along with the dominant ideology. This is the challenge of the preexilic prophets: to speak for God on behalf of the weak in spite of hardness of heart and persecution. The challenge to speak truth to mainstream America, even when people harden their hearts and close their ears, is the task of a new generation of Isaiahs and Jeremiahs. A willingness to accompany the weak as equals, as people of unclean lips living among a people of unclean lips, has never been more important, as partisan divisions have people on the defensive, closed to dialogue. Isaiah and Jeremiah invite a resistance alongside oppressors on behalf of the oppressed to the point of even going down with them into exile. For those already in exile, a whole other model exists for prophetic ministry to those in exile. Isaiah 40–55 offers an empowering image of ministry that recruits the downtrodden as God's change agents.

Isaiah 40–55: God Recruits Exiles

When reading from the prophets with people, we must give great care to discerning which prophetic message applies best to contemporary communities. Prophetic messages announcing good news to the "damned" abound in the prophetic literature coming out of Israel's exile. These texts must be searched to locate appropriate messages to the many exiles at the margins of today's Babylon equivalents.

Isaiah began his prophetic school long before Nebuchadnezzar invaded Palestine with a huge army in 587, carrying off into exile everyone but the poorest people.[1] Isaiah appears to have raised up a prophetic community that actualized his original teaching and received new prophetic oracles. It was likely disciples of Isaiah who are directed by the Lord to offer a radically different message than Isaiah's original words of judgment in Isaiah 6:9–10.

> Comfort, O comfort my people,
>   says your God.
> Speak tenderly to Jerusalem,
> . . . .
> that she has served her term.
>   (Isa. 40:1–2)

These opening verses to Isaiah's words to the exiles offer words of comfort, not punishment or condemnation. God's spokespersons are told by a voice to prepare a way in the wilderness so that people can see God's revelation, using language that evokes the memory of Sinai, where God first met Israel outside the land of slavery.

> In the wilderness prepare the way of the LORD,
>   make straight in the desert a highway for our God.
> Every valley shall be lifted up,
>   and every mountain and hill be made low;
> the uneven ground shall become level,
>   and the rough places a plain.
> Then the glory of the LORD shall be revealed,
>   and all people shall see it together,
>   for the mouth of the LORD has spoken.
>   (Isa. 40:3–5)

The Lord reveals his person to them in the wilderness—not in the temple, synagogue, or in any religious place, but in exile. This comfort comes out of the blue: no prerequisites for receiving comfort, for being the addressees of good news, for seeing God! Isaiah's prophetic community need only work to prepare the way, removing obstacles (mountains, hills, uneven ground) to people's seeing God. God is described as coming, as becoming visible to the battered people and their once glorious Zion and Jerusalem (Isa. 40:9). Preparing the way for people to look for and see God includes confronting the dominant theology.

To exiles who likely felt overwhelmed by the superior strength of their captors, the prophet presents an image of God as still more powerful: "See, the Lord GOD *comes with might,* / and *his arm rules* for him" (40:10, italics added).

To downtrodden exiles still uncertain that a God who led them into exile could be trusted to really offer them comfort, the prophet presents a nurturing image of God:

> He will feed his flock *like a shepherd;*
>   he will gather the lambs in his arms,
> and carry them in his bosom,
>   and *gently lead* the mother sheep.
>   (Isa. 40:11, italics added)

To people inclined to be impressed by the might of the surrounding nations, God speaks a word that relativizes their power (40:15–17). The prophetic word unmasks the reigning powers as overpowered by God's superior presence: idols (40:18–20), governing authorities (40:21–24), the Mesopotamian celestial deities (40:25–26). To those for whom the political and religious system appears more powerful than YHWH, the prophet assures them that this is not the case: YHWH will bring rulers to nothing! In a worldview where the stars were Babylonian deities on the side of their oppressors, God is declared as the creator of them all.

The final theological mountain that functions as an obstacle to faith is the belief downtrodden people often hold that God has forgotten them and that they are unworthy and therefore unnoticed or completely ignored. God directly confronts this interpretation as a lie, offering a countervision designed to subvert and shift their way of negative perception to a true, hope-inspiring one.

> Why do you say, O Jacob,
>   and speak, O Israel,
>   "My way is hidden from the LORD,
>   and my right is disregarded by my God"?
> Have you not known? Have you not heard?
> The LORD is the everlasting God,
>   the Creator of the ends of the earth.
> He does not faint or grow weary;
>   his understanding is unsearchable.
> He gives power to the faint,
>   and strengthens the powerless.
> Even youths will faint and be weary,
>   and the young will fall exhausted;
> but those who wait for the LORD shall renew their strength,
>   they shall mount up with wings like eagles,
> they shall run and not be weary,
>   they shall walk and not faint.
>
> (40:27–31)

The coastlands are addressed by God, who announces to them the reality of his total sovereignty and his designs to bring down the reigning nations and kings (Isa. 41:1–4). They are described as pathetically seeking refuge in their idols. Then God addresses the exiles themselves, the faint and powerless. The weak ones are promised empowerment to prepare them for their high vocation as God's agents of liberation.

> But you, Israel, my servant,
>   Jacob, whom I have chosen,
>   the offspring of Abraham, my friend;
> you whom I took from the ends of the earth,
>   and called from its farthest corners,
> saying to you, "You are my servant,
>   I have chosen you and not cast you off";
> do not fear, for I am with you,
>   do not be afraid, for I am your God;
> I will strengthen you, I will help you, I will uphold you
>   with my victorious right hand.
>
> (41:8–10)

Before leading a Bible study on Isaiah 42:1–8 I ask a group of inmates a question that prepares the way for hearing God's words about the servant as good news.

"When you guys are out on the street, do you feel as if you are free? Or do you feel as if you are serving someone else or some force?" I ask.

"No way am I free," says Victor, a young, goateed Chicano man. "I'm enslaved to drugs, alcohol, to my anger."

"I serve my own self, I do what I want," says someone else.

"I serve the image that I want others to have of me," someone else adds.

"When we get in trouble, and end up in here or in prison, we're the servants of the system, and they're making money on us."

Others are nodding their heads. People mention other forces and institutions that they serve, including money, employers, their probation officer, sex, methamphetamines, DSHS—which garners their wages for child support, and the courts.

I briefly introduce the Bible text that we are about to read, telling the people that God's people were often not living in freedom, but were slaves to Pharaoh, to idolatrous practices, or to other empires like the Assyrians or Babylonians. I invite someone to read the entire first Servant Song of Isaiah 42:1–8, before taking them through a more detailed verse-by-verse discussion of the meaning of these verses for their lives.

Before asking a volunteer to reread Isaiah 42:1ff., where God formally presents his servant, I ask: "So what kind of people do you think God would choose to be his servants or representatives? Do you think they would have to be people who knew a lot about the faith, who were formally trained as priests or pastors and could see what God was doing and hear God's voice?"

I know that people all assume that God's agents would have to be holy-roller intimates with God. I can hardly wait to have them read the next reading, regarding servant Israel, and watch them process the surprising news. I invite a volunteer to read Isaiah 42:18–20:

> Listen, you that are deaf;
> and you that are blind, look up and see!
> Who is blind but my servant,
> or deaf like my messenger whom I send?
> Who is blind like my dedicated one,
> or blind like the servant of the LORD?
> He sees many things, but does not observe them;
> his ears are open, but he does not hear.

"So, what do we know about God's servants here? Were they people who were especially close to God and understanding his ways?" I ask.

"They are blind, they are deaf. They are like us," someone says with a smile.

"So we know that people do not have to be in the know, but where do you think God draws the line?" I ask, preparing people for the next reading. "Do you think God would choose sex offenders, domestic violence perpetrators, felons, drug dealers, people skilled at stealing car stereos, men with anger problems, drug addicts, or alcoholics?"

I ask this question because I know that most people on the margins assume that God prefers to call only smart, together, successful, educated white people. God is viewed as on the side of power and privilege. This "high theology" is accompanied by a correspondingly "low anthropology." The homeless, and people in jails, migrant labor camps, and other situations of social marginalization often feel small and unworthy of any vocation that looks in any way important or valued. They consider themselves to be the last that God would ever call. They feel unusable except for minimum-wage jobs: insignificant, uneducated, unable to speak, explain, or in any way minister. Many people on the margins see themselves as unworthy, and often as failures—far from God because of their unholy behaviors: drinking, drugs, infidelity, criminal activities. They see professional clergy and righteous churchgoers as the called ones, and themselves as the passive beneficiaries of help or active avoiders of charity. God and the church are way up in an unreachable place.

The men agree that most people do think this way. One man surprised me by saying:

"I think it would be better for God to choose someone like me, who has sinned a lot and knows firsthand all that the people have been through. They'd listen more to someone who had experienced what they had."

With men and woman who often feel hopelessly disqualified from any sort of value before God because of their messed-up lives, I find great pleasure when they discover the good news that God is committed to calling and empowering them. Introducing them to servant Israel in exile increases their confidence that God really does like and love people like them.

"You are definitely on to something," I say to the man with the surprising comment. "We'll see that this is in fact God's agenda."

I tell the men that what the servant Isaiah talks about is the people of Israel—exiled from their homeland to a life of servitude to a foreign and very dominant power, the Babylonians. The Israelites who were carried off to Babylon were from *the dominant social class of Israel*—the mainstream people, those in power. They had been warned by the prophets that their attention to wealth accumulation, their own pleasures, and other idols would lead to exile, and it did. Their church, the temple, was leveled, and they were carried off in chains as slaves. In exile they experienced brokenness. They became poor and marginalized—equal to or lower than the broken whom they had once oppressed in their own land. They were servants of the Babylonians, weak slaves with no voice, no citizenship, no vote. God's servant, then, is none other than Israel, a downtrodden, exilic community[2] who likely felt small, insignificant, trapped, like failures. The men look intrigued, and I invite the reader to read Isaiah 42:22:

> But this is a people robbed and plundered,
>   all of them are trapped in holes
>   and hidden in prisons;
> they have become a prey with no one to rescue,
>   a spoil with no one to say, "Restore!"

The men looked pleased and more hopeful. Since we read this in Spanish and then English, there is time for this unexpected word to sink in. We read this verse twice before continuing our discussion.

"So what do you think, you guys?" I ask. "What kind of people does God need to accomplish his mission? Let's check out again how God views people the world sees as worthless."

I invite someone to read Isaiah 42:1–4, reminding them that the servant mentioned here is the same blind and incarcerated one who looks like and probably feels like a loser.

> Here is my servant, whom I uphold,
>   *my chosen*, in whom my soul delights;
> I have put my spirit upon him;
>   he will bring forth justice to the nations.
> He will not cry or lift up his voice,
>   or make it heard in the street;
> a bruised reed he will not break,
>   and a dimly burning wick he will not quench;
>   he will faithfully bring forth justice.
> He will not grow faint or be crushed
>   until he has established justice in the earth;
>   and the coastlands wait for his teaching. (italics added)

We read verse 1 twice, in Spanish and in English, before continuing our discussion.

"So how does God view the servant here?" I ask the men.

"God upholds him, he calls him 'my chosen,'" someone notices, intrigued.

"So, do you think that this could mean that God had a lineup of potential servants, and deliberately preferred this incarcerated, downtrodden servant to other more 'together' types?" I ask. "What else does God say about this people?" I continue.

"God is delighted in him," says someone else.

The notion that the Lord actually delights in servant Israel, and in themselves as near equivalents, is more than anyone can fully take in during one Bible study. Yet the good news penetrates, and some of the men are visibly delighted that God is not ashamed of the servant in his unfit state. The Lord's deliberate placing of God's own Spirit upon the servant shows an intimacy and a willingness to identify that is closer than people had imagined.

I can see a mixture of delight and awe gradually winning over the unbelief, the deeper we probe into the text. God is not ashamed to be closely identified with a humiliated slave. This is good news to people who feel unworthy, insignificant, invisible. God says: Behold my servant! The Lord even proudly presents his people as "my servant." This is good news to someone who feels as if he is possessed by the Babylonian sovereign,

Nebuchadnezzar. You are not the servant of the Babylonians! You are the servant of the living God! You are not the servant of the courts, cocaine, Budweiser, the American dream, an employer: "Here is my servant!" "Here is my inmate," "Here is my illegal alien," says the Lord of history.

The servant apparently did nothing extraordinary to deserve a call. Yet God entrusts these people with a critical mission. I invite someone to read the rest of the poem:

> Thus says God, the LORD,
>   who created the heavens and stretched them out,
>   who spread out the earth and what comes from it,
> who gives breath to the people upon it
>   and spirit to those who walk in it:
> I am the LORD, I have called you in righteousness,
>   I have taken you by the hand and kept you;
> I have given you as a covenant to the people,
>   a light to the nations,
>   to open the eyes that are blind,
> to bring out the prisoners from the dungeon,
>   from the prison those who sit in darkness.
> I am the LORD, that is my name;
>   my glory I give to no other,
>   nor my praise to idols.
>
> (42:5–8)

"So, what is the mission that God has entrusted to his humble servants?" I ask.

The men go through the verses and lift out the particular tasks, mentioning then one by one.

"He will bring justice to the nations" (v. 1), says one. "He'll establish justice in the whole earth" (v. 4), he continues.

"It says God gave him to be a covenant to the people and light for the nations, here in verse 6," says someone else.

"The servant who's blind and deaf himself will open the eyes of the blind!"

"The people who've been in jail are going to bring prisoners out of jail," someone else paraphrases.

"God has taken the servant by the hand and kept him!" (v. 6).

Finally, people note that the servant does not have to do it alone. God has taken the servant by the hand and protected him. People are struck again by God's close identification with the servant in verse 8's "My glory I [will] give to no other."

In this particular study we do not venture into a discussion of the humble means that servant uses: not yelling, but faithfully bringing justice to the land, for example. Nor do we go into detail about the evolution of the description of the servant in the three remaining poems (Isa. 49:1–7; 50:4–11; 52:13–53:12). While I often lead Bible studies on each of these remaining poems, we end the study by reading Isaiah 61:1–3 and then Luke 4:16ff., where Jesus is described as preaching on these Scripture readings in his first sermon in his hometown.

> The spirit of the Lord GOD is upon me,
>   because the LORD has anointed me;
> he has sent me to bring good news to the oppressed,
>   to bind up the brokenhearted,
> to proclaim liberty to the captives,
>   and release to the prisoners;
> to proclaim the year of the LORD's favor,
>   and the day of vengeance of our God;
>   to comfort all who mourn;
> to provide for those who mourn in Zion—
>   to give them a garland instead of ashes,
> the oil of gladness instead of mourning,
>   the mantle of praise instead of a faint spirit.
> They will be called oaks of righteousness,
>   the planting of the LORD, to display his glory.
>   (Isa. 61:1–3)

The men are pleased to see that God is so totally for the likes of them. Even more startling is that God would call them to become agents of liberation to others like themselves. When I ask them to summarize what they have learned, I am surprised at their level of understanding. One by one the men speak their thoughts:

"The servant can be any one of us—José, Pedro," says one Mexican inmate. "He is like any humble person. Because God addresses people who are the smallest and most humble and raises us up. All the time, God addresses people who suffer the most and makes us know his love. He makes us bigger, because we suffer a lot."

"God works through the Holy Spirit, through humble people," says José, "people despised, people who have been submerged in vices and drugs and have suffered a lot. I have even spoken with white people about the love of Jesus Christ, and some even pay attention. I feel very happy, because it is time to change, since the life that we live is not leading anywhere good, only to perdition."

God's pursuit of humble slaves as the preferred mediators and agents of liberation surprises and empowers broken people. In Isaiah 40–55, God shows radical faith in people viewed by the dominant society and themselves as damned losers. God's belief in the weak ones and commitment to not give divine glory to another (Isa. 42:8) reveals a humble God willing to identify with the servant to the point of persecution and death. Jesus' identification by New Testament writers as the individuated servant, whose suffering redeems servants past and present, realizes these poems, and offers a call to discipleship and empowerment by the Holy Spirit to all. Isaiah and Jesus offer a way of liberation through the liberation, healing, and total transformation and empowerment of the least. This is the very best of news to today's damned, who long for a meaningful vocation.

Chapter Seven

Reading and Praying the Psalms

Difficulties due to Negative Images of God

People's vision of God as a cosmic law-enforcement chief or judge will inevitably affect their prayers. Those who are overtly breaking civil laws or rules they think are God-ordained may well avoid any kind of religious encounter. Driven to prayer by a crisis, people in the jail often communicate with God very cautiously, crafting the words to say what they believe will be most pleasing to an easily insulted and volatile God. Prayer is undertaken with great caution, for fear of saying the wrong thing. Fear of God prevents vulnerable people in need of God's favor and immediate help from saying their true feelings. The wrong thing might slip from their lips, leading to disaster. Fear of upsetting God functions like a self-censure, which keeps the fearful from being real. Perceived distance leads the supplicant to use extreme care and formality in addressing the Deity (like the accused before a judge, a job hunter before a potential employer, or a lover who tries to impress the beloved). The more unfamiliar and uncomfortable you are before someone, the less honest you may feel permitted to be.

The men and women I visit with in jail often feel blocked when it comes to prayer. They feel unworthy to approach God until they can first get their life together. Inmates who do come to the Bible study tell me that they are judged by others in their pods who refuse to come.

"You hypocrite," say the critics. "You only seek God when you are in trouble. Why don't you pray and go to church when you're out on the street? You go to church when you're here in the jail, but as soon as you get out you'll go back to the same crazy life. Me, I know that I will go back to drinking and drugging. I'm not ready to go to church on the outside. If you are not ready to change when you're outside, then you shouldn't be a hypocrite and come crying to God when you're in trouble."

According to this logic, you should not pray or attend a Bible study or church unless you can first change your behavior. Since people are unwilling or unable to leave their addictions, they stand perpetually condemned and silent before an impossible-to-please God. These ways of thinking inhibit people from finding their true voice before God.

When an image of God as all-powerful dominates the human image of an incarnate God in Jesus Christ, prayer will also be deeply affected. An all-powerful God demobilizes the communicator, who has no need to tell the all-knowing Deity what he already knows. Even when people have evolved in their perception of God to the point of feeling and believing God to be closer, they often feel insecure in their communication. People know little about prayer, and often feel inadequate praying.

The long, eloquent prayers of more experienced religious people, or the impressive prayers of formal liturgies, often disempower people on the margins. Outsiders are often impressed and intimidated by the religious language of insiders, to the extent that they are demobilized to the point of silence.

The Psalmist Shows Honesty and Intimacy with God

One of my highest priorities is to initiate the people with whom I minister to the psalms, first as spiritual reading and then as prayers. I regularly invite people to follow along with me in their Bibles as I read a few carefully selected verses or entire psalms before a Bible study. This introduces the participants to a new psalm and clears their heads, helping them to calm down and center for the Scripture reading and discussion.

As people enter into the language of the psalmist, the alienating distance and fear they once felt with God is gradually subverted by the psalmist's surprising honesty and intimacy. The psalms articulate a wide range of uncensored sentiments and thinking before God, from frustration, outrage, anger, and unbelief to thankfulness, love, and adoration. The psalms often guide the reader through a liturgy that begins with anguish and ends with a newfound confidence. When I read psalms of personal lament with despairing people who expect no comfort from the Bible, they are often shocked by the depths out of which the psalmist cries. How does the psalmist have the nerve to be that real before God? They expect language that is "sucking up" to a delicate deity, and highly crafted, understated supplication conditioned by self-denigrating promises of reform. The rawness of emotion and reckless pleas and the graphic description of hardship make these prayers credible to those who are submerged in difficulties.

The psalms articulate cries for help, feelings of abandonment, and confession of sins with language that desperate people can relate to.[1] The psalmist makes requests that hurting people can easily identify with. That the following cries are in the Bible at all helps a marginalized reader trust the Scriptures. I sometimes begin a Bible study by inviting people to pray with me one or more of the following lines.

> Why, O LORD, do you stand far off?
>> Why do you hide yourself in times of trouble?
>>> (Ps. 10:1)

> My God, my God, why have you forsaken me?
>> Why are you so far from helping me, from the words
>>> of my groaning?
> O my God, I cry by day, but you do not answer;
>> and by night, but find no rest.
>>> (Ps. 22:1–2)

> Rouse yourself! Why do you sleep, O Lord?
>> Awake, do not cast us off forever!
>>> (Ps. 44:23)

If the psalmist can pray like this, maybe I can dare to express my true sentiments.

The psalms often describe my people's hardship in such detail that they can see the authenticity of the psalmist's struggle and difficulty. This helps them trust that the psalms may be for them too (and not just for the successful religious types or people with middle-class, manageable lives). When people hear the Bible describing oppression, it helps them trust that the Bible is about their reality, and not just about realities they can't relate to or ever hope to experience (e.g., that of a successful religious person, rich person, or "insider").

Marginalized people are surprised when the psalms use language and images that evoke their life situations of oppression. Undocumented immigrants in my jail Bible studies are surprised to find a psalm that articulates their plight before the Border Patrol and INS.

They sit in ambush in the villages;
    in hiding places they murder the innocent.
Their eyes stealthily watch for the helpless;
    they lurk in secret like a lion in its covert;
    they lurk that they may seize the poor;
    they seize the poor and drag them off in their net.
They stoop, they crouch,
    and the helpless fall by their might.
They think in their heart, "God has forgotten,
    he has hidden his face, he will never see it."
Rise up, O LORD; O God, lift up your hand;
    do not forget the oppressed.

                                          (Ps. 10:8–12)

The psalms' many descriptions about human life (Ps. 39:2–11), exploitation (Ps. 53), and the rich and the poor (Ps. 49) lend credibility to the Bible among suffering people.

In my one-on-one counseling, I have initiated many sex offenders facing new charges in our county to praying the psalms. They experience ridicule and persecution from other inmates to such an extent that they are usually held, in isolation or together with others with similar charges, in a pod separate from the rest of the jail population. They are among the most marginalized people in our society. While some find refuge in denial, others despair to the point of attempting suicide. A surprising number of these men have independently told me of their discovery of Psalm 31, which they laud as expressing their situation and desires—giving them hope.

Be gracious to me, O LORD, for I am in distress;
    my eye wastes away from grief,
    my soul and body also.
For my life is spent with sorrow,
    and my years with sighing;
my strength fails because of my misery,
    and my bones waste away.
I am the scorn of all my adversaries,
    a horror to my neighbors,
an object of dread to my acquaintances;
    those who see me in the street flee from me.
I have passed out of mind like one who is dead;
    I have become like a broken vessel.

For I hear the whispering of many—
  terror all around!—
as they scheme together against me,
  as they plot to take my life.
But I trust in you, O LORD;
  I say, "You are my God."
My times are in your hand;
  deliver me from the hand of my enemies and persecutors.
Let your face shine upon your servant;
  save me in your steadfast love.

(31:9–16)

I often hand out to inmates a list of psalms under categories, so they can find prayers that may be especially helpful to them. This list includes personal laments (Pss. 13, 35, 86) and communal grievings (Pss. 74, 79, 137), prayers from the depths (Pss. 88, 109), calls to repentance (Pss. 50, 81), the seven psalms of penitence (Pss. 6, 32, 38, 51, 102, 139, 143), psalms of thanksgiving after a crisis (Pss. 49, 73, 90), and psalms of the pilgrim or sojourner (Pss. 120–134). I introduce them to psalms that are thought to be prayers of the accused, offered in temple where fugitives found asylum from hasty, arbitrary justice (Pss. 7, 26, 35, 57, 59, and maybe 139).

I encourage individuals that I am counseling to read specific psalms in their homes or cells. I show people the great diversity of genres of prayer (complaint, lament, supplication, thanksgiving, worship), and occasionally give them some psalms in each of these categories to help them choose prayers that may best reflect their desire or mood.

For those looking for more advanced practices, I inform them about liturgical use of psalter. I initiate them to monastic usages of the psalms, giving them the numbers of psalms traditionally recited in remembrance of Jesus' passion on a daily (noon, three o'clock, evening, morning), weekly (Thursday, Friday, Saturday, Sunday), and seasonal basis (Advent, Christmas, Epiphany, Baptism, Transfiguration, Holy Week, Pentecost).

I teach people the close relationship between prayer and meditation in daily contemplative reading of the Bible. Those who are condemned to months or years of jail or prison need constant encouragement and practical teaching to help them surmount the many impasses in prayer and other spiritual practices. Some find it helpful to learn to distinguish between prayer, which is direct address to God, and meditation, which is reflecting on God in the third person. For example, Psalm 25 begins with prayer (vv. 1–7) and moves to meditation (vv. 8–10), confession of sin

(v. 11), and back to prayer (vv. 12–22). Consciously moving in and out of prayer and meditation when reading the psalms, or anything in the Scriptures, helps combat distraction.[2] There is extra motivation to do this for people who are seeking to practice the twofold call to "meditate day and night" (Ps. 1) and to "pray without ceasing" (1 Thess. 5:17).

As people begin reading and praying the psalms for themselves, they make their own discoveries and begin to share with me and each other verses they find especially helpful. People are especially attracted to the many prayers for deliverance (Pss. 7; 9; 12; 40:11–17), which become more and more believable in the light of psalms statements in favor of the weak and oppressed.

> The LORD is a stronghold for the oppressed,
>   a stronghold in times of trouble.
> And those who know your name put their trust in you,
>   for you, O LORD, have not forsaken those who seek you.
> Sing praises to the LORD, who dwells in Zion.
>   Declare his deeds among the peoples.
> For he who avenges blood is mindful of them;
>   he does not forget the cry of the afflicted.
>
> (Ps. 9:9–12)

> O LORD, you will hear the desire of the meek;
>   you will strengthen their heart, you will incline your ear
> to do justice for the orphan and the oppressed,
>   so that those from earth may strike terror no more.
>
> (Ps. 10:17–18)

> "Because the poor are despoiled, because the needy groan,
>   I will now rise up," says the LORD;
> "I will place them in the safety for which they long."
>
> (Ps. 12:5)

> For you deliver a humble people,
>   but the haughty eyes you bring down.
> It is you who light my lamp;
>   the LORD, my God, lights up my darkness. . . .
> This God—his way is perfect;
>   the promise of the LORD proves true;
>   he is a shield for all who take refuge in him.
>
> (Ps. 18:27–28, 30)

The God who gave me vengeance
　　and subdued peoples under me;
who delivered me from my enemies;
　　indeed, you exalted me above my adversaries;
　　you delivered me from the violent.
For this I will extol you, O LORD, among the nations,
　　and sing praises to your name.
(Ps. 18:47–49)

I waited patiently for the LORD;
　　he inclined to me and heard my cry.
(Ps. 40:1)

People on the margins find these statements deeply encouraging. Not only do they subvert the reigning theology of fate, they strongly state God's special help for the downtrodden. These statements in favor of the weak are further reinforced by lists of psalms that call on God to fight for the oppressed.

Using the Psalms in Spiritual Combat

The Psalms are filled with strong words against enemies and the wicked.[3] These words can confirm people's most negative images of God as judge, and may at first be interpreted as addressed against them. At the same time, since many people on the margins have personal and institutional enemies, these psalms can be empowering. I often lead a study in the jail or in Tierra Nueva's storefront ministry on these psalms.[4]

I begin by asking how many of the people have had an enemy or currently have an enemy. Most everyone admits to having an enemy, but few want to talk publicly about the details. I broaden the discussion by asking people to name some of the groups or forces that they feel are against them. Here the discussion gets rolling, as people feel freer.

"*La policia*," says Andres, a young undocumented guy in his mid-twenties, with shifty eyes and a recently shaved head. "They stop us for nothing, just because of the color of our skin and hair. They hate Mexicans."

Others in the group nod their agreement, and specify the police forces of particular towns in our county. I often meet Hispanic men in my jail Bible study who were brought in on a trumped-up charge, most likely because the officer suspects they are illegal. The young Mexican immigrants tell me that the officer asks them for their *mica* (slang for green card, or permanent resident card). Since there are often no current charges and a Border Patrol hold, I know they are telling me the truth.

"*La migra*," says Refugio, a farmworker in his late thirties. "They say they are going to build two walls along the border," he continues. "But there are not *gabachos* willing to pick strawberries. Let them build three walls!" he challenges. "Nothing will stop the *raza*!"

"The prosecutor!" says Israel, a guy facing charges for delivery of a controlled substance, facing forty-two months in prison. "They say I did this five years ago, and I'll tell you the truth, I was into drugs back then. But I've since given my life to Jesus Christ. For the last three years I haven't done any drugs. But I did not do what they are saying I did. The prosecutor has it in for me. I think he considers me an enemy."

From my previous dealings with Israel, I can almost sympathize with the prosecutor. Israel and I had been enemies ourselves, until the day when I began visiting him one-on-one. He had requested a visit after a Bible study where some reconciliation had happened. I had been feeling bad about the way I had been confronting him, and had begun to pray for him, as he was often such an irritating representative of the very theology I most detested. He was surprised and pleased by the visit.

I asked him to tell me what he thinks is the heart of the good news. He thought for a while and then responded.

"Total dedication to God. We have to be consecrated," he told me.

"OK, this is clearly important, I agree. Are there other things that come to mind?"

"Holiness," said Israel.

I prod him on to say more. What other things are important about this message of salvation? He went on to list a number of other qualities: faith, discipline, sacrificing all, separateness from the world. When he ran out of words, I asked him what he thought about forgiveness, or love. What about grace and mercy? Israel looked at me emptily. I told him that, for me, the love and grace of God visible in Jesus are at the heart of the gospel. I could be wrong, I insisted, but invited him to read and pray about two passage that I write down and give to him: 1 Corinthians 13 and 1 John 4:7–21. We prayed together and shook hands warmly. A tenuous friendship had begun.

So there we are in a Bible study regarding praying psalms against enemies. Israel is especially angry about the prosecutor. He has hatred for this county official written all over his face. I suggest that we read selections from some of the psalms against the enemies. I invite the men to find and read aloud the following passages.

> You have rebuked the nations, you have destroyed the wicked;
>   you have blotted out their name forever and ever.
> The enemies have vanished in everlasting ruins;
>   their cities you have rooted out;
>   the very memory of them has perished.
>
>   (Ps. 9:5–6)

> Draw the spear and javelin
>   against my pursuers;
> . . . .
> Let ruin come on them unawares.
> And let the net that they hid ensnare them;
>   let them fall in it—to their ruin.
>   (35:3, 8)

> For the cursing and lies that they utter,
>   consume them in wrath;
>   consume them until they are no more.
>   (59:12b–13)

> Let their table be a trap for them,
>   a snare for their allies.
> Let their eyes be darkened so that they cannot see. . . .
> Pour out your indignation upon them,
>   and let your burning anger overtake them.
> . . . .
> Add guilt to their guilt;
>   may they have no acquittal from you.
> Let them be blotted out of the book of the living;
>   let them not be enrolled among the righteous.
>   (69:22–24, 27–28)

> May his children be orphans,
>   and his wife a widow.
> May his children wander about and beg;
>   may they be driven out of the ruins they inhabit.
> May the creditor seize all that he has;

may strangers plunder the fruits of his toil
. . . .
May his posterity be cut off;
    may his name be blotted out in the second generation
. . . .
[A]nd may his memory be cut off from the earth.
                                                    (109:9–15)

O daughter Babylon, you devastator!
    Happy shall they be who pay you back
    what you have done to us!
Happy shall they be who take your little ones
    and dash them against the rock!
                                        (137:8–9)

Let burning coals fall on them!
    Let them be flung into pits, no more to rise!
Do not let the slanderer be established in the land;
    let evil speedily hunt down the violent!
                                        (140:10–11)

After we finish reading this last selection, I ask the men whether they think they could pray these psalms against their enemies.

"They are very strong," says one man. "I could not pray these psalms."

Some of the other men appear to agree. They may feel ashamed to admit any attraction to these psalms. I tell the men that "the wicked" in the Old Testament are often overtly described as the rich, or as those who oppress the poor (Ps. 10). The psalmist then shows God as being for the poor and the "sinner," not for the "successful." I know that this message will be heard as good news to most of them, who tend to interpret every calamity as God's will or judgment.

"I like this last psalm [140:7–13], because the justice of God is equal," says Andrés. "God is presented as on the side of the needy and as doing justice for the poor. It is not only the poor who are punished."

Before moving on to the New Testament teaching on enemies, I briefly present the different ways that Christians have interpreted these psalms. I tell them that some see these psalms as part of the Old Testament viewpoint, which they see as based on the Mosaic law and an understanding of God as harsh and vengeful, a God of retribution. Many people see this Old Testament God and the laws of the Old Testament as having been superseded by the New Testament and the teaching of Jesus. I tell them that this approach does not satisfy me.

I review with them a second way of dealing with these psalms, which is to embrace them thoughtfully, not appropriating them until they are understood rightly. I suggest that this approach may be preferable to reading them literally against personal enemies, which could lead us into error. On the other hand, I suggest that even in error, when we pray to God against flesh-and-blood enemies, at least we are addressing God and crying out for God's help. This is better than taking action ourselves: "Vengeance is mine, I will repay, says the Lord."

I go on to describe how the enemies in the psalms most often do not refer to people's personal enemies, but to adversaries of God's reign in the world. Israel's enemies are spiritual enemies, insofar as they oppose Israel's true vocation to usher in the kingdom of God on earth. Pharaoh, the Amalekites, and the Edomites are examples of physical enemies who are also spiritual enemies. These enemies may even include religious enemies, like the false prophets or Israelite priests who sided with the wrong people (Amos 7:10–17).

At this point I present the greatest difficulty related to praying the psalms against flesh-and-blood enemies: the teaching of the apostle Paul and Jesus to love and pray for our enemies. Together we read the key Scripture passages that present this apparently counterteaching.

> Bless those who persecute you; bless and do not curse them. (Rom. 12:14)

> Beloved, never avenge yourselves, but leave room for the wrath of God; for it is written, "Vengeance is mine, I will repay, says the Lord." No, "If your enemies are hungry, feed them; if they are thirsty, give them something to drink; for by doing this you will heap burning coals on their heads." Do not be overcome by evil, but overcome evil with good. (Rom. 12:19–21)

> You have heard that it was said, "An eye for an eye and a tooth for a tooth." But I say to you, Do not resist an evildoer. But if anyone strikes you on the right cheek, turn the other also; and if anyone wants to sue you and take your coat, give your cloak as well. (Matt. 5:38–40)

> You have heard that it was said, "You shall love your neighbor and hate your enemy." But I say to you, Love your enemies and pray for those who persecute you, so that you may be children of your Father in heaven. (Matt. 5:43–45)

But I say to you that listen, Love your enemies, do good to those who hate you, bless those who curse you, pray for those who abuse you. (Luke 6:27–28)

After the last reading I ask the men what they think of the difference between the strong words of the psalms against enemies and Jesus' teaching. They are surprised by this apparent contradiction, finding both the psalms and the teaching of Paul and Jesus difficult to practice. We talk about how often Jesus is seen as the nice guy compared to his strict, vengeful father, the God of the Old Testament. I stress that Jesus, like the prophets, has strong words against the religious establishment (Pharisees, scribes . . .) and the rich. Yet both Jesus and Paul call us to show love for our flesh-and-blood enemies, whom they clearly distinguish from spiritual enemies, which must be combated.

For the next thirty minutes we look together at the New Testament's many strong words against spiritual forces. We read together a number of passages where enemies are described as being conquered and destroyed, using violent, aggressive vocabulary that contrasts markedly with Jesus' teaching about flesh-and-blood enemies. I talk about how the New Testament talks about at least two categories of spiritual force: principalities and powers, and passions.

The principalities and powers include social, structural, and political powers (empires, nation states, armies), organizations (INS, U.S.A., DSHS, Department of Corrections, Skagit County, WTO [World Trade Organization], IMF [International Monetary Fund], U.S. dollar), ideologies (nationalism, ethnocentrism, capitalism, communism), along with powers like death, disease, hate, and many others. Religions and Christian denominations can be included as well, such as the Roman Catholic Church, Presbyterian Church (U.S.A.), Evangelical Lutheran Church in America (ELCA), the Pentecostal Church, and every other name.[5] We read together a number of texts that demonstrate violence that is being promoted against spiritual enemies.

We interpret Psalm 110's strong words about enemies' being put under the feet of the Messiah in the light of Paul's reflections on Jesus' victory over the principalities and powers in 1 Cor. 15:24–27.

Then comes the end, when he hands over the kingdom to God the Father, after he has destroyed every ruler and every authority and power. For he must reign until he has put all his enemies under his feet. The last enemy to be destroyed is death. For "God has put all things in subjection under his feet." But when it says, "All things are put in subjection," it is plain that this does not include the one who put all things in subjection under him.

The men are fascinated to see Jesus associated directly with strong language like "subjected" and "destroyed," especially related to forces like authorities, rulers, and death, which they normally see as God-ordained. Ephesians 2:14–16 is especially impressive:

> For he is our peace; in his flesh he has made both groups into one and has broken down the dividing wall, that is, the hostility between us. He has abolished the law with its commandments and ordinances, that he might create in himself one new humanity in place of the two, thus making peace, and might reconcile both groups to God in one body through the cross, thus putting to death that hostility through it.

The inmates interpret the dividing wall of hostility that Jesus breaks down as being discrimination and racism. They are amazed that Paul describes Jesus as having abolished the law, with its commandments and ordinances.

I continue leading them through passage after passage that describe God's violent actions against spiritual enemies. We read that Paul tells the Romans the God of peace will crush Satan under their feet (Rom. 16:20), that Jesus sees Satan fall from heaven like a flash of lightning (Luke 10:18). We read together how Babylon, symbol of the power of the state, will be destroyed (Rev. 18) and how the beast and false prophet are thrown alive into the lake of fire that burns with sulfur (Rev. 19:20). Other Scripture passages, which describe angels, authorities, and powers made subject to Jesus (1 Pet. 3:22) and enemies put under the Messiah's feet (Matt. 22:42–44), further convince the men that there is a difference between physical and spiritual violence.

I continue leading the group to see how the Scriptures distinguish between spiritual forces and people. We note together how Jesus' temptations in the desert are depicted as being done by the devil (Luke 4:13a), who waits for an opportune time (4:13b), coming back to enter into Judas as Satan (Luke 22:3). Jesus names the devil as the enemy who plants weeds (Matt. 13:39). Luke calls the spiritual forces "the power of Satan" (Acts 26:18), or the "power of darkness" (Luke 22:53), like Paul: "[God] has rescued us from the power of the darkness" (Col. 1:13). Jesus rebukes Satan in Peter, and not Peter himself (Matt. 16:23). Finally we end this brief survey with a text (Eph. 6:10–12) that is one of the most popular among the men and women with whom I minister.

> Our struggle is not against enemies of flesh and blood, but against the rulers, against the authorities, against the cosmic powers of this present darkness, against the spiritual forces of evil in the heavenly places. (Eph. 6:12)

"So if the New Testament distinguishes between enemies of flesh and blood and spiritual enemies, how might this affect our praying of the psalms against enemies?"

We wrap up our discussion by talking about how we can pray psalms against enemies most beneficially by trying to separate in our minds the human beings (INS agents, prosecutors, drug task force informants, etc.) from the deeper spiritual force that they represent to us (discrimination, the law). Jesus teaches us to pray for and love our flesh-and-blood enemies even as we cry out to God to combat the deeper spiritual enemies.

God, Not We, Responsible for Our Enemies

I try to avoid leaving people with the feeling that there are right and wrong ways to pray the psalms, as this could easily demobilize them. I stress that we still may find ourselves desiring the destruction of our enemies, and we may pray the psalms more literally against them. I emphasize that what is most important is that we cry out to God, asking God to take responsibility for our enemies. When we are in communication with God, God may teach and correct us, as Jesus did his disciples.

Jesus often corrected his disciples when they came to him desiring vengeance. Jesus corrects his disciples when they want to wipe out Samaritans (Luke 9:51–56), and the Pharisees who want to stone the adulterous woman (John 8:1-11). Jesus responds, "No more of this!" to the disciple who cuts off the high priest's servant's ear (Luke 22:47–53), and calls upon his Father to forgive his enemies, for they do not know what they are doing (Luke 23:34).

"As Christians we can pray these psalms against spiritual enemies, but we must remember that before God there is a difference: these are distinct from actual people, whom Jesus invites us to love," I conclude.

"Wow, this is important for me," says Israel. "I have had a hard time not hating the prosecutor and the judge, who seem to be against me. Even if they are my flesh-and-blood enemies, I am to love them and pray for them."

A week later Israel reported that he had been praying for the judge and the prosecutor every day. On the Monday before Israel's day in court, his public defender called me and asked me to talk with Israel, who was despairing.

"Tell him that he's just going to have to accept forty-two months in prison. Even though it's for a crime five years ago, there is nothing more I can do. He will have to pay," said the public defender.

I asked whether there was anything I could do. His attorney said: "Well, you could try talking with his prosecutor."

That afternoon I called Israel, told him to say a prayer, and walked across the street to talk with the prosecutor about my impressions regarding Israel's change of heart.

"Thanks for your impressions," said the prosecutor. "All I had were the police reports."

Two days later Israel's charges were unexpectedly dropped way down. He was given three months, which he had already served. He wept with joy that evening at his final Spanish Bible study with us.

"God is big. God heard me. God is pure love," he said.

Unfortunately, Israel was then picked up by the INS to face charges of illegally returning to the United States after four prior deportations. He sat for months in federal detention until his day in federal court, where he faced a five-year sentence if convicted. I wrote a letter to the judge on his behalf, and accompanied his pastor and wife to the court. The judge unexpectedly gave him just two years in prison. I visited Israel several months later in federal prison. He told me that since I had given him 1 Corinthians 13 to read over a year before, until that afternoon, he had read this passage every day.

"Now I know that the good news is all about love, Roberto. It is all about love!"

Psalm 8: Crushing Or Being Crushed by Nature

During our second year of theological studies in Montpellier, I worked on my master's thesis, on Psalm 8. I explored the place of humans vis-à-vis God and the creation. I sought to develop a theology that leads to care of nature, recognized both as vulnerable and as highly threatened, and at the same time menacing and destructive.

In Central America I had witnessed firsthand how the fragile tropical ecosystems are highly threatened. Deforestation, erosion, burning of valuable organic matter, and pollution from smoke are rapidly destroying rain forests. Ecological destruction threatens valuable water sources, turning vast areas into waterless deserts. The traditional use of slash-and-burn farming methods is ruining the delicate tropical and subtropical ecosystems needed for survival. Foreign mining companies exploit mineral resources with few restrictions, contaminating groundwater and rivers in delicate tropical regions. Overpopulation puts increasing pressure on limited land and other resources. Daily scavenging for firewood strips fragile forests and watersheds. People hunt nearly every bird and wild animal for food or sport. The natural world is vulnerable and threatened, and needs aggressive protection.

On the other hand, nature itself wreaks havoc on subsistence farmers. Underbrush, weeds, insects, and disease invade the people's food crops. People must combat these forces in a life-and-death battle for survival, eking life out of the all-consuming jungle. Naive views of nature as human-friendly, or calls to return to ancient cosmologies that deify nature, are not solutions. North American and European–originating theologies of creation that depict nature as revealing God or as being inhabited by the Divine often unknowingly endorse the most demobilizing images of God. These theologies emphasize God's magnificence through nature, reinforcing the dominant perception that all natural events, especially natural catastrophes and death, are God's sovereign will.

For subsistence farmers who struggle to survive off the land, nature and God are together viewed as unpredictable adversaries. Heavy or prolonged rains, outbreaks of fungi or insect hatches, often wipe out entire fields of corn, beans, or rice. Malaria, hepatitis, dengue, amoebic dysentery, and other tropical diseases hit unexpectedly, killing the young and old. Nearly every family we know has lost brothers and sisters and their own children to curable sicknesses. Flocks of birds descend on and pick clean unguarded corn and rice plots. Rabbits munch bean fields. Despite the best erosion-control methods, Hurricane Mitch demonstrated Mother Nature's power to kill.

The image of God communicated through the tropical and subtropical Central American environment is one of a scorching, raging, decaying, death-dealing, ever-menacing, unpredictable, all-powerful tyrant who favors the fittest and crushes the weak. While God is combated with machete, hoe, ax, and fire, nothing can finally overcome the ever-victorious death that finally conquers through disease, hunger, or calamities. Poverty keeps people from benefiting from technology and medicine that would shelter them from nature, providing them with the luxury of time and protection to form a more positive creation spirituality.

The "Gore-Tex theology" of the north is unaffordable to the poor, who see nature more as a combat zone, where they are losing. Identifying a beautiful and comforting God in creation is easy when you are hiking in the forest for pleasure with all the right gear, food, water filter, and first-aid kit. God in creation looks far less attractive and positive when you are slogging barefoot up a muddy hill under the scorching tropical sun, with a five-gallon plastic canister full of contaminated water or a heavy load of firewood. Theologians in the north who venture into wilderness lie in state-of-the art sleeping bags on comfortable pads that protect them from uneven rocky ground, behind mosquito netting in their high-tech tents. Meanwhile, most Honduran peasants sleep packed beside children or siblings atop thatched grass mats over sagging, string bed frames, or in hammocks that reek of urine from infants that are rocked to sleep in them by day. Most of the world's poor live close to nature that is forever encroaching on their personal space. Cockroaches scurry about. Fleas breed on dirt floors and bite at people's gnarled ankles. Malaria-carrying mosquitoes suck blood from their skin, which lacks the special nontoxic repellents that I use.

Creation spirituality done from behind the shelter of privilege, whether those privileged are North American, European, or third-world theologians, will rarely speak to the hearts of the world's damned, who are often at the same time among nature's destroyers. The people urgently need a way to think theologically about conservation that also works for them. A myriad of forces threaten the fragile natural environment that sustains them. Among these forces are multinational corporations that take advantage of lax environmental-protection laws and people's desperation, exploiting nature and cheap labor for their profits.

When I was working with the Hondurans, a North American mining company had been drilling in the mountains above Minas de Oro to determine where to locate an open-pit mining operation for gold and copper. The North American miners told people they were only exploring, but according to a report we were able to obtain from the project's U.S. fundraisers, the mine was much farther along. They had already determined that there were 0.80 percent copper and 0.04 ounces of gold per ton. To recover these minerals would involve excavating and crushing the rock. Cyanide would then be used to leach out the gold.

The probable site of the mine was a heavily forested mountain above the town—the source for springs that feed gravity-flow water projects for at least eight large villages. The damage caused by erosion, and the pollution from the cyanide leaching process and sulfuric acid byproduct, would foul local water supplies and could well destroy the surrounding villages. The mining company workers insisted that a mine would be a boost to the local economy, but they were currently paying only $3 a day to laborers and $6 a day to a much smaller group of skilled workers. Tierra Nueva former trainers (known as *promotores*) and others in Minas de Oro had been concerned about the negative environmental and social effects of this mine and had begun to organize to oppose it.

Nature, Humans, and God

We decided with the Tierra Nueva *promotores* to spend three days together talking about nature, humans, and God. Psalm 8 and its usages in the New Testament will help guide our discussions.

We begin by listing the forces that threaten nature, and come up with the expected list, including the campesinos themselves, Kennicott Copper Corporation, foreign logging companies, insecticides, and herbicides. We go on to discuss the underlying forces that drive people to abuse the earth, coming up with things like fear of death, insecurity, greed, envy, love of money, desire for power, pride, and other motivations.

Next I invite the group to reflect together on how Psalm 8 may respond to some of these issues. We read together my own translation of the entire psalm.

> O LORD our Lord, how magnificent is your name in all the earth!
> I will sing your majesty, which is above the heavens.
> Out of the mouth of babies and sucklings you have established power
> because of your adversaries: to silence the enemy and the avenger.
> When I look at your heavens, the work of your fingers,
> the moon and the stars that you have set in place,
> what is humanity that you remember them?
> And the son of Adam that you visit him?
> But you have made him a little less than God,
> and you have crowned him with glory and honor.
> You have caused him to have dominion over the works of your hands.
> You have placed all things under his feet,
> sheep and oxen, all of them, and even the beasts of the field,
> the birds of the air and the fish of the sea
> and everything that passes through the paths of the sea.
> O LORD our Lord, how magnificent is your name in all the earth!

I read over the first verse, which I describe as probably the refrain of the psalm, which was likely sung after every verse in this hymn:

O LORD our Lord, how magnificent is your name in all the earth!

The group is quick to note that the Lord's name is praised as magnificent in (or on) the earth. This name of God is described as separate from the earth, which is the theater wherein this name is lauded in concurrence with the many names competing for greatness.

"What are other names or forces that are praised as magnificent in Honduras?" I ask.

"The politicians!" says one man.

"The rich!" states another.

"The Kennicott!" is quickly named.

We list the names that compete for magnificence, including: lempiras (Honduran money), dollars, the U.S.A., Tierra Nueva, the Catholic Church, ourselves, and other institutions and powers. We discuss how other names or forces can function as "idols" before which we sacrifice forests, mineral resources, and our own lives.

"So where is God according to this psalm?" I ask.

We observe that the psalmist depicts God's majesty as being set "above the heavens." Does this reflect a cosmology that locates God outside of nature? We discuss the likelihood that the psalmist understands that God is not contained in the natural world, but is separate from the "creation." If the psalmist viewed God as everywhere or specifically within nature, this could have been easily communicated. In actuality, several details in the text distinguish God from creation. God's name, YHWH, is praised *on* the earth by creatures, showing this name is both distinct from the earth and not contained within the earth as nature's essence. In addition, the psalmist specifies the location of God's majesty as being "above the heavens"—a way of differentiating nature from the creator. These affirmations differ radically from the cosmology of the Mayan ancestors of the Honduran people, who viewed nature as sacred, God-indwelled, and ordained.

The *promotores* are intrigued to see this proposed differentiation between God and nature. Their traditional understanding of natural events and nature itself as God's will has never kept them from slashing and burning—how else could they survive? The people hear this desacralizing word regarding nature as good news, not because it gives them license to further rape and pillage the environment. Rather, once the link is broken in their minds between God's will and whatever happens to them (fatalism), they can begin to envision God freshly.

The union between God and nature is broken in people's minds through both social analysis and study of Scripture that speak to these questions. If nature is separate or in some way independent from God, functioning according to its own laws of cause and effect, then God is no longer seen as automatically to blame for catastrophes or for even human abuses of nature. Nature must be recognized as finite, bound to the laws of decay and death, acknowledged as the status quo. Nature is not deified, nor is it demonized. Nature is distinguished from the adversaries and from God. The next line of the psalm presents God at work to combat adversaries, which are described as the enemy and the avenger that are distinct from both nature and God.

> Out of the mouth of babies and sucklings you have established power because of your adversaries: to silence the enemy and the avenger.

"What might be some of the adversaries of God's reign, who might oppose God's name as magnificent in the whole earth?" I ask.

The *promotores* are quick to rename the list they had already come up with as competing for their names to be magnificent: they include themselves in their slavery to tradition, and go on to name Kennicott, the U.S.A., money, the rich, the Honduran government. Someone even mentions the IMF.

We look at how the psalmist both acknowledges the adversaries and declares them silenced/vanquished.

"How are God's enemies conquered?" I ask the group.

"Here it says through the mouth of babies and breast-feeding infants," someone notices.

"How could this be possible?" I ask. "How might the mouth of infants vanquish the powerful? What do the mouths of babies and suckling ones do?" I ask the group.

Nobody has difficulty answering this final question. Babies nurse away on nearly every Honduran woman between fifteen and forty. The *promotores* conclude that the baby's mouth indicates the baby's total dependence. We discuss together how praise of God, rather than allegiance to money, the state, a company, or anything other than God, subverts the reigning idols. Just as the early Christian slogan "Christ is Lord" countered the reigning "Caesar is Lord," so our heartfelt praise and cries to God might lead us to freedom from the powers. Rather than looking to money, the rich, the U.S.A., foreign companies, and such, as God, the psalmist portrays the praising infants as exemplary in their radical dependence on YHWH.

We sit in amazement together as we contemplate how the weakest images (mouths of babies and nursing ones) are used to describe power over the most powerful enemies. The next day in a Bible study, on the use of Psalm 8 in Matthew 21, we see this enacted. The blind and the lame come to Jesus in the temple, where they are healed. Children recognize Jesus as the Messiah in the temple, singing hosanna to the Son of David (Matt. 21:14–16). All of this is done in the presence of the amazed and then angry religious leaders (chief priests and scribes). Their image of God and their own power are subverted by the children who come freely to Jesus. They are scandalized that Jesus would let them bypass the prescribed path to God through the religious establishment's highly controlled system. The repeated refrain, "O LORD our Lord, how magnificent is your name in all the earth!" with an emphasis on *our*, presents a counterallegiance that silences the counterreign of the adversaries. God does not belong only to the powerful.

Silvano, a thin, enthusiastic Tierra Nueva *promotore* in his late twenties, leads us in singing before a group lunch of chicken, rice, beans, and tortillas. We gather together after lunch for a second study on the psalm.

Nature's Threats

We begin our second session by listing ways in which people are threatened by nature, and come up with a long list, including drought, floods, insects, disease, death, earthquakes, and hurricanes. The campesino *promotores* can fully relate to the psalmist's feelings of smallness before all-powerful nature.

> When I look at your heavens, the work of your fingers,
> the moon and the stars that you have set in place,
> what is humanity that you remember them?
> And the son of Adam that you visit him?
>
> (Ps. 8:3–4, au. trans.)

We discuss together the psalmist's surprise and awe before the awareness that God has not abandoned fragile humans to an overwhelming and often hostile universe. I present background information on the heavens, the moon and stars, which for the people of ancient times were powerful, capricious deities that needed to be appeased through elaborate religious rituals. Their depiction here as "the work of [God's] fingers," which God has established, strips them of their threatening nature, representing them as fellow creatures.

God elevates human beings both in this psalm and in the stories that the psalm evokes in ways that surprise my Honduran companions. We look at examples of God's remembering and visiting: Noah and the ark above the floodwaters, infertile Sarah and Rachel, the children of Israel in Egyptian bondage. I point out that the Hebrew term for the human whom God remembers, often translated "man," comes from the verb "to be weak." The son of Adam reflects people outside the garden, the first of whom was the murderer, Cain. God elevates the "weak one" in a way distinct from the rest of creation, making him "a little less than God," and crowning him "with glory and honor" (Ps. 8:5).

We agree that the continual remembrance that God has not forgotten us, and can be expected to visit, strengthens our faiths. Faith in a remembering and visiting God is offered as a new security. This good news undercuts reliance on and allegiance to other "gods," and might keep us from nature-destroying practices based on our fear and insecurity. After all, according to this text, it is God who is the subject of all these verbs. God remembers, visits, crowns with glory and honor. If this is true, then there is no need to actively seek these things for ourselves. If the psalmist is right, we are passive beneficiaries of God's actions, which are finally described with language of total victory:

> You have caused him to have dominion over the works of your hands.
> You have placed all things under his feet.
>
> (Ps. 8:6)

We discuss at length how in ancient times the list in Psalm 8:7–8—sheep, oxen, beasts of the field, birds of the air, fish of the sea, and whatever passes through the paths of the seas—included both domesticated and wild animals. The psalm's declaration that all these things are under the feet of the human one/son of Adam gives people license to subsist off the natural world. In addition, they could be assured that predators were not to be seen as exercising spiritual power over people or reflecting God's menacing actions against them. Human domination over "everything that passes through the paths of the sea," the mythic Leviathan, is a declaration of victory over death itself. At the same time, the list begins with things on the earth, the location of human life and the place where the name of the Lord is proclaimed as excellent and is surrounded by the heavens above and the seas below, showing the human as a fellow creature endowed with unique authority in the middle of the universe. The fact that fellow humans are not included in the list, and that all things are placed under all, provides the basis for an egalitarian society where everyone rules.

My Honduran friends are also surprised at how positively the psalmist describes human beings. Among people with an image of God as holy and distant, humans are usually viewed as lowly and even degraded. A "low anthropology" usually goes hand in hand with a "high theology." Here in Psalm 8, humans are viewed as "a little less than God." I present this psalm as likely being written before Genesis 1:26–30, which goes even farther. In Genesis 1 humans, male and female, are depicted as being made in God's image and likeness. They are given dominion over the creation in a way that is even more all-encompassing than in Psalm 8. In a country where doctrines of original sin and the total depravity of man have beaten people's already shattered self-esteem into the ground, this suggesting that humans are like God and "very good" is empowering.

Victory over Adversaries

Over the course of the following two days we discuss at length our keen awareness that, while this psalm is a declaration of victory over antagonistic forces and a pronouncement regarding human equality, victory is far from being realized.

"In what ways can we say victory has been accomplished now?" I ask. "How are we to benefit from this victory in our lives here and now?"

These questions are the most difficult, and appear to inspire at least a skeptical interest.

I present the results of my research on the singular "human," and son of Adam, who can be interpreted both as a collective singular that includes all humans and as an actual singular. The "weak one" and "son of Adam" both can be read as referring to the coming Messiah. The New Testament usages of Psalm 8 bring clarity here, showing how the early Christians saw this Scripture as being realized in Jesus Christ's victory over the principalities and the powers.

First Corinthians 15:24–28 and Ephesians 1:20–23 both see Psalm 8's declared victory over the adversaries and dominion over nature as finally realized in Jesus. According to 1 Corinthians 15, every ruler, every authority, and every power replaces the domesticated and wild animals, which are placed under the feet of the Weak One/Son of Adam. First Corinthians 15 appears to identify the ruling forces of this world as the adversaries, enemy, and avenger that are silenced, and nature that is subjugated. Yet Paul goes much farther than Psalm 8 by describing the destruction of rulers, authorities, powers, and death itself by Christ.

Ephesians clarifies that the resurrected Christ's reign from "the heavenly places, far above all rule and authority and power and dominion, and above every name that is named," is a victory that will benefit the church. Paul's emphasis that Christ is "head over all things for the church" (1:22), assures that Christ's "body" (v. 23) benefits directly from the subjugation of the powers. Christ's victory for actual humans as distinct from a "body," which could be misread as only referring to the institutional church, is announced clearly in Hebrews 2's read of Psalm 8:

> Now God did not subject the coming world, about which we are speaking, to angels. But someone has testified somewhere,
>
> "What are *human beings* that you are mindful of them,
>   or *mortals*, that you care for them?
> You have made them for a little while lower than the angels;
>   you have crowned them with glory and honor,
>   subjecting all things under their feet."
>   (Heb. 2:5–8a, italics added)

In addition, what follows in Hebrews 2:8 speaks a desperately needed word to Honduran faith communities. While it declares victory now in Christ, like 1 Corinthians 15 it is clear that much of God's reign remains "not yet" fulfilled.

> Now in subjecting all things to them, God left nothing outside their control. As it is, we *do not yet see everything in subjection to them.* (Italics added)

Finally, Hebrews 2:9–10 also depicts humanity's victory over death as being accomplished by Jesus, and takes matters another step farther. Hebrews directly incorporates Jesus' sufferings and death into its theology by presenting Jesus' being "crowned . . . with glory and honor" and "bringing many children to glory" as the direct result of his suffering of death.

> But we do see Jesus, who for a little while was made lower than the angels, now crowned with glory and honor because of the suffering of death, so that by the grace of God he might taste death for everyone.
>   It was fitting that God, for whom and through whom all things exist, in bringing many children to glory, should make the pioneer of their salvation perfect through sufferings.

The depiction of Jesus' very human sufferings and death as redemptive is a new idea for Honduran peasants, accustomed to seeing suffering as the result of deserved punishment for being inherently flawed. Hebrews's description of Jesus' suffering on behalf of "many children," in a way that makes them holy children of the same Father, is a powerful affirmation of passive sanctification and unconditional adoption!

> For the one who sanctifies and those who are sanctified all have one Father. For this reason Jesus is not ashamed to call them brothers and sisters, saying,
>
>> "I will proclaim your name to my brothers and sisters,
>>   in the midst of the congregation I will praise you."
>
> And again,
>
>> "I will put my trust in him."
>
> And again,
>
>> "Here am I and the children whom God has given me."
>>   (Heb. 2:11–13)

It is through the total solidarity in the human condition of the "weak" one that all are made holy. Finally, it is through death that Hebrews depicts Jesus as destroying the devil:

> Since, therefore, the children share flesh and blood, he himself like-wise shared the same things, so that through death he might destroy the one who has the power of death, that is, the devil, and free those who all their lives were held in slavery by the fear of death. For it is clear that he did not come to help angels, but the descendants of Abraham. (Vv. 14–16)

In destroying the source of death, Jesus frees people from the fear of death. This freedom from fear comes as a result of hearing and believing the good news of Christ's victory. The passage from unbelief to a living faith must happen in the face of widespread suffering and premature death.

Silvano joyfully sang out about this victory, writing many songs that announced good news to campesinos and lauded changes that Tierra

Nueva promoted. He put Psalm 8 to the music of an upbeat ranchero tune, which we all sang heartily at the end of the course and over the remaining weeks of our visit. He wrote the chorus in the light of the New Testament's perspectives on Psalm 8, which we sang between verses made up from the body of the psalm: "O Jesus, our Lord, how wonderful is your name in all the earth!"

Later that year, our beloved Silvano died unexpectedly at the age of twenty-nine as he was leading a Bible study and celebration of the Word in his isolated community of Alta Mira. Silvano left his wife and fellow Tierra Nueva *promotora* Alejandra, and five young children. Silvano's enthusiastic presence had lifted the spirits of Tierra Nueva. His unexpected death hit my wife Gracie, me, and the entire group of Tierra Nueva *promotores* harder than any of the many obstacles that we had confronted. This premature death was likely due to a condition that doctors would likely have diagnosed early and treated with ease in a North American or European context. Yet in technologically deprived Honduras, life is both heartier and more fragile. The weak eventually die off, leaving only the fittest to survive.

It will be hard for people in a Central American context not to see a theology embracing God in creation as promoting a God of natural selection, on the side of the strong, of predators, disease, and natural disasters; an enemy to the weak, the preyed on, diseased, and oppressed. An ecotheology of the reign of God must elevate the weakest members of the system, standing with them before the strong in a highly unnatural way. The ecology of the reign of God will appear "not of this world." The people will consequently find it difficult to believe, and so to resist the status quo. The reign of death imposes itself, leading people to act to protect themselves with or without God's help. Nature's deathblows to the weak and even the strong happen with enough regularity that people are quick to sacrifice nature to gain some greater security. This became evident as the mining project above Minas de Oro advanced in spite of the protest of an increasingly minority opposition.

Tierra Nueva *promotores* became actively involved in opposing the mine, together with a local environmental group and two American nuns who had recently taken responsibility for the parish. The movement focused on educating the people about the impact of open-pit copper and gold mines. The anti-mine activists organized public meetings, disseminated information, and organized to the best of their ability. Kennicott Copper Corporation's claim changed hands several times, finally ending up in the possession of Vancouver, B.C.'s Tombstone Mining Company.

The mining company countered local opposition with an aggressive public relations campaign and behind-the-scenes politicking that gradually won over the community's power brokers and eventually conquered the community. The company started with the municipality, offering money for special projects and help conditioning roads. They approached influential families, offering supervisor positions to their grown children. They donated money to help the local high school, and set up grants so people could send their children to the high school and university. Gradually the opposition was reduced to Tierra Nueva and a few scattered activists, by benefits that people found hard to turn down.

The North American nuns and our group struggled to decide how much to work to mobilize international opposition to the mine. If the local people lack the economic base and spiritual resources to struggle against the mine, international action looks like paternalistic meddling. I felt challenged to understand the spiritual underpinnings of passive and active compliance with oppression, with hope of coming to greater clarity regarding a theology of creaturehood and a spirituality of resistance.

Chapter Eight

Reading the Gospels with
Tax Collectors and Sinners

M inistry to inmates in county jails is like working with people from beside a queue that is constantly moving. People at the front are being released or sent to prison or to the Department of Homeland Security for deportation. Those at the end of the line are people recently arrested or transferred in from other counties to take care of local warrants. While some people move through quickly, bypassing others, some may stay a year or even longer. Consequently, there is nearly always a core group of individuals who have attended my Thursday evening and Sunday afternoon studies for weeks or months. Many have come to believe and are growing in their newfound faith. The initiated need more advanced Bible studies and mentoring. Sometimes the majority of my core group will all leave within a few weeks, making way for a new group of people who have never opened a Bible. I almost always introduce newcomers to the Bible through stories in the Gospels.

I seek to help people recognize the distinct characters and their role in the story, their social class, location, and other factors in the biblical narrative, as a basis for getting people to look for equivalents in their lives and in their society. Discussion of our own lives first often makes it easier to note equivalents in the Scriptures. In this way the text informs our lives, and our lives shed light on the text. The primary character in the Gospels is Jesus. Each of the Gospels uniquely shows God's identity as Jesus, Jesus' identification with the Father, the Spirit's witness to both.

Since many people on the margins envision God the Father as more wrathful and distant than Jesus, one of my first strategies is to help people see that Jesus came to reveal the Father's love. I often begin a Bible study with a new group by taking them through the beginning of Mark or John, looking at these Gospel writers' claims regarding Jesus' identity. Mark 1:1–3 provides an excellent introduction to Jesus' identity as "Christ"—that is, the one anointed by God; as "Son of God"—one fully identified with the Father; and as the coming "Lord"—understood as the YHWH/*Kyrios* of the Old Testament before whom John the Baptist prepares the way. Mark's insistence that stories about Jesus are good news prepares readers to look for good rather than bad news in the stories that follow.

Teaching regarding Jesus' identification with God prepares the way for people's negative images of God to be transformed as they meet Jesus in the Gospels. John's prelude identifying Jesus as the Word, with God, God's very person (John 1:1–2) who becomes flesh and lives among us (1:14), and later teachings in John 14:5–11 most clearly show the identification between Jesus, the Father, and the Spirit in ways the new readers find helpful and exciting.

In my years of reading the Gospels with people on the margins, we have been delighted together to notice how consistently the marginalized characters of Jesus' times were the beneficiaries of his healing and words of comfort. I often challenge people to find a single negative word coming out of Jesus' mouth toward the people on the margins of his day. Jesus' rebukes and stronger admonitions are always addressed to religious and political insiders: scribes, Pharisees, Sadducees, and disciples. I regularly point this simple truth out to inmates when I introduce a biblical story, knowing that they assume that God has nothing but harsh rebukes and moral imperatives for people like them and words of encouragement and delight for the "good guys."

The genealogy of Matthew disarms moralism, subverting people's shame regarding their often seemingly illegitimate births. Matthew's account of how God came to earth in Jesus is nothing less than shocking. I take people through Matthew 1:1–17, pointing out the inclusion of marginalized women (Tamar, 1:3; Rahab, 1:5; Ruth, 1:5; Uriah's wife, 1:6) and notorious men (Jacob, Judah, David, etc.) among Jesus' ancestors.

People are shocked to find Mary as the fifth and final woman on the list, and to see that the circumstances surrounding Jesus' birth suggest that Mary got pregnant with someone other than Joseph. God's birth into the world does not appear "proper," but conspicuously scandalous. The men can relate to Joseph's initial reaction to Mary's pregnancy. They laugh and shake their heads when I ask them what they would think if their girlfriends were said to be pregnant by the Holy Spirit. They are especially surprised to see that the Holy Spirit can even be identified with Old Testament lawbreakers sentenced to die by stoning for sleeping with a virgin betrothed to another man (Deut. 22:23–24). That God would take responsibility as Father, identifying with women and men in unseemly circumstances, makes God seem close and human. Joseph's righteousness consists in both his decision to put her away quietly rather than denounce her as a lawbreaker (Matt. 1:19) and his willingness to believe a revelation that it was OK to ignore the law and take Mary as his wife even though she was pregnant with someone else's child (1:24). That Jesus becomes a descendant of David not through legitimate biological procreation, but by an adoption irrespective of the law's demands, is certainly good news to undocumented aliens and people who do not know their biological fathers. The angel of the Lord's revelation of Jesus' name as meaning "he will save [heal] his people from their sins" (1:21) and the consequent identification as Emmanuel—"God with us"—leaves people hungry to delve into the Gospel stories that follow, with hope of hearing news that is even good to them.

Jesus' location when he is speaking or healing is also important to point out to people, who often assume that their absence from mass, church, or other religious places when they are out on the streets marks them as hypocrites who seek God only when in trouble. People are surprised and delighted when I give quick overviews of Jesus' itinerary. In the Gospels, Jesus spends most of his time on the road, in fields, on mountains, along the sea, in homes, in forsaken Galilee, incarcerated, and on the cross, rather than in traditionally holy places like the temple, Jerusalem, or synagogues.

People's assumptions that God prefers powerful people,[1] the good guys, and those who seek him over "bad guys" who don't is challenged by many texts.[2] Jesus heals and calls marginalized people without conditions, and often requires nothing of them.[3] Jesus is one who elevates infants (Matt. 11:25) and invites the downtrodden to come to him:

> Come to me, all you that are weary and are carrying heavy burdens, and I will give you rest. Take my yoke upon you, and learn from me; for I am gentle and humble in heart, and you will find rest for your souls. For my yoke is easy, and my burden is light. (Matt. 11:28–30)

While Jesus does frequent synagogues and the Temple, usually he gets into trouble in religious-insider hangouts, confronting or being confronted by religious authorities.[4] Jesus' strong words are never to the "sinners," but rather to the religious establishment and disciples that exclude them.[5] At the same time, Jesus continually invites religious insiders to join him in extending God's embrace to the excluded other.

Jesus' Call of Matthew, the Tax Collector

Careful reading of the narrative detail of biblical texts can help people hear good news in a way that inspires confidence. This is because careful reading shows a high respect for the text, which many people on the margins still consider sacred. Attention to what the text does not say is also highly important, since absences often reveal a lack of concern for particular assumptions considered important by religious people and traditions. The text can even become a refuge, for people on the margins, from the dominant theology. A jail Bible study on Jesus' call of Matthew the tax collector illustrates both the power of character and place for marginalized readers and the stumbling block this can be for people who hold to the dominant theology. After an opening prayer, I ask the men to take turns telling me what they do to earn a living.

The men go around the circle, naming their occupations: farmworker, construction, mechanic, seafood processor. Some of the men begin to snicker, and one of them points to three of the others and tells me that they sell drugs. I acknowledge this with a respectful nod, and we've soon completed the circle. A Mexican inmate named Timoteo then reads Matthew 9:9–13.

"So where was Matthew when Jesus called him?" I ask. "What was he doing? Was he praying? Was he at mass or in a church?"

"He was collecting taxes. He was doing something bad," responds Timoteo.

"He was just sitting there doing his job like José here, *ese*, selling dope and shit," someone comments, eliciting smiles and nods from some of the men.

"So where was Jesus? How does Jesus respond to him?" I ask.

"It says Jesus went along and saw him sitting there, and then said, 'Follow me!'" someone says.

"So, did Jesus scold him for his bad behavior? What sort of requirements did Jesus have for someone following him?" I ask.

"Nothing," said Timoteo. "And he wasn't even baptized!"

"So Jesus didn't say: 'No, Matthew, you have to get your act together first—you must repent, stop drinking, selling drugs, and stealing from people. You do all this, then I'll come back to see if you are ready'?"

"No, Jesus just called him," repeats Timoteo, eliciting an angry response from a Mexican man named Israel. Israel is a fervent evangelical convert who has been announcing to everyone that they can be cured instantly from their alcohol problems if they just have faith and repent, like he did. Israel had done a good job of continually arguing for the dominant street theology during the previous two Bible studies, confronting me as a heretic for talking so much about grace. He had even opposed my offer of Communion on Sundays.

"So you are saying that it doesn't matter what you do? You don't have to repent? You can follow Jesus and still be into the bad things of this world?" interrogates Israel, who interprets my questions and comments as a frontal attack on his theology.

"No, I'm not saying this, and neither is the text talking directly about this. Israel, I am not directing this at you. I'm not here to give you correct answers. My goal is to help you become a more careful reader of the Bible, and to help you learn how to think about the implications of this story for our lives. Let's look closely at the text.

"Where did Jesus go after he called Matthew?" I ask, inviting people to reread the story in their Bibles.

"He went to eat at his house, and a bunch of tax collectors and sinners came to sit with him," someone responds.

"So, how did the Pharisees respond?" I ask.

We read about their negative reaction to Jesus' presence with sinners when they say: "Why does your teacher eat with tax collectors and sinners?"

We discuss how the Pharisees likely saw themselves as better, and how Jesus' words show that they excluded themselves from his work by not including themselves among the sick and sinners. A man named Fidel tells how all the pastors he knows scold people.

"They talk only about all the rules that have to be followed. They are not like you. You discuss these things, you don't scold and lay down rules. Scoldings don't work," he concludes.

Jesus' words provide the perfect conclusion to our gathering:

> Those who are well have no need of a physician, but those who are sick. Go and learn what this means, "I desire mercy, not sacrifice." For I have come to call not the righteous but sinners. (Matt. 9:12–13)

I tell the men that I know that I am a sinner. I find that I am a slave to ways of being that I want to change, but that I am still sick and in need of healing. So, Jesus has come for me. At this point Israel really starts to calm down and listen. We end with a prayer. Israel surprisingly asks me to pray for him and even to visit him one-on-one. Some walls may have come down, and a friendship begins.

Encounters with the Gerasene Demoniac

Another story regarding walls' coming down through Jesus' crossing forbidden borders to reach out to notorious bad guys is the story of the Gerasene demoniac, in Mark 5. I begin a Thursday evening discussion in the jail by asking the following question:

"Do you think there are people who are too far gone, or too bad, to be able to be saved?" I ask a group of Mexican men.

I explain that I've run into many individuals who have told me that there was no hope for them. I tell the story of a Honduran man, a neighbor of ours in Minas de Oro, who told me insistently that he was too bad to be saved.

"I have done too many bad deeds for God to forgive me," said Moncho one evening, as I sat on my idling motorcycle on the trail up to our farm. "No, Roberto, God is not going to protect me. I have to protect myself. That's why I carry a gun. My pistol will protect me. My pistol is my God."

I tell how Moncho had later broken into our home as we slept to rob us, and then, later on, stole our calf. I ask a Honduran colleague who is accompanying me in the jail that evening, David Calix, to share the tragic story of how Moncho was finally killed in El Porvenir, shot by a man in a bar as he waved his gun in a drunken rage.

After an opening prayer, I invite the group to turn to Mark 5. I introduce the text as a story about a man who everyone thought was too far gone to be saved.

We note that the man was living in the cemetery and bruising himself with stones.

"Why was he hurting himself?" I ask.

"He probably didn't like himself," a man says.

"Clearly it looks as if he did not respect himself," I agree.

"Everyone probably rejected him, so he rejected himself," says another.

"Do people hurt themselves these days, or is this story only about people two thousand years ago?" I ask.

"Well, I don't know anyone who lives in a cemetery," says Juan, "but we all do things to hurt ourselves."

"Like what? In what ways do we harm ourselves today?" I ask.

"We stick ourselves with needles," says one man.

"We do drugs and other shit," says another.

"We don't use condoms," says Juan.

"So what happened to this guy?" I ask. "How did he respond to Jesus?"

"The man ran to Jesus and told him not to mess with him," says an inmate.

"Did Jesus leave him alone, or dismiss him for rejecting him?" I ask.

"No. Jesus rebuked the spirit in him. He sent the unclean spirits into pigs."

"So what happened to those bad spirits?" I ask.

"They went into the pigs, which ran into the water and were drowned," someone responds.

"So it looks as if Jesus is hard on the bad spirits. What about the man?"

We look together at how Jesus heals the man by separating the bad spirits from him. He loves and helps the man, but destroys the bad spirits that are in him.

"So if the courts were to deal with bad spirits and sin like Jesus, how would that affect the way they dealt with you guys?" I ask.

We talk about how incredible it would be if the courts punished the addictions, anger, hatred, greed, jealousy, resentment, and other forces that cause people to commit crimes by destroying them, letting the men and women go free. We laugh together about how they would need lots of pigs outside the courthouse to drive the spirits into.

We continue our discussion by reading Romans 7:14–8:3, which describes Paul's struggle with sin. Paul clearly differentiates between his will to do good and the tendency to do what he does not want to do. Paul stresses that it is not he who wills the bad, but the sin in him that holds him captive. "Wretched [person] that I am! Who will rescue me from this body of death?"(Rom. 7:24). We can conclude that, like the Gerasene demoniac, only Jesus can free us from the sin that enslaves us. We end the study talking about how Jesus restored this man to his family and community, sending him back to tell them about what Jesus had done. Jesus loves us sinners, but is out to cast out and destroy the sin that oppresses us.

Reading Luke 15 with Lost and "Other" Sheep

Since nearly everyone I read with has experienced judgment from religious people, my favored Scriptures to read with first-time Bible-study participants are the parable of the Pharisee and the publican in the temple (Luke 18:9–14), the great banquet (Luke 14:15–24), or Luke 15's three-part parable of the lost and found coin, sheep, and son, which Jesus tells to Pharisees and teachers of the law who criticize him for eating with tax collectors and sinners. The following brief account of a jail Bible study shows how Luke 15 can serve to open people up to expecting God's healing presence.

As I entered the jail's multipurpose room one Thursday night, my eye immediately noticed Zack, a strapping thirty-one-year-old, Anglo man who stands six feet seven. His shaved head, mustache, mischievous face, and heavily tattooed neck and forearms make him look intimidating. About ten other Anglo guys sat around him to my right. A dozen Mexican men sat across from them to my left. After shaking hands with everyone I took a seat in the circle to begin the Bible study.

"Tonight, I don't want to impose my particular choice of a Bible study on you guys," I state in Spanish and then English, looking around at each man around the circle. "People are always imposing their agendas on you. I'd like to know if there's any particular question or biblical story *you* want to look at." Immediately Zack speaks up.

"These Mexicans all think I'm a racist, and maybe they're right. I do get into my fair share of fights and can be hard to live with. I just want them to know that I respect a lot of things about them and their culture. The way they value family, their willingness to work hard. I guess I'd like to learn how to get along."

The Mexicans look a little uncomfortable as I translate Zack's words into Spanish. There have been some tensions with Zack, so they seem wary of his advances. I welcome the comment, and then formally begin the Bible study with a prayer inviting the Holy Spirit to be present as our guide and to bless each person. Thinking quickly of an appropriate text, I reach for Luke 15, about the judging attitude of the Pharisees toward Jesus for eating with tax collectors and sinners and his parable in response.

Together we read through the three stories that make up one parable: the story about the finding of lost sheep, the lost coin, and the lost son. The men become noticeably more relaxed and even happy as they see Jesus comparing God or himself to a pastor who leaves the ninety-nine compliant sheep who have their acts together to search for the one lost sheep who's in trouble—*until* he finds it! They seem moved when we read about the woman who, after losing one of her precious coins, turns the house upside down. Here, God is revealed as not like the masked and heavily armed drug-task-force officers who scour apartments searching for illegal drugs—but like a lover looking for something precious that symbolizes *them!* Their growing amazement turns to joy as we read about the son who, after hitting bottom partying, staggers back in humiliation, willing to do time in servitude, only to find the father running to embrace him before a confession even leaves his lips. As I wrap up our time together by inviting people to stand for a time of prayer, something surprising happens.

Zack jumps up from his seat and runs toward me, blurting out his conviction that he thinks God wants us to pray that Fabiano's liver will be healed. Fabiano, a large, heavily tattooed Mexican man with a shaved head—the most likely man in the room to have a racial run-in with Zack—looks shocked.

"Is it true that you have a problem with your liver?" I ask. He tells me that he's been experiencing sharp pains for a while, and they're getting worse and worse. "Do you mind if we pray for you?" I ask. He politely agrees.

"Don't you have a liver problem too, Zack?" I ask, knowing from a previous encounter that his seventeen years of heroin addiction have taken a heavy toll on his liver and kidneys. Zack's hands are swollen to nearly twice their normal size.

"Yeah, but listen, Bob. I'm always thinking about Zack, about me and my problems. I think God wants me to focus on others, like Fabiano here."

He agrees to let me pray for him too, as we gather in a circle and hold hands. I place a hand on the two men's shoulders and we pray: for God's Spirit to come to bring healing to Zack's and Fabiano's livers. We pray too for people's legal problems, and their families, then that we'd all experience a greater thirst for God, and that God would fill us with faith, hope, and love. God's Spirit is all around us in the room. I feel it pulsing through my hands in our circuit of solidarity. There's a warmth of Presence that lingers as we finish praying and say our good-byes.

Fabiano and Zack don't show up for the next study, but a week or so later Fabiano takes his seat with a now mostly Mexican group. I ask him how he's feeling, and he tells me there's no more pain in his liver. I call Zack later that day, but he says he's still feeling bad. We pray over the phone for healing, and a few weeks later he attends our study. "Everything seems to be better," he tells me. "The doctor's tests have even come out giving me a clean bill of health." Zack tells me he's been praying for lots of people, and God's been answering prayer after prayer.

While there were not overt, verbal links between Zack's actions and our Bible study on Luke 15, I believe that Zack saw himself both as one of the sinners with whom Jesus ate and as a discriminatory Pharisee to whom Jesus addressed the parable. In any case, Zack exercised a bold freedom to reach out beyond barriers, much like Jesus, in response to the reading of Scripture and the presence of the Spirit in our Bible study.

Jesus' Surprising Offer in John 4

In my Bible studies on John 4 with people who consider themselves excluded by the church or dominant culture, I typically begin either with a first question regarding their lives and world, or with a brief question regarding the narrative detail of the text—specifically, the characters and geography. When people are newcomers or appear wary of anything religious, I usually begin with a question about their lives and values. In the following composite of two different jail Bible studies with Latino inmates, as the text introduced the well it appeared to provide an ideal jumping-off place to talk about our lives.

After beginning with a prayer for God to send the Holy Spirit to open our hearts and minds, I invite a volunteer to read John 4:1–4, before briefly commenting on Jesus' passing through Samaria. I give them a brief description of behind-the-text information about Samaria, its location outside of acceptable Jewish religious places, and the religious and ethnic divisions that existed between Jews and Samaritans, which do not keep Jesus from showing up.

I ask another volunteer to read John 4:5–8, then ask some basic questions to get people to pay attention to some of the narrative detail in this evolving story.

"Who are the characters in this story, and what do we know about them up to this point?" I ask.

"There's Jesus, who has been passing through Samaria and sits by a well, tired and thirsty," someone says.

"Then who comes along?" I probe, inviting the men to look back down at their Bibles.

"There's a Samaritan woman who comes to draw water," someone responds.

I talk briefly about the importance of wells for people in the first century. "Everyone needed water to meet their most basic needs: to quench their thirst, water their animals, irrigate any crops, wash their clothes and bodies," I say.

"Do any of you go to wells to meet your most basic needs?" I ask, a question that I know will acknowledge our distance from the world of the text.

They shake their heads and someone answers the obvious. "None of us."

"So where do you go when you are thirsty for something, or when you are seeking to meet your most urgent needs?" I ask, seeking to inspire reflection on possible contemporary equivalents.

"I go to church," says a man who is a newcomer to our jail Bible study group. While this may indeed be where he would go, I suspect that he is trying to please me and God by giving what he considers the spiritually correct answer.

Since people look uncertain about what I am trying to ask or are not feeling enough trust to answer honestly, I rephrase the question several ways.[6]

"What do people you know do, or where do they go, to find satisfaction, to meet their needs?" "If you were released right now for twenty-four hours, where are the first three places you'd go?"

"To the bar," says a Mexican farmworker in his early thirties. People smile, and some nod.

"I'd go to my girl's place, man," says Neeners. Neeners has 666 tattooed under his lower lip and the names of past girlfriends tattooed on his neck. People laugh and nod their agreement.

"To the crack house," says a heavily tattooed Chicano man. A number of men rock back in their plastic chairs and laugh.

"Hey, wait a minute," interjects Neeners. "You may not believe this, but I go to jail to get my real needs met. This is the only place, right here, where I feel like I can think straight and get my shit together. Coming in here to study the Bible and shit helps me gain a new perspective," he says.

These answers loosen up the group, and men mention other places they frequent or things they do: the mall, heroin, sex, music, family, dealing drugs, cars, work, partying, dancing.

"So do these places and activities give you total satisfaction?" I ask. "Do you feel as if you are able to meet your needs?" I continue.

"No way, homes," says a man named Ben. "Look, here we are, all of us stuck in here. I ain't satisfied by my life, not out there, not in here. None of us are."

Ben's answer seems to resonate with most of the men, who nod their agreement that nothing really satisfies them.

"I've had everything money can buy: cars, women, drugs, clothes, jewelry. I've never been satisfied," says someone. "I know that I'm still thirsty for something."

Others nod their heads in agreement.

"So, the woman from Samaria shows up at the well to get the water she needs to survive, and Jesus is already there," I summarize. "What might this mean for us?" I ask. "If this story tells us where Jesus hung out back then, what does it suggest about where we might run into Jesus now?"

The men are tentative in responding to the obvious. They look at me and then down at their Bibles awkwardly, afraid to say something blasphemous. They start with safer responses.

"Could this be saying that Jesus may come to us when we are out working?" someone asks.

"Well, if that is a place where you are seeking to meet your needs, the place where you work would be a sort of well. Where else do you go to satisfy your needs, to quench your thirst?" I probe.

Eyebrows are raised and I see some slow nods and slight smiles. However, at this point I am aware that I am running into serious resistance from a deeply ingrained dominant theology, which envisions God as residing in Catholic or evangelical churches and other religious places, or far away in heaven, looking at the earth from a distance. Some may envision God as being near a religious shrine in the corner of their home, when candles are lit before the Virgin of Guadalupe or other saints. No one would naturally envision God as meeting them at the above-mentioned places, which they would actually frequent to meet their actual physical and psychological urges.

The Bible is another place that people would naturally view as a sacred site for God's presence. Most inmates assume, however, as already mentioned, that the Bible is too holy a place for them to feel welcomed into. Many Latino inmates fear that the Bible will confirm their worst fears: that they are damned because they cannot succeed at obeying the rules or because they avoid exposing themselves to new demands. Do this, believe that—change, or else. The Bible is not viewed as offering anything that would meet any of their most pressing needs. Consequently, whoever facilitates the Bible study is viewed as someone who invites them into a foreign, irrelevant place associated with guilt and punishment for crimes committed.

"If today's wells are places where we go to quench our thirst, like bars, crack houses, and meth labs, what do you think of Jesus' request to the woman: 'Give me a drink'?" I ask, inviting a direct confrontation with the dominant theology.

This question, overtly inviting people to interpret Jesus' presence in a way that challenges the dominant theology, directly parallels Jesus' provocative request to the Samaritan woman: "Give me a drink" (John 4:7). My inmate Bible-study participants often fear departing from the official transcript, especially when they are detained by the state, which appears to have received power sanctioned by the all-powerful God. Standing with Jesus, whose request shows total solidarity with them in their thirst, is a challenge to the entire system. Embracing this challenge appears risky. What if God in fact legitimates and upholds the power of the state? Their embracing of a God with them right where they are, rather than renouncing their wells in breast-beating repentance, may be perceived to lead to further sanctions in the form of more jail time or a guaranteed deportation.

The woman's response to Jesus parallels inmates' gut response to the interpretation I suggest. I ask a volunteer to read John 4:9.

> The Samaritan woman said to him, "How is it that you, a Jew, ask a drink of me, a woman of Samaria?" (For Jews do not share things in common with Samaritans.)

The woman's questioning of Jesus' openness to her reflects both her and the inmate-equivalent Samaritans' recognition that they are being called to ignore traditional boundaries. She reflects a hesitancy to move beyond the official transcript. At the same time, her hidden transcript apparently is not as risky as Jesus'. Jesus, a Jewish male who would normally view himself as superior to and forever separate from an unclean Samaritan woman, is willing to receive from her and drink her water.

"Let's see how Jesus responds to the woman," I suggest, inviting someone to read John 4:10.

I invite the men to imagine what Jesus' offer of living water might sound like to them if he were to actually meet them at their particular wells, where they actually go to quench their thirst.

Knowing full well that I am inviting people to risk blasphemy, I myself suggest a contextual rereading of this verse based on one of the men's identification of the crack house as his well.

"Is it possible that Jesus' answer might sound something like this," I ask: "'If you knew the gift of God, and who it is who says to you, "Give me some cocaine," you would have asked him, and he would have given you living cocaine'?"

The men smile hesitantly at first, and then begin to see that, indeed, Jesus is not taking the expected sermonizing, judging tone they assume he would have. Nor am I. When we read on in John 4:13–14: "Everyone who drinks of this water will be thirsty again, but those who drink of the water that I will give them will never be thirsty. The water that I will give will become in them a spring of water gushing up to eternal life," the men can see that Jesus is talking about more than actual water, cocaine, or whatever the contemporary equivalent of the contents of the well might be. At the same time, to help people identify God's surprising presence there outside the religious spaces where they would least expect God, I ask another question.

"Have any of you experienced God as being present with you in a positive, helpful way while you were drinking or doing drugs?"

Several men start talking at the same time, feeling permission to express a hidden transcript that they had never expressed publicly to anyone. Arnold tells of how he would often drive home after drinking and doing drugs and that he never got in an accident, even though in the morning he would have no memory of having driven his car the night before. Another man tells about how God speaks to him when he is high, making him feel a hunger for God's presence and for reading the Bible. Neeners tells about how, as a teenager, while he was stealing car stereos he prayed to God that he would not be caught, and how he felt God's protection. Another man mentions that it is a miracle that he and many of them are alive at all. He went on to tell the group how he is sure that if the police had not arrested him and brought him to the jail this time, he would be dead from an overdose: "God allowed me to be arrested to save my life and bring me here to get closer to God." Through these stories the men identify God as a gracious presence, who accompanies them in spite of their crimes and brokenness.

When we read together Jesus' order for her to return for the living water with her husband, and note that Jesus' offer was given with full knowledge that she had had five husbands, the men become more confident that this new theology may be believable.

"So if Jesus reveals God's true identity, as it says in different places in John's Gospel, what is God like, according to this story?" I ask, inviting the men to summarize this positive theology for themselves.

"Jesus comes to people right where they are, no matter what they're doing, even if they're messed up and shit," says Neeners.

"He offered living water to the woman, even though he knew she'd lived a bad life and without making her change first," says someone else.

The men are visibly moved as we glimpse together Jesus' startling solidarity with people as apparently messed up as this Samaritan woman. Jesus seems more approachable now that they have seen his offer of living water, no strings attached, to an undeserving woman.

I ask the men how many of them feel thirsty, desirous of this living water that Jesus offers. Everyone raises his hand or nods. An idea pops into my head that seems rather extreme, but still appropriate.

I invite the men to imagine a "forty," the slang for a forty-ounce can of the least expensive and highest-alcohol-content malt liquor preferred by people on the street. I invite them to imagine that it contains the living water that Jesus offers, which will permanently quench their thirst instead of the old, well-known malt liquor. At this point everyone is clear that the living water Jesus offers is not actual water, just as the malt liquor equivalent I invite them to drink is not literal malt liquor. I invite them to pop off the top and raise it up and drink freely together as I pray. Everyone pops the tops and we raise up our imaginary cans together over our mouths while I pray: "Jesus, we receive your gift of living water. We drink it down into our beings. Satisfy us with your loving, gracious presence."

Everyone makes the sign of the cross over himself in a way that I have come to recognize means they have been deeply touched. I leave for home feeling as if I have shared living water at a place that functions regularly like a life-giving well for me: Skagit County Jail. I return again the next Sunday, hoping that trust has grown between them and God, one another, the Bible, and myself as pastor and facilitator. My hope is that my presence, however directive or incomplete, would somehow fit within the company of Jesus and the woman, who both in their own ways bring people into authentic encounters with the source of living water.

Every Sunday I routinely use either the Old Testament or Gospel reading from the Revised Common Lectionary for our jail service. It is important for people on the margins to be brought into the larger body of Christ through reflecting on Scriptures that are being studied and preached on around the world. This commitment means that we are often forced to deal with more difficult texts. It is important that people newly initiated to the Bible not be overly protected from difficult texts, but be helped to interpret them in liberating ways, so their confidence will grow. On a Sunday afternoon on the First Sunday of Advent I ask a volunteer to read the first few verses of the lectionary reading, Luke 21:25–26, in Spanish and then in English:

> There will be signs in the sun, the moon, and the stars, and on the earth distress among nations confused by the roaring of the sea and the waves. People will faint from fear and foreboding of what is coming upon the world, for the powers of the heavens will be shaken.

I'm sheepish about this Scripture reading's end times feel, but decide to be bold and assume these men will somehow see its relevance and even helpfulness. So I blurt out a challenge: "OK, you guys, I need some help here. You all have been through way more than I have. You've known suffering, you know dark sides of this world. Do you see any of the signs that Luke talks about here?" I ask.

"Oh, for sure. They're all over the place," says a big, tall Caucasian guy to my left, confidently.

I nod and brace myself for some holy-roller hype that inmates-turned-religious sometimes get into to try to get back onto God's good side, and then invite him to say more.

"Well, just look at global climate changes," he began, raising my eyebrows. "Temperatures are rising everywhere, glaciers are melting, places that used to be lush and green are drying up. Even around here, remember how last summer it only rained three times? And then we just had a massive flood."

The Mexican men to my right are nodding. They talk about how droughts in parts of Mexico have led whole villages to migrate to the U.S.A.

I give the men a brief overview of Luke 21:1–24, which describes conflict and destruction related to the major powers of Jesus' time: the Temple, the nations, nature, kings, governors, and synagogues, family, and Jerusalem. I then ask them if they feel the distress and fear these verses describe, and if they feel more or less secure now.

"Man, yeah, we feel more stress. Everything is getting harder," says another Caucasian guy. "It's especially hard when you get into trouble with the legal system. Doing time, fines, probation, there's no relief. And then you look at how our country doesn't face these problems—we're stuck fighting way over in Iraq."

"We feel less secure than before," says a Mexican man. "It's getting harder to find jobs, pay rent, survive."

The men talk frankly about their addictions to drugs and alcohol and need for treatment, difficulties crossing the U.S.-Mexican border, and surviving on minimum wage. I summarize our discussion up to this point: "OK, so here in Luke, Jesus is alerting his disciples to signs that we can expect to come upon the world. Anxiety and fear are very normal reactions. Yet, in the next verses, Jesus says something surprising. Could someone read the next few verses in Spanish and in English?" A volunteer reads Luke 21:27–28:

> Then they will see "the Son of Man coming in a cloud" with power and great glory. Now when these things begin to take place, stand up and raise your heads, because your redemption is drawing near.

"When bad, depressing things are happening around us, getting us down, how does Jesus call us to respond?" I ask.

We talk about how, in the face of all the chaos of the failing systems, Jesus calls us to stand up tall, because we can expect him to come to deliver us soon. Jesus challenges us to do the opposite of what comes naturally. To those feeling stressed, downtrodden, and hopeless he says: "Stand up and raise your heads."

"How do we normally react when we're anxious and overwhelmed?" I ask.

"We go out and drink and do drugs," says a Latino guy, stirring the whole group to nods and smiles.

"We commit crimes. We sell drugs, or get violent on our women," says a white guy.

"Well, these seem to be fairly normal reactions. Check this out, you guys—Luke 21:34–35 seems to be reading our minds!" I say, inviting volunteers to read in Spanish and English.

> Be on guard so that your hearts are not weighed down with dissipation and drunkenness and the worries of this life, and that day does not catch you unexpectedly, like a trap. For it will come upon all who live on the face of the whole earth.

"Man, did I need to hear this today. And I wasn't planning on coming tonight. I'm not religious, and never go to church, but something was pushing me to go, and boy, am I glad," said the man who'd first raised my eyebrows. People are inspired by the call to stand up and lift up their heads when things get bad, expecting God to show up. The final verse clinches their resolve:

> Be alert at all times, praying that you may have the strength to escape all these things that will take place, and to stand before the Son of Man.

I invite the men to gather in a circle and join hands for a closing prayer. "OK, you guys, stand tall and lift up your heads." I'm deeply moved when everyone takes my admonition literally. People raise their heads upward when I pray. "Come, Lord Jesus, deliver us from all the dark forces that oppress us. Help us to escape the troubles that overwhelm us. Help us to watch for you and welcome you as the one who can comfort, heal, and liberate us." I leave the jail inspired by how those guys soak up the good news. I drive home wanting to watch and pray for our liberator to come and save us. When things look dark, we all need to lift up our heads and expect the presence. Being in touch with people on the edge can awaken in all of us our need for Jesus.

Why Did Jesus Have to Die?
Suffering, Election, and the Atonement

Many people with whom I read struggle to understand the significance of the death of Jesus for themselves. Traditional understandings of the atonement as "penal substitution" are well known on the street. Nearly everyone has heard statements like "Jesus paid the price to set you free," "He died for you so that you don't have to die," or "Jesus has taken your punishment upon himself." These traditional formulas ring hollow to inmates, farmworkers, and peasants who are sentenced to time in jail or prison, are unable to find work, or experience crop failures regardless of their belief in this teaching. A lot of work is still needed to help people come to a more helpful understanding of Jesus' passion. I begin a Bible study on Matthew 20 by inviting a volunteer to read Matthew 20:17–19:

> While Jesus was going up to Jerusalem, he took the twelve disciples aside by themselves, and said to them on the way, "See, we are going up to Jerusalem, and the Son of Man will be handed over to the chief priests and scribes, and they will condemn him to death; then they will hand him over to the Gentiles to be mocked and flogged and crucified; and on the third day he will be raised."

I ask the men what they think about Jesus' words to his disciples, and am surprised by their response.

"Jesus is just telling them what he had to do. He didn't have any other choice. He came for that, to fulfill what was written, and his time had come. He was just telling them what was ordained for him," someone says matter-of-factly.

The others nod their heads in approval, as if this was a no-brainer. While there is certainly some truth to this, the fatalism was reminiscent of explanations I hear over and over for people's suffering.

"I was caught by the police, and here I am. But God set it up that way," I have heard over and over from Latino immigrant inmates. Other common statements that reveal a view of God as hypersovereign and humans as predetermined puppets include: "What can we do? It was the will of God." "That's the way God wanted it." "It was all in God's plan." "God knows everything that he has for us. Everything that is written for us must be fulfilled. All we can do is be in agreement." Before a distant God who predetermines everything and carries it out exactly as planned, human beings are reduced to either automatons or outlaws seeking to get by with whatever is possible before destiny catches up with them. Accordingly, Jesus' death and all human suffering are nothing more than our unavoidable fate.

In an attempt to move past this impasse, I invite the men to think of other explanations. "Why would Jesus tell the disciples what was to happen to him?" I ask. When nobody ventures another answer besides the one already given, I ask the men whom the text blames for Jesus' death. To help the group grapple with this question, I ask more pointed questions regarding the narrative detail of the text.

"What exactly did Jesus say would happen to him?" I ask the men, looking down at my Bible.

We notice together that Jesus says he will be handed over to the chief priests and scribes, condemned to death, handed over to the Gentiles, mocked, flogged, and crucified, and then be raised from the dead.

"Who will do these things to Jesus?" I ask, hoping that this question will get us beyond attributing everything to God's sovereign will.

We notice together that Jesus was handed over to the Jewish religious authorities by Judas, one of his very own disciples, present with him. The chief priests and scribes were the ones who condemned him to death and handed him over to the Romans. The Romans were the ones who mocked, flogged, and crucified Jesus. The men are surprised when they notice that the only thing that God does in this account is resurrect Jesus!

We talk together about how, rather than attributing their legal troubles to God's will, perhaps we should all look closer at who actually is responsible for the abuses of the criminal and immigration legal systems. The American public votes in its representatives, who make the laws. Law-enforcement officers and prosecutors enforce these laws, while public defenders and other attorneys defend the accused. The judge sentences people, while the jail and prison officials and guards mete out the sentence. Based on parallelism with Matthew 20:17–19, God is the one who brings about the liberating outcome. "On the third day he will be raised." When I ask the men if this is encouraging to them, I am surprised by one man's honest quandary.

"This does not comfort me. It doesn't matter that Jesus was raised after three days. He could have been raised after twenty-four hours, two days, one week, one month. God has the power. We don't have the power. Jesus goes to the cross and knows he'll be resurrected, whenever he wants. He was righteous, so of course God would resurrect him. But us, we are not righteous, so we cannot expect to be resurrected like Jesus."

Before directly responding to this difficult question, we talk briefly about why Jesus told his disciples what would happen to him. We talk about how Jesus may have been alerting his disciples—and readers like us—to what they and we too may expect as we willingly pursue our vocations as agents of liberation. Betrayal by confidants can be expected. The guardians of the dominant theology may become extremely antagonistic and condemning, to the point of denouncing followers of Jesus as subversives before the state. The powers, too, will act violently and unjustly, in compliance with the religious establishment. Finally, though, God will vindicate Jesus' followers just as he did Jesus, resurrecting them from the dead. This strips the powers of their worst weapon, emboldening disciples to be steadfast to the end. While this is good news to disciples, the question as to who are included with Jesus needed to be pursued if the men were to experience comfort from this story.

I invite a volunteer to read Matthew 20:20–23, and after asking the men to identify the different characters in the narrative, I ask them what is happening in this story. A man reads the first few verses again:

> Then the mother of the sons of Zebedee came to him with her sons, and kneeling before him, she asked a favor of him. And he said to her, "What do you want?" She said to him, "Declare that these two sons of mine will sit, one at your right hand and one at your left, in your kingdom." But Jesus answered, "You do not know what you are asking. Are you able to drink the cup that I am about to drink?" They said to him, "We are able." He said to them, "You will indeed drink my cup, but to sit at my right hand and at my left, this is not mine to grant, but it is for those for whom it has been prepared by my Father." (Matt. 20:20–23)

I remind the men that these are special disciples of Jesus, some of the first people he called (Matt. 4:21).[7] We talk about how the mother's special request probably shows that she and her sons envision Jesus as coming to power soon, and they want high positions in his government. "Do they think they deserve a special favor from Jesus, since they are his close followers?" I ask.

"He doesn't give them what they want," someone says.

I agree, and further complicate the discussion by alerting them to three texts that Jesus appears to contradict. In Matthew 7:7–8, Jesus teaches, "Ask, and it will be given you; search, and you will find; know, and the door will be opened for you. For everyone who asks receives . . ." Later, in Matthew 18:19, Jesus says "if two of you agree on earth about anything you ask, it will be done for you by my Father in heaven"; and in Matthew 21:22 Jesus says, "Whatever you ask for in prayer with faith, you will receive."

"How many of you have asked God for something in prayer and he hasn't answered your prayer as you'd hoped?" I ask.

Nearly everyone nods or raises his hand.

"So how did Jesus respond to his followers? 'You do not know what you are asking. Are you able to drink the cup that I am about to drink?'"

We talk about how Jesus appears to know something about which the sons of Zebedee and their mother appear ignorant. The men can all see that the disciples appear to accept Jesus' question as a challenge to prove their worthiness. "We are able," they say. We talk about spiritual machismo—the human tendency to demonstrate to God or others our worthiness to receive blessing, forgiveness, or any privilege through striving to fulfill what we think is required of us. People all agree that the cup is a reference to Jesus' suffering. We read Jesus' response again in the following verse before continuing our discussion.

> He said to them, "You will indeed drink my cup, but to sit at my right hand and at my left, this is not mine to grant, but it is for those for whom it has been prepared by my Father." (20:23)

I ask the men when they think the sons of Zebedee drank of the cup. I invite them to turn to Matthew 26:36–43, and a volunteer reads:

> Then Jesus went with them to a place called Gethsemane; and he said to his disciples, "Sit here while I go over there and pray." He took with him Peter and the two sons of Zebedee, and began to be grieved and agitated. Then he said to them, "I am deeply grieved, even to death; remain here, and stay awake with me." And going a little farther, he threw himself on the ground and prayed, "My Father, if it is possible, let this cup pass from me; yet not what I want but what you want." Then he came to the disciples and found them sleeping; and he said to Peter, "So, could you not stay awake with me one hour? Stay awake and pray that you may not come into the time of trial; the spirit indeed is willing, but the flesh is weak." Again he went away for the second time and prayed, "My Father, if this cannot pass unless I drink it, your will be done." Again he came and found them sleeping, for their eyes were heavy.

We agree together that the cup that Jesus says they will drink may not, then, be their suffering. I ask them, then what cup did they in fact drink? I invite a volunteer to read Matthew 26:26–28:

> While they were eating, Jesus took a loaf of bread, and after blessing it he broke it, gave it to the disciples, and said, "Take, eat; this is my body." Then he took a cup, and after giving thanks he gave it to them, saying, "Drink from it, all of you; for this is my blood of the covenant, which is poured out for many for the forgiveness of sins."

The men are all moved as they can see that Jesus was telling the sons of Zebedee that they would do nothing heroic to save themselves or merit positions of privilege. Rather, they like the "many" would be passive beneficiaries of Jesus' suffering and death for them. The identity of those who would sit at his right and his left still is unknown.

"So when do you think that Jesus entered his kingdom?" I ask.

"After he dies and goes to heaven," says a man. Nobody challenges this answer.

I invite the men to turn in their Bibles to Matthew 27, and ask people to read aloud verse 11, where Pilate asks Jesus whether he is "the King of the Jews," and verses 28–29, where more references to Jesus' being king are visible:

> They stripped him and put a scarlet robe on him, and after twisting some thorns into a crown, they put it on his head. They put a reed in his right hand and knelt before him and mocked him, saying, "Hail, King of the Jews!"

These verses are enough to convince the men that, according to Matthew's Gospel, Jesus enters his kingdom when he goes to the cross. The final clincher, though, comes when I ask someone to read Matthew 27:35–38:

> And when they had crucified him, they divided his clothes among themselves by casting lots; then they sat down there and kept watch over him. Over his head they put the charge against him, which read, "This is Jesus, the King of the Jews." Then two bandits were crucified with him, one on his right and one on his left.

The men are shocked to see how clearly Jesus identifies with people like them.

"What did these bandits have to do to merit this place beside Jesus in his kingdom?" I ask.

"They committed crimes!" someone says.

We talk together about how the sons of Zebedee and their mother really did not know what they were asking. I invite a volunteer to read Matthew 27:55–56, where the mother of the sons of Zebedee is mentioned as looking on from a distance, likely understanding something new about the way of Jesus.

We return at this point in our discussion to Matthew 20:24–28, and talk about how the other ten disciples were angry with the two brothers for trying to get special favor from Jesus. None of these insiders understood what Jesus was about. Jesus' words to them invite them to a similar path of pouring out their life:

> You know that the rulers of the [nations] lord it over them, and their great ones are tyrants over them. It will not be so among you; but whoever wishes to be great among you must be your servant, and whoever wishes to be first among you must be your slave; just as the Son of Man came not to be served but to serve, and to give his life a ransom for many.

People in the jail are always very touched by this Bible study, which fully subverts their preconceived notions about worthiness and who are included as beneficiaries of Jesus' life and death. They can see themselves as among the many who benefit from Jesus' shed blood and life given as ransom. Others identify fully with the robbers, and find comfort in this image of Jesus' presence between them in their suffering and death. Paul's statement that those who die with Christ will live with Christ (Rom. 6:8; 2 Tim. 2:11) offers them new hope.

At times we focus some discussion on the role of God in Jesus' suffering. As we saw above, most people assume that Jesus had to die because God had planned it all out, requiring it because he needed a blood sacrifice. Once again, careful attention to detail in the text sheds light on the meaning of Jesus' death, suggesting that humans, not God, are the ones in need of blood.[8]

"God didn't need Jesus to die, we needed him to die," says Carlos, a Chicano man who's been attending my recent series of jail Bible studies on the death of Jesus. "God wants us to enter the kingdom. He needs all of us. No, he doesn't need us, he wants us," he concludes.

❧❧❧❧❧❧❧❧❧

In the Gospels it seems clear that God did not need Jesus to die. Those who plot his death are consistently the religious authorities. Jesus' conscious and willing taking up of his cross is best interpreted as God's total solidarity with human beings and willingness to identify fully with the victims of human violence and injustice. Could the death of Jesus be interpreted as God's offering Jesus as a willing sacrifice to human beings? This is a question I am anxious to pursue in future studies with inmates.

When we look at the notion of Jesus' life given as ransom, or bail, it is clear from an inmate perspective that bail would not be posted to God, but is required by the state. Jesus does not give his body and blood to God in a way that would be in keeping with penal substitution. Rather he gives his body to his disciples, saying, "This is my body, broken for you." Jesus offers the cup for his disciples to drink, not to his Father, saying, "This is my blood of the covenant, which is poured out for many for the forgiveness of sins." Jesus' offer of his very life to humans is certainly a precious gift that is nothing less than astounding. When people begin to glimpse God's vulnerable love, true change of the heart begins.

Chapter Nine

Following Jesus, the Good Coyote

Reading Paul with Undocumented Immigrants

R eading Paul's epistles with people in the jail requires constant creativity. The fact that most were written from jail gives them special
credibility among inmates. However, Paul's letters present a special challenge because, unlike narrative texts, they lack characters, places, and
actions that can serve as launches for contextual readings. People's own
lives must serve as the primary narrative, which can then be read in the
light of Paul's theology.

Most often I end up reading selections from Paul's writings during
group discussion of an Old Testament or Gospel story, where a question
comes up that appears to be addressed by a famous passage like Romans
5:6–11, where Paul describes God's love for sinners, or Romans 7:14–8:4's
description of the difficulty of doing the good one truly desires. Paul's
descriptions of the chosen as the nobodies of his day in 1 Corinthians
1:26–31, and of himself as a notorious blasphemer and all-out bad guy in
1 Timothy 1:12–17, always deeply encourage people who feel too unimportant and unworthy for God to call them to active ministry. Other popular Scripture passages include 1 Corinthians 13's description of love,
Galatians 5's description of the struggle between the flesh and the spirit,
and the passages describing struggle against the principalities and powers
already treated in my presentation above on Psalm 8 and praying the
psalms against enemies.

Most often I invite people to read the epistles in rapport with a particular question coming out of pastoral counseling or a group's struggle with
a particular question. Reading Jesus as a coyote who brings us into God's
reign against the law at no charge, or presenting baptism as making us all
equally "wetback" strangers and aliens, are understandings coming directly

179

out of years of working with undocumented immigrants struggling with the constant reality of possible deportation.

Problems Facing Undocumented Immigrant Families

I drive my Isuzu Trooper over the bridge crossing the Skagit River from my house, and head out across fertile farmland on my way to visit Feliciano, a Mixteco farmworker who also pastors a Mixteco-speaking congregation called Iglesia de Jesucristo. I have been thinking of this pastor and his family ever since I dropped eighteen plump white chickens by their place a few months back. A local poultry farmer had called me, wondering if she could get a tax receipt for donating sixty-five free-range hens she'd raised to sell. "No problem," I said, and made four separate trips to ferry the chickens in cardboard boxes out to migrants living in several of the area camps. I had received chickens on many different occasions from other local farmers, and always love the opportunity to give them to peasant folk who relish the opportunity to slaughter birds for fresh pozole (a corn and chicken or pork stew), or chicken enchiladas.

People look insecure and somewhat depressed on this rainy October evening, when I ferry my first two carloads of live chickens to farmworkers in large migrant camps across the valley from Feliano's. The blueberry harvest had ground to a halt, and people were looking for apartments or preparing to head south to California or back to Oaxaca for the winter. I feel joy as I hand out the squawking birds to the smiling women and children who line up. I am especially warmed by a six- or seven-year-old girl who firmly clutched a struggling bird after dutifully ordering "*uno para mi mama*" (one for my mommy). We had carried the eighteen chickens for Feliciano's family and parishioners into a shed beside their run-down trailer atop a forested hill in the middle of cornfields. Now I am returning in hopes of finding Feliciano. I had heard he was having terrible headaches, and I wanted to encourage him.

I drive across the flats past wintering snow geese and recently harvested potato fields, taking a right onto a heavily potholed dirt road that divides a cornfield from a potato field, and mount the pine-forested hill to where more cars are parked beside three run-down trailers. At least forty vans are parked alongside the road, alerting me that some sort of gathering is going on. As I walk up the dirt driveway toward Feliciano's trailer with my two sons, Isaac (thirteen) and Luke (twelve), I notice the movement of women and children working around fires and camping stoves under a big plastic awning. When they see me they look a bit nervous, until a man recognizes me and tells them something in Mixteco that appears to put everyone more at ease. We walk under the smoky awning past big aluminum pots full of meat simmering over flames. It's cold outside and some are huddling close to the fire. A woman points beyond her, where a group of men are gathered around some task. We make our way past the fires and the women and come upon a group of twelve to fifteen men atop a big blue plastic tarp, cutting away at slabs of meat from the carcass of a big cow, whose head lies already skinned. The men chatter away in Mixteco, and someone tells me in Spanish that Feliciano is not here. An older man, who speaks Spanish haltingly, escorts us past another group of men hard at work digging a big hole that will soon be filled with firewood, lit, and heaped with rocks. They are preparing for the wedding of Feliciano's daughter the next day. The meat will go into the pit atop hot rocks and be buried until the next morning, when it will be unearthed for the fiesta.

The older man leads me into the family trailer, past chickens that roost on the railing. My sons check out a video game with Feliciano's sons on their PlayStation. They show the Mixteco kids their new Nintendo DS, as the older man awkwardly enters numbers on his cell phone and Feliciano answers. He's at the Kmart and won't be back for a few hours. We plan to meet later in the afternoon. Before we leave, the people insist that we all join them for a bowl of broken rice and chicken with broth and whole chiles and slabs of thick, rust-colored chile paste. We head home with warm stomachs.

When I return, it is near dark and there are still more cars. Feliciano meets me at the door. He's a dark, weather-beaten man in his late fifties, dressed in humble attire: polyester pants, muddied work boots, insulated nylon jacket. He tells me that his living room is too crowded with guests for us to converse in peace. He escorts me into his son's bedroom and has me sit on the bed. I tell him that I have been thinking of him often. He looks worried, tired. He tells me that it has been difficult pastoring people—forty-eight families—while still working full-time as a crew boss for a local farmer. "*Mucho problema*—the people don't understand," he tells me in broken Spanish. "I visit families. Lots of drinking, violence between spouses. It's difficult." On top of that, he has six children still living at home. "*Mucha responsabilidad.*" He tells me about his terrible headaches, which have kept him in bed for the last four days. I offer to pray for him. Feliciano first wants me to pray for his son Antonio, and calls him in.

Antonio appears in the doorway, wheeling himself into the narrow room on his wheelchair. Antonio's legs are badly deformed. In his late twenties, he spends much of his time there in the trailer. He tells me about the burning pain in his stomach, which sounds to me like acid reflux. He tells me he has been suffering for over a year. Big tears tumble down as he describes his pain. He tells me he has been trying everything: avoiding greasy food, meat, coffee, and soft drinks. He's been to several doctors, but medicines are not helping.

"There are people who tell me I should fast, and I have been fasting," he tells me. "I want to serve God," he says as he cries.

I happen to have a bottle of a homeopathic remedy, nux vomica, and offer to leave it with him, showing him how to take them as a remedy for indigestion. Antonio is eager to try the remedy but also desires prayer. He immediately bows his head, and his father and I pray over him. I anoint him with oil and pray in the name of Jesus that the comforting presence of the Holy Spirit would replace the pain in his stomach. I pray in every way I know how, so desperately do I want him to experience relief. Then I offer to pray for Feliciano's headaches. The whole time I pray Feliciano, too, is praying simple prayers, "Yes Jesus, help me, help me, help us."

After I anoint him with oil and bless him, he sits and tells me how all his people are illegal, and that this is the greatest problem that they have been facing. "Pray, Roberto, that God will help us get papers." He tells me how the American "*hermanos*" (brothers) from other churches he knows have been telling him that it is wrong to break the law.

"This makes me feel bad. What do you think, Roberto? All of us are illegal. When you wanted to talk with me, I thought at first that maybe you too were coming here to tell me that this is wrong that we are illegal," he says. Even pastor Feliciano is living under the shadow of the dominant theology, which views God as cosmic Border Patrol chief and church as his deputies. I lament his correct perception that the mainstream church, much like the scribes and the Pharisees of Jesus' time, takes the side of state and the law, rather than that of the people and God's kingdom.

I tell him that I believe that in the kingdom of God there are no borders, and that God views us all as his beloved children. If salvation were the result of obeying the law, then all of us are damned. I tell him that I've been seeing Jesus more and more as our *Buen Coyote*. Jesus crosses us over into the kingdom against the law, by grace. We cannot save ourselves through observing laws. Jesus liberates us, Jesus saves us. He doesn't even charge, he just wants us to trust him and follow. This delights Feliciano and Antonio, filling them with joy and encouragement in ways that are more visible than my prayers. We laugh together, and they invite me to the wedding the next day. A month later I meet him by chance in a local café. He tells me with a smile that his headaches have disappeared since the day I prayed. He is in full rain gear ready to pick daffodils with his crew. "Let's organize a healing service at my church," he says as we part.

I have always been attracted to coyotes, the wild dogs that wander under cover of darkness throughout Skagit County. This group of clever, wary migrant Mixtec farmworkers gathering on the wooded hill makes me think of a pack of coyotes surviving resourcefully on the margins of our county. I regularly hear real coyotes howling in the woods just outside our home on the Skagit River. A chill goes up my spine as their wild yelps penetrate through my consciousness. Though they have attacked and eaten four of our sheep, I cannot help admiring their wily, streetwise nature. They have learned to survive at the edges, much like the outlaws and indigents with whom I minister. My ministry parallels the work of another sort of coyote, who serves my Latino sheep.

Smugglers who lead people into the United States through the U.S.-Mexican border are named after coyotes. Immigrants from Mexico and Central America who do not qualify for visas nearly all have had to hire "coyotes" to smuggle them into the United States. Coyotes, also known as "*polleros*" (chicken carriers), meet their clients, "*pollos*" (chickens), in border towns or barrios of large border cities like Tijuana and Ciudad Juárez. They take their cash, U.S.-dollar down payments and set up the time and place to begin the perilous journey through the hills or deserts into the United States. In many ways they function like priests for the underdogs—offering them a rite of passage into the land where tangible salvation is possible.

Most every immigrant can tell you both good and bad coyote stories, much as they have good pastor/priest and bad pastor/priest stories. Bad coyotes may knowingly lead people into bands of robbers, rape women, or abandon their charges in the desert. Some will hold people hostage in safe houses until family members pay their fees. Others are known to lock people into trucks or boxcars and even abandon them to their deaths. Good coyotes treat people respectfully and fulfill their obligations to guide people securely into the country. This includes guiding people to safe houses where they can eat, bathe, and rest. They may carry children, rescue lost immigrants, or provide food and water to stranded travelers. Coyotes all function to lead immigrants who lack legal immigration documents into the United States, against the law—a role that provides a strong contemporary metaphor to Jesus' role as Savior, according to Paul's theology.

In harmony with Paul's theology, Jesus can be viewed as comparable to a coyote in his embracing and symbolically crossing people who cannot fulfill the legal requirements to enter legitimately into the reign of God.

Jesus' eating with tax collectors and sinners, healing on the Sabbath, touching lepers, speaking with Samaritans, and countless other actions mark him as an alien smuggler. The Pharisees, scribes, and other religious authorities neatly parallel the Border Patrol and other law-enforcement agents, who consider it their job to keep "illegal aliens" out.

Most of the immigrants with whom we work do not have the luxury of legality. They work using counterfeit residency and Social Security cards, drive without valid driver's licenses and insurance. In addition, many struggle with addictions to alcohol or drugs. Consequently, they are constantly living in a state of legal and spiritual insecurity. Andrés and María are typical of the people whom Tierra Nueva serves.

I first met Andrés in the jail when he was twenty-two. He participated in my weekly Spanish Bible studies there over periods of three or four months while he did time on at least three occasions. Deported by the Border Patrol to Mexico, he returned illegally each time. Andrés is short and muscular, with dark skin and hair that have earned him the nickname "el Negro" (the black one).

Andrés was an orphan at an early age, learning to fend for himself on the streets of Mexico City. He has scars on his face and elsewhere on his body to show a life marked by struggle. He crossed the border illegally in his late teens to work in the fields in California. Eventually he made his way to the Skagit Valley and found work on a construction crew. His eyes reveal both a life of suffering and a readiness for unlimited levels of illegal adventure. He looks expectant and prepared to face any kind of fun or trouble, and can invent brilliant lies, which he tells unflinchingly to police detectives, judges, and also to public defenders that are ready to represent him, whom he does not trust. At the same time he weeps the moment he talks about the ones he loves. He adores his partner María and their four young children, though he is constantly separated from them due to his perpetual troubles with the law.

María was also in her early twenties when I first met her. She has a dark, beautiful face and long black hair. In spite of her difficult life, she is unusually quick to smile, revealing slightly crooked, protruding teeth that do not detract from her beauty but give her a slightly mischievous, fun look. She had two young children when she met Andrés. When I first visited her, she and Andrés also had a one-year-old and María was pregnant with their second. She lived on the second floor of a rickety, cockroach-infested house beside the railroad tracks with her children, struggling to make it with no income since Andrés went to jail.

María herself is one of nine children, born to a poor young woman in Tijuana, who carried her across the border when she was several months old. María has lived her entire life moving from farm labor camps to flophouses and the lowest-level apartments, eventually earning money in ways that have led some to gossip. Andrés's adoration makes him ready to pick a fight with anyone who questions her past or shows the slightest disrespect. Since she has spent all but three months of her life in the United States, she speaks English better than Spanish, and considers herself more American than Mexican. Yet, since her mother never was functional enough to apply for her permanent residence, she is in the United States illegally, and has already been deported once. Her problems are compounded by the fact that she has no Mexican papers. Her mother has no memory of having a birth certificate for her, cannot remember in which poor barrio in Tijuana María was born, and is unsure whether she ever officially registered her. Consequently María has no identification of any kind. When she and Andrés came to me asking me to perform their wedding, I could not legally marry them because she lacked the necessary ID to obtain a marriage license.

As her advocate and pastor, I worked long and hard with María to pull together documents that might work to prove her identity so she could measure up to the demands of the law. The only proof we could dig up was her mug shot and personal information on file in the jail from an arrest the year before. María was unwilling to request a copy of this herself, for fear that the sheriff's office would notify the Border Patrol that she was back. Her false immigration papers and Social Security card would have to do until someone figures out a way to help her become an official person.

Andrés and María are somewhat typical of people on the margins with whom I read Scripture. They, like so many others from places all over the world, are accustomed to rejection by the powerful. Their spiritual outlook is subsequently impacted, as they do not naturally expect God to call them or give them any special attention. They have accurately observed that their race, social class, nationality, and other factors destine them for what they consider irremediable, permanent exclusion.

Andrés has been arrested, jailed, deported, and returned at least three times in the seven years that I have known him. Each time in the jail he progresses farther in both his self-understanding and his faith and love for God. He participates actively in the Bible studies, talking honestly about his temptations and failings. He welcomes any good news he can get in ways that have been contagious for the others. Each time I have watched him prepare to leave jail to be deported by the Border Patrol he appears more committed to María and their children. Andrés's risky illegal returns for María qualify him as a sort of *buen coyote* figure—willing to break the law and face federal prison time if caught. Each time he returns to warrants for failures to appear in one court or another, which we help him quash with the required fifty dollars cash. This beautiful young couple and their children are "damned" to an underground life, driving without driver's licenses, working with false papers—always on the lookout for law-enforcement agents of every variety who could temporarily end their happiness at any time. Yet Andrés talks of feeling God's presence beside him in ways that are tangible and subversive.

Andrés's most recent return involved crossing alone through the desert of Arizona, since he and María had no way to pull together the $1,400 needed to pay a coyote. He tells the story of praying without ceasing as he crossed the border, and of how the Border Patrol drove right past him without stopping as he entered a border town on foot.

"It was like God made me invisible or something," said Andrés. "It was a miracle, Roberto! God helped me."

I do not doubt Andrés's perception that God had helped him. He is full of faith wrought from the furnace of his recent suffering, which always burned away all the distractions and left him glowing. I had visited him and María in the months after this incident. I watched him struggle with the temptation to do unnecessary illegal actions, which he carefully sought to distinguish from the necessary illegalities. Being caught driving without a license for his fifth or sixth time would most certainly land him in jail and into the hands of the Border Patrol. Yet when his ride did not show up, he would take the calculated risk rather than lose his hard-to-come-by construction job. Working with counterfeit immigration papers and Social Security number was no different than Jacob's covering his arms and neck with goatskins and lying to his blind father. Was I willing to be a Rebekah-like accomplice?

One afternoon when I show up unexpectedly at Andrés's marijuana-smoke-filled apartment living room, I worry that he might be slipping into an old pattern that included justifying more and more unnecessary and risky behaviors. Andrés was eventually arrested on suspicion of knowingly using and selling counterfeit twenty-dollar bills and possession of stolen property—crimes for which he may well have been guilty. After the prosecutor was unsuccessful in convicting him, the jail turned him over to the INS for deportation. Since he was undocumented and had numerous prior deportations, the INS decided to prosecute Andrés for illegal reentry, and sentenced him to two years in federal prison. Andrés called me collect from prison on numerous occasions. He was going through a dark period of worry and doubt. He asked me how María was doing, since she had long since had her phone service disconnected because of her inability to pay her phone bill. Meanwhile, María surprised him by preparing to move back to Mexico to start a new life with, hopefully, fewer troubles. When Andrés was recently deported, María left the country she considers home to join him in Mexico, where they have been reunited with their four children.

God is with Andrés and María in the land of their dreams or in exile, as God is with my inmate brothers in Skagit County Jail. Not long ago I heard that they have crossed back over and are living somewhere in Texas.

Inspired by my visit with Feliciano and memories of people like Andrés and María, I decide to further explore the image of Jesus as Good Coyote with inmates in the Skagit County Jail. I begin a Sunday afternoon Bible study with a group of twenty-five Latino, Native American, and Caucasian inmates with the question: "Do you feel as if you are unable to cross from where you are in your life right now to the new place or way of being that you desire?"

Nearly everyone says, "Yes," "*Sí*," or in some way shows his agreement. I then ask what blocks them from being able to move.

The men share about their difficulties in being able to live the way they desire. Some talk of difficulties in stopping smoking weed, using harder drugs, or drinking. Others talk about their failures with child support, court-imposed fines, or complying with the Probation Office. I invite a reader to read Romans 7:15–24, which describes the experience of failure to live up to the law:

> I do not understand my own actions. For I do not do what I want, but I do the very thing I hate. Now if I do what I do not want, I agree that the law is good. But in fact it is no longer I that do it, but sin that dwells within me. For I know that nothing good dwells within me, that is, in my flesh. I can will what is right, but I cannot do it. For I do not do the good I want, but the evil I do not want is what I do. Now if I do what I do not want, it is no longer I that do it, but sin that dwells within me.
>
> So I find it to be a law that when I want to do what is good, evil lies close at hand. For I delight in the law of God in my inmost self, but I see in my members another law at war with the law of my mind, making me captive to the law of sin that dwells in my members.

Wretched man that I am! Who will rescue me from this body of death?

Everyone relates readily to this realistic description of their struggles.

"If change or salvation depends on our efforts to be good, then we're clearly screwed," I suggest.

To bring this home again, I ask whether there are any people there in the room who have tried over and over to change in some area of their lives but have been unable to. Everyone raises his hand.

For the benefit of the Americans, and to draw in a social dimension regarding the near-impossibility of changing from a place of hopelessness to a place of new possibility, I ask the Mexican men whether there are barriers that keep them from coming to El Norte (North America). Since most are undocumented, they talk freely about how it is nearly impossible to get permission to enter the United States legally unless you are a university student, from a wealthy family, or have a U.S.-citizen family member who can qualify to sponsor them. They share how it costs between fifteen hundred and three thousand dollars to cross the border with a coyote. We talk about how impossible it often feels to achieve your dreams or change your life through your own effort alone, and how easy it is to give up and assume you must be damned. I then invite a volunteer to read Galatians 3:10:

> For all who rely on the works of the law are under a curse; for it is written, "Cursed is everyone who does not observe and obey all the things written in the book of the law."

"What do you think it means to be under the curse of the law?" I ask the men.

"Here we are, experiencing it," someone says. "We can't leave here."

We talk about how their red uniforms, plastic identity bracelets, criminal records, sentences, pending court appearances, detention, and undocumented status mark them as cursed under the law.

"When we leave here, the Border Patrol will deport us," says a Mexican man. "Then we'll have to come up with money to pay a coyote to cross back over."

"So if we cannot change our ways, or find insurmountable obstacles to getting out of debt, getting a driver's license, a job if you are a felon, or acquiring legal immigration status, what hope is there for us?" I ask the men.

When no one can think of a compelling answer, I invite a reader to read Paul's answer to his own question in Romans 7:24: "Wretched man that I am! Who will rescue me from this body of death?" which is found in the next verse: "Thanks be to God through Jesus Christ our Lord!"

"So how does Jesus do this?" I ask the men. I then propose envisioning Jesus like a Good Coyote who brings us into the kingdom of God, in spite of the law, against the law. Before fleshing out the details of this analogy, I invite a volunteer to read Galatians 3:11–14:

> Now it is evident that no one is justified before God by the law; for "The one who is righteous will live by faith." But the law does not rest on faith; on the contrary, "Whoever does the works of the law will live by them." Christ redeemed us from the curse of the law by becoming a curse for us—for it is written, "Cursed is everyone who hangs on a tree"—in order that in Christ Jesus the blessing of Abraham might come to the Gentiles, so that we might receive the promise of the Spirit through faith.

For people unfamiliar with Paul's theological world, this language clearly requires some brief but careful explaining. My first attempt to make this language more relevant is to summarize Paul's arguments for the men.

"According to Paul," I begin, "nobody can be justified, that is, become law-abiding, righteous, or successful by complying with the law. Paul had been a holy roller for years," I continue, "and lists all his religious and social merits in Philippians 3:4–6. As a Pharisee he had attempted to be perfect through obeying the Jewish law, but in the end actually says he recognizes that his righteousness ain't shit compared to knowing Jesus."

The men are surprised that I swear, but I assure them that the Bible actually uses this word in Philippians 3:8–9, when Paul says:

> More than that, I regard everything as loss because of the surpassing value of knowing Christ Jesus my Lord. For his sake I have suffered the loss of all things, and I regard them as rubbish [literally, shit],[1] in order that I may gain Christ, and be found in him, not having a righteousness of my own that comes from the law, but one that comes through faith [of] Christ,[2] the righteousness from God based on faith.

"According to Paul," I continue, "we are saved only through faith in Jesus and what he has done. What has he done, according to Galatians 3:13?" I ask the men, who look down at their Bibles.

"He has redeemed us," says one of the men.

Since nobody knows exactly what "redeemed" means, I briefly describe posting bail as a kind of contemporary equivalent of redeeming that I know the men can relate to.

"How does he do this exactly?" I ask, inviting the men to keep examining Galatians 3:13.

"He became a curse for us," a man reads. "It says that cursed is anyone who hangs on a tree. He became a curse for us when he was hung on the cross."

We talk about how during the first century the cross was the equivalent of the electric chair, lethal injection, or any form of capital punishment.

"If this is true, then can we say that Jesus is like a coyote who crosses us into the kingdom of God, brings us into favor with God even though we cannot legally do this ourselves?"

While I wonder to what extent the men are grasping my argument, I have their full attention, and they are visibly intrigued enough to make an effort to understand. When I continue by describing how Jesus actually gets caught, detained, and sentenced, assuming the curse that is upon us because of the law, people are all ears. Jesus is such a good coyote that he actually gets caught by the Border Patrol agents of his time, while the law-breakers run free.

We talk about how it is by faith in Jesus that we become justified, an idea that can discourage people who struggle to believe.[3] I invite a volunteer to read further in Galatians 3:23, to deepen our understanding of how Jesus crosses us into a place of blessing.

> Now before faith came, we were imprisoned and guarded under the law until faith would be revealed.

"What do you think Paul is talking about when he writes of faith 'coming' and 'being revealed'?" I ask the men.

"Faith is Jesus himself," says one of the men matter-of-factly.

I agree, and ask the reader to continue reading Galatians 3:24–26, in hopes of penetrating this mystery:

> Therefore the law was our disciplinarian until Christ came, so that we might be justified by faith. But now that faith has come, we are no longer subject to a disciplinarian, for in Christ Jesus you are all children of God through faith.

We discuss together how Jesus' action on behalf of lawbreakers makes him a truly subversive coyote. Jesus' work undoes the legal basis for us-them distinctions and borders or barriers of any kind. Jesus brings about a leveling that destroys any distinctions based on compliance with laws. Jesus makes all people children of God. Faith comes in the flesh to accomplish what humans could not do. I invite the men to turn to Ephesians 2:13–16, which I hope will bring further clarity:

> But now in Christ Jesus you who once were far off have been brought near by the blood of Christ. For he is our peace; in his flesh he has made both groups into one and has broken down the dividing wall, that is, the hostility between us. He has abolished the law with its commandments and ordinances, that he might create in himself one new humanity in place of the two, thus making peace, and might reconcile both groups to God in one body through the cross, this putting to death that hostility through it.

Our heads are reeling as we contemplate Jesus as a coyote who actually breaks down the borders through abolishing the law. By reconciling humans to God through the cross, Jesus brings about a new society with no distinctions between us and them. I ask the reader to continue reading Ephesians 2:17–20:

> So he came and proclaimed peace to you who were far off and peace to those that were near; for through him both of us have access in one Spirit to the Father. So then you are no longer strangers and aliens, but you are [*fellow*] *citizens* with the saints and also members of the household of God, built upon the foundation of the apostles and prophets, with Christ Jesus himself as the cornerstone.

I sit amazed at the power of these words there in the heart of the jail and migrant farmworker communities where I serve. The men look both perplexed and comforted. In an attempt to invite active response from the men while at the same time holding them in a place of grace, I ask the men a question: "How do we come to embrace the benefits of what Jesus has done?"

Armando, a Pentecostal pastor in his fifties facing a 115-month sentence, is tracking fully. He says:

"People at the border have to look for a coyote to cross them. And we also have to look for Jesus so that he can pass us."[4]

I agree with Armando, and then ask the question, "What does Jesus the Good Coyote charge to cross us into the reign of God?"

"*Nada,*" says an inmate. "He does not charge."

"That's true, I believe," I respond. "Yet perhaps there is something that is necessary as we contemplate following Jesus. When you go with coyotes, even if you pay them, you put your trust in them, don't you?" I ask.

The Mexicans all nod their heads. For the others there in the group who have never had to cross a border illegally, I point out that when they buy and use drugs or drink a Budweiser, they are putting their trust in the dealer or company that they will not die when they smoke, snort, inject, or drink.

"All Jesus wants from us is our faith," I say, reminding the group of Paul's words in Galatians 3:14, "that in Christ Jesus the blessing of Abraham might come to the Gentiles, that we might receive the promise of the Spirit *through faith*" (italics added).

I talk briefly about how in our baptism we enter into a death, leaving our distinctions based on the law behind in the water. On the other side of baptism we are a new community marked by solidarity. I invite a volunteer to read Galatians 3:27–29:

> As many of you as were baptized into Christ have clothed yourselves with Christ. There is no longer Jew or Greek, there is no longer slave or free, there is no longer male or female; for all of you are one in Christ Jesus. And if you belong to Christ, then you are Abraham's offspring, heirs according to the promise.

To conclude, we discuss together how, according to Paul, in our baptism we enter into and become beneficiaries of Jesus' death on our behalf. In the waters of baptism into Jesus' death and resurrection the borders are brought down, and there are no longer distinctions between the law-abiding and criminals, U.S. citizens and foreigners, legals and illegals, brown and white, chemically dependent and clean and sober, poor and rich, male and female—all are one in Christ Jesus. On the other side of baptism we are members of one human family, not by right but because Jesus has brought us into the kingdom. We're all wetbacks, and must even count ourselves as fellow "criminal aliens." Paul certainly did in his humble confession in 1 Timothy 1:12–16, which never fails to shock people in its radical inclusiveness of the bad guys:

> I am grateful to Christ Jesus our Lord, who has strengthened me, because he judged me faithful and appointed me to his service, even

though I was formerly a blasphemer, a persecutor, and a man of violence. But I was received mercy because I had acted ignorantly in
unbelief, and the grace of our Lord overflowed for me with the faith
and love that are in Christ Jesus. The saying is sure and worthy of full
acceptance, that Christ Jesus came into the world to save sinners—
of whom I am the foremost. But for that very reason I received mercy,
so that in me, as the foremost, Jesus Christ might display the utmost
patience, making me an example to those who would come to believe
in him for eternal life.

Knowing that inmates might miss the power of this text when they
notice that Paul is thankful to Christ for having appointed him in spite of
his *past* behavior as a blasphemer, persecutor, and violent man, I invite a
volunteer to reread verse 15, where Paul speaks of himself in the present:
"Christ Jesus came into the world to save sinners—of whom I *am* the foremost" (italics added).

On this particular afternoon, I ask the men how many of them feel
attracted to Jesus the Good Coyote enough to desire to follow him. Nearly
everyone expresses agreement, and I invite people to stand, gather in a circle, and hold hands for a closing blessing and prayer.

"How many of you desire to follow Jesus, and receive his gift of crossing you from where you've been unable to succeed through obedience, to
making it through his grace?"

I hear many "I do's" and "*yo sí's*" as I repeat the question in English and
Spanish.

"In putting our faith in Jesus, the blessing of Abraham is available to
us," I announce.

"Let's pray that God would pour out blessing on us through filling us
all with the Spirit, as Galatians 3:14 mentions," I say. "God's blessing is a
gift. All we need to do is humbly receive," I continue.

The men close their eyes and wait expectedly as I pray for God to pour
out the Spirit on them, filling each man with a special blessing. As I pray,
I notice many faces lifted up with great openness. People appear to soak
in God's love and blessing as I continue to pray for God's mercy as they
face their court hearings during the coming week, relate to family who
visit them or whom they are able to phone, and as some are released. We
pray for a man who'll be off to twenty-one months in prison two days later,
and for Mexican guys awaiting deportation. I pray that God would free
each man from the curse of the law, touching the hearts of the prosecutors and judges so that mercy would win over justice. We close with the

Lord's Prayer. "Let your kingdom come, your will be done, on earth as in heaven" has fresh meaning as I leave the jail that afternoon, thinking of Feliciano's pain from American Christians' criticisms of the immigration status of his congregation. We are people of another kingdom, whose allegiance to Jesus the Good Coyote causes us to walk by faith and not by adherence to the law. Our higher allegiance to God's reign marks us as strangers and aliens, wetbacks. This is a call to live outside the camp, in solidarity with those who truly suffer exclusion, regardless of their circumstances. Clearly stated and boldly lived solidarity brings great hope to people on the margins. Yet it must be announced, practiced, and celebrated over and over in order for it to become believable as it becomes incarnate.

⁂

I regularly have opportunities to announce, practice, and celebrate Jesus as the Buen Coyote who brings outlaws into the kingdom by grace. During another Sunday afternoon bilingual Bible study, I invite the men to celebrate Communion. We gather in a big circle, where I take them through a simple liturgy. Two Chicano men from California, Julio and Seferino, are among those gathered. Julio has been coming to the Bible study regularly for months after yet another DV (domestic violence) conviction, participating with intelligence and wit. Julio often talks about his addiction to crack cocaine and his temptation to sell drugs to make quick money. He complains about not being able to sense God's presence with him, until one day he tells me it's happened.

"God came to me, man, in the middle of the night. It was so good. I felt all warm and shit. I was tripping out," he announces to the group.

Seferino is in his mid-thirties, a battered heroin user from East Los Angeles who had been living on the streets of Mount Vernon when he was not in jail or in the hospital. The last time he did heroin his kidneys shut down. The doctors told him that if he used again he would probably die.

As I am on the verge of offering each person the body of Christ, Julio stops me and asks a question: "Hey, Pastor, I probably shouldn't take this if I know that I might not be able to resist drugs and shit when I get out, should I?"

"Do you need and want God's help, Julio?" I ask.

Julio nods his assent, and I tell him and the others that Christ's body and blood are the food and drink that they really need, to heal and strengthen them. I move toward the first man to offer him the body of Christ, when Seferino stops me with a question.

"Hey, Pastor, maybe Julio is right. He probably shouldn't take the Eucharist. What he's saying is that he's probably going to go back to using drugs when he gets out of here. He's telling you the truth, man."

Slipping into my coyote role, I remind the men that on the night when Jesus was betrayed, he gave his body and blood to all his disciples. He gave it to Judas, who he knew would betray him. He gave it to Peter, who he knew would deny him. He gave it to the rest of his disciples, who he knew would abandon him. Jesus said, "I came for sinners, not for the righteous." From the cross he cried out: "Father, forgive them; for they do not know what they are doing." Finally, I ask Julio to read Romans 5:6–8:

> For while we were still weak, at the right time Christ died for the ungodly. Indeed, rarely will anyone die for a righteous person—though perhaps for a good person someone might actually dare to die. But God proves his love for us in that while we still were sinners Christ died for us.

My explanation and the reading from Romans appeared to be enough to appease Seferino, and I begin serving the men. Halfway around the circle, an Anglo guy meekly asks me:

"I was baptized in the Mormon Church. Can I still take Communion?"

I assure him that I believe Jesus died for him too, and he assents. I leave the jail in amazement, glad that Christ's body and blood were able to freely make their way into the drug-craving bodies and bloodstreams of these spiritually starved men.

Reading Paul with undocumented immigrants, inmates, and "criminal aliens" can clearly bring new life to worn-out texts. Reading these Scripture passages in a way that holds onto the radical grace that infuses them requires faith and risk. Though I am fully aware of other texts that emphasize the importance of being subject to governing authorities (Rom. 13:1–7) and of walking by the Spirit and not by the flesh (Gal. 5:16–26), I do not believe that people always need to be presented with the "whole picture." Most people on society's margins assume the Scriptures are only about lists of dos and don'ts and calls to compliance. Reading with people whose social standing, family of origin, addictions, criminal history, and other factors make compliance with civil laws or scriptural teachings impossible requires a deliberate reading for and acting by grace. The good news alone must be seized by faith as having the power to save, heal, deliver, and liberate. This good news is no one other than Jesus Christ himself, who meets us through the words of Scripture and the sacraments, and through the flesh of his beloved family of *buen coyote* followers. My own attempt to follow Jesus through accompanying today's Samaritans, lepers, tax collectors, and sinners has shown me the necessity of switching sides and changing allegiances. Pledging allegiance to Jesus above all other authorities and powers comes about as a result of repentance, understood as having another mind, or after-mind.[5] Paul's words in Romans 12:1–2 point to this notion of repentance when he writes:

> I appeal to you therefore, brothers and sisters, by the mercies of God, to present your bodies as a living sacrifice, holy and acceptable to God, which is your spiritual worship. Do not be conformed to this world, but be transformed by the renewing of your minds, so that you may discern what is the will of God—what is good and acceptable and perfect.

Transformation through the renewal of our minds happens in the process of conversion, which means literally to change direction, or turn around. Reading Paul with undocumented immigrants and inmates invites us to a radical reorientation away from total allegiance to the state, denominations, and other principalities with their laws and doctrines, toward a 100 percent following after the One crucified outside the camp. Baptism into Christ's death as a lawbreaker is necessary if one is to effectively serve as a bearer of good news to people like Feliciano, Antonio, Andrés, María, Julio, and Seferino, and any of today's undocumented immigrants and outlaws.

Notes

Preface

1. My reading partners include, among others, a Cuban Jew, Guatemalan university students, Honduran campesinos, Chicano gang members, drug dealers, incarcerated heroin and crack and meth addicts, and undocumented farmworkers.
2. I use the terms "good news" and "gospel" interchangeably to refer to the heart of the Judeo-Christian kerygma, the *evangelium* announced and embodied by Jesus of Nazareth.
3. I have taught this twelve-week course several times at Regent College in Vancouver, BC, and presented shorter versions of it during numerous retreat and shorter courses for congregations.
4. I borrow this word from Ken Auletta's *The Underclass* (New York: Vintage Books, 1983).
5. An exhaustive theology of ministry or biblical grounding for ministry of the Word is beyond the scope of this book.
6. The Greek word for this (*metanoeo*) can be translated "change your way of thinking/understanding," which happens in part through ministries of the Word.

Chapter 1: Reading Scripture for the Liberation of the Not-Yet-Believing

1. From unpublished journal entry after a conversation with Daniel Lys at l'Institut Protestant de Théologie in Montpellier, France, September 1990. Lys goes on to point out that later, in Jeremiah, the prophet is unable to find even one righteous one in all of Jerusalem.
2. Daniel Lys offers his own set of pitfalls and helpful reflections on liberating reading of the Bible. See Daniel Lys, *Comprends-tu ce que tu lis? Initiations au sens de l'Ancien Testament* (Paris: Ediciones du Cerf, 1972); *Au Claire de la Bible: Essais et transformations* (Paris: Les Bergers et les Mages, 1999).
3. Reading widely in the Bible rather than sticking to safe or favored texts can be a first step. Reading early Jewish translations and interpretations, the early church fathers, and diverse exegetical and theological approaches is another. Reflect in dialogue with the wider ecumenical church body. Draw on the riches of the church's diverse traditions (e.g., Catholic, Reformed, Lutheran, Orthodox, Methodist, Pentecostal). Reflect in tension with and dialogue with the powers (courts, immigration, police, politicians). Let your

reflection be in active dialogue with the social sciences (psychology, sociology, political science) and with the treatment community.

4. Carlos Mesters, *Defenseless Flower: A New Reading of the Bible*, trans. Francis McDonagh (Maryknoll, NY: Orbis, 1989); *God, Where Are You? Rediscovering the Bible*, trans. J. Drury and F. McDonagh (Maryknoll, NY: Orbis, 1995).

5. Ernesto Cardenal, *The Gospel in Solentiname*, vols. 1–4 (Maryknoll, NY: Orbis, 1976, 1979).

6. Countless others are working in the trenches to facilitate *lectura popular*. Most have not published and many have been martyred.

7. Paulo Freire, *Pedagogy of the Oppressed*, trans. Myra Bergman Ramos (New York: Seabury, 1970); *Education for Critical Consciousness*, trans. Myra Bergman Ramos (New York: Continuum, 1974). See also Daniel S. Schipani, *Paulo Freire: Educador cristiano* (Grand Rapids: Libros Dasafio, 2002).

8. See Freire's account of the empowerment of marginal communities through their reading the Gospels, under the military dictatorship in Brazil in the 1970s, in Paulo Freire and Antonio Faundez, *Learning to Question: A Pedagogy of Liberation*, trans. Tony Coates (Geneva: WCC Publications, 1989), pp. 63–64.

9. See Stanley P. Saunders and Charles L. Campbell, *The Word on the Streets: Performing the Scriptures in the Urban Context* (Grand Rapids: Eerdmans, 2000), Gerald O. West, *The Academy of the Poor: Towards a Dialogical Reading of the Bible* (Sheffield: Sheffield Academic Press, 1999), Hans de Wit, Louis Jonker, Marleen Kool, Daniel Schipani (eds.), *Through the Eyes of Another: Intercultural Reading of the Bible* (Elkhart, IN: Institute of Mennonite Studies; Amsterdam: Vrije Universiteit, 2004), for helpful discussion regarding hermeneutical issues related to reading Scripture.

10. The determined "heart of the matter" in a text is best held lightly. The "heart" or "good news" of the text from the perspective of the margins is often quite different than what is visible from a mainstream perspective. Often in the midst of a dialogical Bible study I witness a shift in my own perception. Most of this paradigm shift is initiated by an untrained reader's reaction to the story. Gerald West goes into great detail regarding the "hidden transcript" of marginalized readers— interpretations that are only disclosed in an environment of total trust.

11. When I begin with issues I seek to address among my parishioners or with their spontaneous questions, knowledge of the Scriptures becomes especially important. The more you know the Bible, the more ready you are to choose the appropriate text for your particular context. Once a text is selected that appears to address a given contemporary situation, the leader can explore the group's question before inviting them to look at the selected Scripture.

12. See note 11 for the importance of knowledge of the Scriptures in helping you choose the appropriate text.

13. West, *Academy of the Poor*, pp. 35–62. See also James C. Scott, *Domination and the Arts of Resistance: Hidden Transcripts* (New Haven, CT: Yale University Press, 1990).

14. In the highly Christianized South African context after apartheid, black South Africans in the churches and even those in grassroots political organizations not tied to the church appear to have drawn from the Scriptures, their faith communities, and positive images of God for strength to resist the status quo in ways that surpass traditional Roman Catholic peasant communities in Central America and a largely unchurched North American underclass.

15. *Examples*: Look at call stories of Abraham (Gen. 11:27–12:4); Moses (Exod. 3); Jacob (Gen. 25); Isaiah (Isa. 6); Jeremiah (Jer. 1); the disciples (Matt. 4:18–22); Matthew (Matt. 9:9–13); Paul (Acts 9). What were the characters doing when they were called? And ask the questions: "What kind of people does God call? What were the persons God called doing when God called them? Where were they? What were the prerequisites required by the caller before the call?"

Chapter 2: New Beginnings Require New Readings

1. Or read: "In the beginning of God's creating of the heavens and the earth, when the earth was chaotic and empty, and darkness was over the face of the deep. . . ."

   For the observations in chapter 2 and accounts of group studies, most Scripture quotations are the author's own translation or adaptation of various versions, words from which may appear in the discussions.

2. Genesis 1 is attributed to the Priestly source, written during the exile in Babylon. Uprooted from their homeland to live as exiles in a foreign place, the Israelites in Babylon likely experienced the chaos and darkness of *tohu va bohu*. The Priestly writer affirms that God is creating, present as the Spirit hovering over the depths. Israel is assured by Genesis 1 that God will speak, and that God's speaking brings light in the darkness, order out of chaos, and life out of death. God is pronounced the creator of all that is visible in the world, including entities that the surrounding culture deified (stars, moon, sun— lights—and sea monsters) and all that made life difficult for humans (birds, creeping things). These are not extensions of the demonic, but part of God's good creation. God's word and work are affirmed as preceding the presence and response of human beings.

3. Desert spirituality, otherwise known as Hesychast tradition, originated in upper Egypt among the desert fathers in the third century. John Cassian brought these teachings to the West in his famous "Conferences." The Cistercian order finds its roots here.

4. In other Bible studies on this passage, people have sometimes asked whether we are still in God's image after Adam and Eve. In response to this, I invite them to turn to Gen. 5:1–2, where humans outside the garden are described as being made in God's image and likeness. We also read Gen. 9:6, where after the flood people are described as being made in God's image.

5. In some Bible studies, when appropriate and important to emphasize woman as made in God's image, I mention that one of God's names in Genesis, El Shaddai, literally means God with two breasts (Gen. 17:1; 28:3; 36:11; 48:3).

6. The Priestly writer announces a "high anthropology" at a time when exiled Israelites are oppressed and consider themselves judged and punished by God for their sins. In spite of the appearances (life in exile), human beings are presented as the pinnacle of creation (according to a structure based on ten words and six days).

7. St. Symeon the New Theologian, "One Hundred and Fifty-three Practical and Theological Texts," *The Philokalia: The Complete Text*, vol. 4, no. 61, comp. St. Nikodimos of the Holy Mountain and St. Makarios of Corinth; trans. G. E. H. Palmer, Philip Sherrard, and Kallistos Ware (London: Faber and Faber, 1995), p. 36.

Chapter 3: Getting Back into the Garden

1. Some inmates express outright disdain for the first woman, and tend to blame all women, whom they see as responsible for moving the human race from being perfect to being in our "fallen," totally depraved current state.

2. Among some questions that help people enter the detail of the text are: What is being said to whom through the detail of the text? Who were the original addressees? What does God do? Who and where is God, according to the text? Who are humans? How are they described? What do humans do? What is the relationship between what God does and what humans/the world does?

3. God's actual first command to humans in Genesis 1:28 "be fruitful and multiply" surprises and delights people even more.

4. In addition, the woman's specifying "of the fruit of the tree" and change of the original second-person-singular command to the man to a second-plural jussive, "You shall not eat," reveals an overly legalistic interpretation.

5. In being vulnerable to the creature and listening to his perverse theology, the woman is no longer "good"—if good is defined by being in relationship with God. However, if "good" is the way God looks at creation/humans, quite apart from humans and creatures, then the woman remains good. She is just disoriented (and spiritually sick).

6. The predicted "pain in childbearing" is not evident from the seemingly painless and victorious births of Cain and Abel. This leads the reader to wonder about the nature of this pain, which is best translated "pain in child raising," especially in the light of Genesis 4:1–16 and the later patriarchal narratives.

7. According to Rachi, an eleventh- to twelfth-century Jewish mystic and Bible interpreter, Abel is "keeper of sheep because the earth had been cursed, he withdrew from working it," cited by James L. Kugel, *Traditions of the Bible: A Guide to the Bible as It Was at the Start of the Common Era* (Cambridge, MA: Harvard University Press, 1999), p. 37. The mention of God's providing clothing for the humans from animals ties Abel's vocation with animals to a moment of grace.

8. The September 17, 1999, jail Bible study.

9. In the Hebrew Bible humans are never the subject of the verb "to be angry," but always the object of this verb. God is the only one who is the subject of this verb, indicating that God's anger is something that God is in control of, unlike humans.

10. Daniel Bourguet offers a helpful study of sin as malady and God as physician in *Les Maladies de la vie spirituelle*, Veillez et Priez (Paris: Réveil, 2000).

11. See especially the story of the paralytic who is lowered through the roof before Jesus.

12. God is the only subject of the Hebrew verb "to heal" (*rafa*). This is also true for the Hebrew verb "to forgive."

13. St. Hesychios the Priest, "On Watchfulness and Holiness," *Philokalia*, vol. 1, no. 6, p. 163.

14. John Cassian, *Conferences*, The Classics of Western Spirituality (New York: Paulist Press, 1985), p. 46.

15. Ibid., 51.

16. Ibid., no. 20, p. 54.

Chapter 4: God Empowers the Down and Out

1. The use of this verb evokes Genesis 2:15, where the Lord God took the human and placed him in the garden, here identified as Canaan.

2. In Genesis 11:27–32 there is very little movement among the characters, who die, are sterile, take, went out, go, came, settled, and died. In contrast, there is abundant movement among the characters in Genesis 12:1–9, who went, departed, took what they had gathered, acquired, set forth to go, came, passed through, built, moved, pitched his tent, built, invoked, and journeyed on.

3. Willie Clenfuegos, "Letters from Jail: Advice about Drugs, Sex, etc." *Tierra Nueva / New Earth News*, Spring 1999, p. 10.

4. Isaac and Rebekah's first encounter supports Isaac's dominance. Isaac brings her into the tent, takes her, knows her, loves her, and is comforted (Gen. 24:26). This contrasts with the betrothal narrative, where Abraham's servant treats her with more respect. In Genesis 26, Isaac continues to treat Rebekah as an object, putting her at risk among the men of Gerar (Gen. 26:6ff.).

5. I told them that in trying to get a job teaching theology it would help me if I were black or Hispanic and female—things I could never be.

6. "*Estamos jodidos.*"

7. "*Portate bien, mi hijo, sino Diosito te va a castigar.*"

8. Bledstein argues that Isaac's name can be translated "trickster" and Jacob "heel," in Adrien Janis Bledstein, "Binder, Trickster, Heel and Hairy-Man," *A Feminist Companion to Genesis*, ed. Athalya Brenner (Sheffield: Sheffield Academic Press, 1999), p. 283. However, the narrator presents an etymology suggesting Jacob means "heel," "supplanter" (Brueggemann), or even "trickster"; though the original meaning of Jacob's name is likely "God protects" (see Nahum M. Sarna, *The JPS Torah Commentary Genesis* [Philadelphia: The Jewish Publication Society, 1989], p. 180), or "God follows after" (see Robert Alter, *Genesis: Translation and Commentary* [New York and London: W.W. Norton & Company, 1996], p. 128).

9. Bledstein's assertion that trickster Isaac knew Jacob's true identity all along and sought to test his "resolve and stamina" before passing on "the mantle to the next-generation trickster" ("Binder, Trickster, Heel and Hairy-Man," pp. 288–89) has little support from the text. Rather, it reflects yet another attempt typical of rabbinic exegesis to deny or in some way justify the weakness of the father(s). This reading disempowers true tricksters, attributing the success of their plots to the patronage of the powerful.

10. The Septuagint's semantic equivalent for the Masoretic Text's *qᵉlālāh* (curse) is *katara*, which links Rebekah's action in this text to Galatians 3:13–14, where Jesus is described as taking on the curse (*katara*) of the law in order that the excluded nations might be brought in. "Christ redeemed us from the curse [*katara*] of the law by becoming a curse [*katara*] for us—for it is written, 'Cursed is everyone who hangs on a tree'—in order that in Christ Jesus the blessing of Abraham might come to the Gentiles, so that we might receive the promise of the Spirit through faith."

11. *The Sayings of the Desert Fathers: The Alphabetical Collection*, trans. and foreword by Benedicta Ward (Kalamazoo, MI: Cistercian Publications, 1975), p. 25.

Chapter 5: Encountering God in Exodus and at Today's Margins

1. Initiative 695 is a 2000 Washington State initiative that repealed the license plate tax, reducing it to a flat fee much less than the value-based tax.

2. Sometimes I invite inmates to read together the places in Genesis and Exodus that support this (Gen. 16:7; 21:14, 17, 20–21; 37:22; Exod. 4:27; 5:1, 3; 7:16; 8:27–28; 13:18, 20; 14:3, 11–12; 15:22; 16:1–3, 10, 14; 17:1; 18:5; 19:1–2).

Chapter 6: God's Empowering Call to the People

1. See 2 Kgs. 24:14.

2. In most occurrences of *eved* in Isaiah 40–55, Israel is clearly the servant (Isa. 44:1, 2, 21, 26; 45:4; 48:20; 49:3, 7; 54:17 pl.).

Chapter 7: Reading and Praying the Psalms

1. Certain psalms describe incredible suffering with physical details (Ps. 22:14–18), psychological suffering (Pss. 22:7–8; 6:7–8).
2. Daniel Bourguet comments on this at length in his book from a Fraternité Spirituelle les Veilleurs retreat, *Méditation de la Bible*, Veillez et Priez (Paris: Réveil, 1998).
3. Lists of psalms considered to regard enemies vary widely. The following list includes psalms most widely included in this category: Pss. 5, 7, 9, 10, 13, 16, 21, 28, 31, 35, 36, 40, 41, 44, 52, 54, 55, 58, 59, 68, 69, 70, 71, 109, 137, 140.
4. I am grateful to Daniel Bourguet for his helpful insights regarding Christian appropriation of psalms against enemies. See Daniel Bourguet, *Prions les psaumes*, Veillez et Priez (Paris: Réveil, 2000), pp. 55–66.
5. See William Stringfellow, *An Ethic for Christians and Other Aliens in a Strange Land* (Waco: Word Books, 1973), and Walter Wink, *Naming the Powers: The Language of Power in the New Testament* (Philadelphia: Fortress Press, 1984).

Chapter 8: Reading the Gospels with Tax Collectors and Sinners

1. The powerful were unaware of Messiah's birthplace and time (Matt. 2:3–4), and the first to receive the birth announcement are the humble shepherds. God chooses the insignificant places and people: "You, Bethlehem, in the land of Judah, are by no means *least* among the rulers of Judah; for from you shall come a ruler *who is to shepherd* my people Israel" (italics added).
2. Light is described as dawning on people who sat in darkness (Matt. 4:16).
3. Fishermen are called as disciples (Matt. 4:18–22), as is Matthew the tax collector (Matt. 9:9–13).
4. Luke 4:16–29; Matt. 21:14–16.
5. The Gospel writers constantly depict Jesus and others as critiquing the dominant theology of their time. John the Baptist's harsh words in Matthew are addressed to the *Pharisees and Sadducees* (Matt. 3:7–12). To *a scribe* Jesus says: "Foxes have holes, and birds of the air have nests, but the Son of Man has nowhere to lay his head" (Matt. 8:20). To *a disciple* who wanted to bury his father, Jesus said: "Follow me, and let the dead . . ." (8:22), and to Pharisees' criticism of his disciples' plucking grain responds: "I desire mercy and not sacrifice" (12:7). Jesus says to Pharisees who say he casts out demons by Beelzebul: every sin will be forgiven except blasphemy against the Spirit: "Whoever speaks a word against the Son of Man will be forgiven, but whoever speaks against the Holy Spirit will not be forgiven, either in this age or in the age to come" (12:32). To Pharisees he says: "You brood of vipers! How can you speak good things, when you are evil? . . ." (12:33–37). To the scribes and Pharisees who want a sign Jesus says: "An evil and adulterous generation asks for a sign" (12:38–42). To Pharisees and scribes who confront Jesus about his disciples' not cleaning their hands before they eat, he responds: "And why do you break the commandment of God for the sake of your tradition?" (15:1–3). "You hypocrites! Isaiah . . . said: 'This people honors me with their lips, but their hearts are far from me; in vain do they worship me, teaching human precepts as doctrines'" (15:7–9). Jesus responds to disciples who tell him that Pharisees were offended by his words: "Every plant that my heavenly Father has not planted will be uprooted. Let them alone; they are blind guides of the blind" (15:12–14).
6. Rephrasing questions happens constantly as I lead Bible studies, based on my sense as to whether or not the question hits home.

7. In other Bible studies on this text we look in detail at the three verbs commonly used when people come to Jesus in this Gospel: *come to*, *kneel*, and *ask*. I argue that the heaping of these verbs represents a sort of pietistic striving, or "sucking up," before Jesus to get a favor.

8. Jesus' prayers in the garden, "Father, if it is possible, let this cup pass from me; yet not what I want but what you want" (Matt. 26:39) and "My Father, if this cannot pass unless I drink it, your will be done" (26:42), do not confirm that it was God's will for Jesus to be crucified. God is silent in the narrative, though God's agreement with Jesus in his death certainly would not support traditional penal substitution theories.

Chapter 9: Following Jesus, the Good Coyote

1. The Greek word *skubilos* literally means excrement or shit.

2. I often point out that the literal Greek genitive here best translates as *"faith of Christ,"* though the standard translation "faith in Christ" is also possible. This notion of Christ's faith making us righteous fits the literary context of Philippians 3:8–9, where gaining Christ is described passively as *being found* in him and as "the righteousness from God." The description of faith as *coming* in Gal. 3:23 supports this interpretation, as does the similar genitive construction in Gal. 2:16, which reads literally: "yet we know that a person is justified not by the works of the law but through *faith of Jesus Christ*. And we have come to believe in Christ Jesus, so that we might be justified *by faith of Christ*, and not by doing the works of the law, because no one will be justified by the works of the law."

3. See note 2, above.

4. *"La gente de la frontera tiene que buscar un coyote para pasarnos. Y nosotros también tenemos que buscar a Jesús para que nos pase."*

5. *Metanoia* literally means after-mind, or other mind.

Tierra Nueva

"New Earth"

Reading the Bible with the Damned has emerged out of the fertile ground of Tierra Nueva (New Earth). Tierra Nueva is an ecumenical ministry dedicated to proclaiming the good news of God's reign (on earth as in heaven) in solidarity with the oppressed for our mutual liberation, healing, empowerment, transformation, and total salvation.

Tierra Nueva's ministry includes five branches:

- Skagit County Jail Ministry
- The Family Support Center
- Road to Emmaus Faith Community
- Tierra Nueva Honduras
- The People's Seminary

Through the People's Seminary, Tierra Nueva offers courses on transformational ministry to people on the margins.

For more information on Tierra Nueva or the People's Seminary or to contact Bob Ekblad for speaking engagements visit our Web site at www.tierra-nueva.org or www.peoplesseminary.org, write info@peoplesseminary.org or P. O. Box 161, Burlington, WA 98233, or call (360) 755–5299.